The Art of Positional Play

The Art of Positional Play

by

Samuel Reshevsky

International Grandmaster

DAVID McKAY COMPANY, INC.

NEW YORK

Library of Congress Cataloging in Publication Data

Reshevsky, Samuel, 1911–
    The art of positional play.

    Includes index.
    1.   Chess.   I.   Title.
GV1449.5.R47   794.1′ 4   76–41038
ISBN 0–679–14101–4

Ninth Printing

To My Wife

Introduction

We often hear the terms "positional" and "tactical" used as opposites. But this is as wrong as to consider a painting's composition unrelated to its subject. Just as there is no such thing as "artistic" art, so there is no such thing as "positional" chess.

The business of the chess player is to conceive practical objectives and to plan and carry out the maneuvers necessary to achieve them; the objectives, the plans, the maneuvers—all must be based on the possibilities inherent in actual positions. Thus chess is *by definition* positional. Tactical play is concerned with the immediate details of executing the maneuvers necessary to the success of the plan and the attainment of the objective.

Example: White sees in a given situation that he would probably obtain a decisive advantage by getting his Rook to the seventh rank; this goal could be achieved if Black's Queen were temporarily diverted and the QB-file opened; he calculates that maneuvering a Knight to Q5 would force Black's Queen to retreat, after which White could push a pawn and eventually open the QB-file. We see in this process three interdependent elements: 1) deciding on a positional objective (getting a Rook to the seventh rank); 2) planning a logical strategy to achieve it (diverting Black's Queen and opening the QB-file); 3) carrying out the strategical plan tactically (calculating the specific moves and variations).

Every position, like the one in the example, contains certain characteristic patterns, which we may call themes. The pawn structure, a weak square, a poorly defended King, an open line, a badly placed piece—all of these, and many more, are positional themes. Recognizing them, and knowing how to use them to plan logically, are as necessary to a chess player as line and color are to a painter.

When a beginner plays P–K4 on his first move he is already playing positionally (although he may not be aware of it): he has begun to occupy and control the center (particularly Q5), and he has opened lines for his King Bishop and his Queen. Center control and open lines are common positional themes.

When a player sacrifices a pawn, or even a piece, to expose the enemy King, the details of the operation are tactical but the conception and the goal are positional. King safety is a positional theme.

For the purposes of this book, I have chosen to concentrate on the most common and easily recognized positional themes, and to illustrate them with actual games selected from recent tournaments and matches. This is the most useful method for the student because he will learn to recognize the themes in their practical settings and how they are handled under tournament conditions by the best contemporary masters. I am sure that the games, chosen for their inherent interest and quality, will also prove entertaining to the casual reader.

It has been known for a hundred years that a positional advantage is a prerequisite for a successful attack. This book was written to show you how to get that positional advantage.

I want to thank Bert Hochberg for editing this book.

Contents

CHAPTER 4   SPACE   116

CHAPTER 5   OPEN LINES   158

CHAPTER 6   TACTICS   195

CHAPTER 7   PIECES, GOOD AND BAD   224

The Art of Positional Play

Chapter 1

Weak Pawns

The pawn, wrote Philidor, is the soul of chess. Although he wrote it some two hundred years ago, and although it remains valid today, many amateurs do not realize just what it means and how they can profit by understanding it.

The pawn formation (or skeleton) that results from the opening is the principal determinant of the further course of the game. The position of the pawns largely indicates where the other forces are best disposed, and it is the clash of unbalanced pawn structures that makes chess a fight. That is why symmetrical pawn structures usually lead to drawish positions.

Furthermore, given the sophisticated technique of today's masters, weak pawns are excellent targets, and the loss of a single pawn can mean the loss of the game. Therefore good players avoid weak pawns assiduously.

What is a weak pawn? A pawn that is exposed to attack and also difficult to defend is weak. There are several varieties: isolated, doubled, too advanced, retarded. An isolated pawn, because it is separated from the neighboring pawns and cannot be supported by them, requires defense by pieces. These pieces are called passive since they must function below their full potential. A doubled pawn is limited in mobility; its weakness is usually felt in the endgame because a group of pawns that includes a doubled pawn is less likely than a healthy group to produce a passed pawn. (However, not all doubled pawns are weak.) A pawn that is advanced too far runs the risk of being cut off from the rest of its army and becoming isolated. A pawn not advanced far enough (or not at all) can get in the way of the other pieces and may become backward and vulnerable.

Weak pawns can be tolerated in certain cases, particularly when you have, or are sure to get, equivalent compensation, like a strong attack or at least the creation of an equally weak pawn in the opponent's camp. Best, of course, is to avoid them.

In game 1 we see an example of weak pawns created by Black's need to keep White's pieces from swarming all over his position. His decision is clearly the lesser of two evils but is an evil nevertheless. His pieces soon become tied up, and he cannot prevent the eventual incursion of the White pieces anyway.

In game 2 Black's advanced QNP becomes a source of trouble when he tries to avoid simplification (for in the endgame weak pawns are fatal because of the reduced opportunities for counterplay), but the sequel produces an even worse endgame for him. Smyslov's technique here, as in most of his games, is worthy of close study.

As noted, pieces which might otherwise be used more profitably must defend weak pawns. Game 3 is an example: Black's QBP is weak because it is isolated and on an open file. The technique is to attack the square in front of the pawn to prevent its advance and keep the defending pieces in their passive positions.

In game 4 Black follows the usual pattern of counterplay: he works on the Kingside while White ought to be occupying himself on the Queenside. White refuses to cooperate, however, and plans to undermine a crucial Black pawn.

Game 1

Consequences of a Weak Pawn

One of the leading exponents of the Gruenfeld Defense, Wolfgang Uhlmann of East Germany, has trouble with his favorite defense when he faces Mark Taimanov of the Soviet Union in the famous match between teams from the Soviet Union and "The Rest of the World." A new idea in an old variation compels Uhlmann to weaken the dark squares in the center so he can castle. When White immediately threatens to exploit those weakened squares, Black is forced to make further concessions. Taimanov handles the entire game extremely well. Note especially how his control of an open file leads to control of the seventh rank and an irresistible assault on the weak KP.

USSR vs. the Rest of the World

Belgrade, 1970

GRUENFELD DEFENSE

M. Taimanov	W. Uhlmann
1. P–Q4	N–KB3
2. P–QB4	P–KN3
3. N–QB3	P–Q4
4. B–N5	. . .

Taimanov chooses a long-discarded line that his opponent could hardly have been expecting.

4. . . .	N–K5
5. B–R4	. . .

A relatively recent idea that seems to give Black difficulty. More usual is 5. PxP NxB 6. P–KR4 N–K5 7. NxN QxP 8. N–QB3 Q–QR4 with even chances.

5. . . .	P–QB4

Also playable is 5. . . . NxN 6. PxN P–QB3.

6. BPxP	NxN
7. PxN	QxP
8. P–K3	PxP

In view of what happens in this game, 8. . . . B–N2 or 8. . . . N–B3!? ought to be considered.

9. QxP!	. . .

By attacking Black's Queen and Rook, White forces the exchange of Queens. The alternative 9. BPxP (9. KPxP? Q--K5ch and 10. . . . QxB) allows Black the possibility of capitalizing on the absence of White's QB from the Queenside. Now White can use the open Queenside files and has pressure against Black's KP, whereas Black's most active piece, his Queen, is back in the box.

| 9. . . . | QxQ |
| 10. BPxQ | . . . |

Opening the QB-file for action by his Rooks. Black now has problems castling because of the pressure against his KP.

10. . . .	N–B3
11. B–QN5	B–Q2
12. N–B3	B–N2
13. O–O	P–K3

A weakening move but necessary in order to be able to castle. If 13. . . . O–O Black loses his KP.

| 14. QR–N1 | O–O |
| 15. N–Q2! | . . . |

White's threat is 16. N–K4, aiming at QB5, Q6, and especially KB6, with a strategically won game. To prevent this Black weakens himself further.

| 15. . . . | P–B4 |

No doubt played reluctantly, for his KP is now very weak and his position precarious. A better try is 15. . . . P-QR3 16. B–K2 N–R4, but after 17. N–K4 White's advantage is clear. The next move prevents N-K4 forever, but it is a major concession.

| 16. N–N3 | . . . |

Headed for QB5, which provokes Black's reply.

| 16. . . . | P–N3 |

Another weakness, this time the QB3 square.

| 17. KR–B1 | QR–B1 |
| 18. B–R6 | QR–K1 |

Black tries to keep his second rank safe from White's Rook by maintaining his Knight at QB3. Nonetheless, after the next move White has his way.

| 19. B–N7 | N–Q1 |

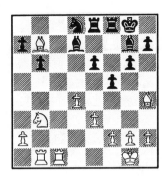

  20. R–B7   · · ·

White's control of the seventh rank leads to Black's downfall.
Now 20. . . . NxB? 21. RxN and White wins a pawn.

    20. . . .   **R–B2**

    21. B–R6   **B–R5**

    22. QR–QB1   **B–B1**

    23. R/1–B4!   · · ·

Unproductive is 23. B–B8 B–Q3 24. RxR (24. BxN? BxR 25.
BxB R/1xB) 24. . . . KxR.

    23. . . .   **RxR**

    24. RxR   · · ·

Thus White takes complete control of the seventh rank.

    24. . . .   **N–B3**

    25. B–B4   · · ·

Black's weak KP cannot be saved. The crushing threats are
26. R–B8, winning the KP, and 26. B–B6, with P–Q4 in the air.

    25. . . .   **B–N2**

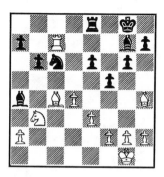

26. R–B8!   . . .

Winning a pawn by force. Black was aware of this possibility but could do nothing to prevent it.

      26. . . .   **RxR**

      27. BxPch   **K–B1**

      28. BxR   . . .

The resulting endgame presents some technical difficulties for White, whose extra pawn is counterbalanced somewhat by Black's potential passed pawn on the Queenside and more active King.

      28. . . .   **N–N5**

      29. N–B1   **K–B2**

      30. B–N3   **B–B1**

Preventing B–Q6 and activating this Bishop.

      31. B–N7   **K–K3**

      32. B–N8   **K–Q2**

      33. B–B3   . . .

Not 33. BxP K–B2 34. B–B3 B–B3 trapping the Queen Bishop.

      33. . . .   **B–N4**

      34. B–Q1   **P–QR4**

      35. P–QR4   **B–B5**

35. . . . B–B3 allows 36. B–QN3 with danger to Black's Kingside pawns. The struggle has been between Black's efforts to mobilize his Queenside and White's efforts to prevent it.

      36. P–N4   . . .

Attempting to weaken Black's Kingside pawn structure and to develop two passed pawns in the center. Black therefore avoids 36. . . . PxP, but his Kingside pawns become weaker.

36. . . .   **P–QN4**

Black's only chance of survival: counterplay with his QRP.

       37. PxBP   **PxBP**

       38. B–K5   **. . .**

Moves to post the Bishop on the important QR1–KR8 diagonal to prevent the QRP from queening.

       38. . . .   **N–B3**

Better chances are offered by 38. . . . N–Q4, threatening . . . N–B6 and keeping White's QB from QR1 by blocking White's QP.

       39. B–R8   **B–R6**

       40. PxP   **. . .**

       40. . . .   **BxN?**

If 40. . . . NxP 41. BxN BxN 42. B–B2 B–K3 43. P–N6 K–B3 44. P–K4 P–B5 45. P–K5 and wins. But Black could put up resistance with 40. . . . BxP 41. N–N3 (41. N–R2 or 41. N–K2 B–N7 would restrict the Knight's activity) 41. . . . K–Q3, and if 42. B–B2 P–R5 (not 42. . . . B–R5? because of 43. NxP BxB 44. N–B4ch) 43. N–Q2 B–N5 with good play.

       41. PxNch   **KxP**

       42. B–R4ch   **K–Q4**

This offers no hope at all, since it gives up any thought of promoting the QRP. Black's effort to contain White on the opposite wing proves futile. Uhlmann should try 42. . . . B–N4: if 43. P–Q5ch K–B4 44. B–Q4ch K–B5 45. B–B2 (45. BxB KxB

poses problems for White to stop the dangerous passed pawn)
45. . . . B–Q2 with good drawing chances; if 43. B–B2 P–B5 44.
P–K4 (44. PxP BxP 45. BxP P–R5 with drawing chances) 44. . . .
P–B6 makes it somewhat difficult for White to score the point.

43. B–B2	K–K3
44. K–N2	B–R6
45. B–K5	B–B1
46. B–B7	B–Q4ch
47. P–B3	. . .

47. K–N3 is more forceful, for if 47. . . . B–N5 48. K–B4.
Taimanov was perhaps fearful of 47. . . . B–Q3ch 48. BxB KxB
49. BxP P–R5 50. BxP P–R6 51. B–N1 P–R7 52. BxP BxB, but
after 53. P-B4, White would have no difficulty scoring the point
since the Bishop would be helpless against the four pawns.

| 47. . . . | B–N5 |
| 48. K–N3 | K–B3 |

If 48. . . . B–Q3ch 49. BxB KxB, and White would not be forced
to continue with 50. BxP, which allows 50. . . . P–R5 (as pointed
out in the last note), but he could safely continue with 50. K–B4
followed by K–N5 and K–R6.

49. B–K5ch	K–N3
50. K–B4	B–K3
51. B–R4	B–KB1

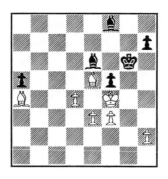

| 52. P–K4 | . . . |

Having neutralized Black's QRP, White now proceeds to take advantage of his two connected passed pawns. Black's defense collapses rapidly.

52. . . .		B–R3ch
53. K–N3		PxP
54. PxP		B–Q7
55. P–Q5		B–K8ch
56. K–B3		B–R6
57. B–K8ch		K–R3
58. B–KB6		Resigns

Black is helpless against the onrushing pawns. An excellent performance by the Soviet veteran.

Game 2

Too Far Advanced

To advance pawns farther than needed merely to develop pieces and to control the center is always a matter of delicate judgment. Pawns insufficiently advanced may become backward and drastically reduce mobility; those advanced too far may exceed the reach of other units and thus become indefensible.

In this game between two Soviet giants, Viktor Korchnoi's risky style gets a little the better of his sound judgment. Considering that his opponent is a former world champion who is justly famed for his merciless exploitation of the tiniest weakness, Korchnoi should not avoid the exchange of Queens on his 22nd move, for the exchange is forced a few moves later under even less favorable conditions. His problem is his advanced QNP, which finally becomes the victim of White's excellent technique. Note how Smyslov coaxes the pawn to advance so that it will become more vulnerable.

Match: Leningrad vs. Moscow, 1967

CATALAN SYSTEM

V. Smyslov	V. Korchnoi
1. P–Q4	N–KB3
2. P–QB4	P–K3
3. N–KB3	P–Q4

Korchnoi, who is extremely enterprising and is always searching for sharp play, avoids the Queen's Indian Defense, 3. . . . P–QN3, which usually leads to a colorless middlegame and a quick draw.

4. P–KN3	. . .

Typical of Smyslov. He prefers simple and safe variations.

4. . . .	PxP
5. Q–R4ch	QN–Q2
6. B–N2	P–QR3
7. QxBP	P–B4
8. Q–B2	P–QN4
9. 0–0	B–N2
10. P–QR4	B–K2

Can Black afford to lose this tempo? Smyslov succeeds in taking advantage of this questionable move. An alternative is 10. . . . R–B1 11. PxNP RPxP 12. Q–N3 Q–N3 13. N–R3 B–B3 with approximate equality.

11. QPxP	BxP
12. B–N5	Q–N3
13. BxN	NxB
14. PxP	PxP

14. . . . QxP 15. N–B3 costs Black valuable time.

15. RxRch	BxR
16. N–B3	0–0
17. P–K3	. . .

To free the Rook for action.

17. . . .	R–B1
18. Q–Q3	. . .

White's strategy is to compel Black to advance and thus weaken his QNP.

18. . . .	P–N5
19. N–QR4	Q–B3
20. NxB	. . .

Stronger than 20. P–N3 P–K4 with the annoying threat of . . . P–K5.

20. . . .	QxN
21. R–Q1	P–R3
22. Q–Q4	. . .

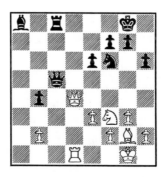

Believing that Black's QNP is a worthwhile target, Smyslov wants to exchange Queens.

        22. . . .   Q–B7

The adventurous Korchnoi always tries to avoid drawish lines. He usually manages to outwit his adversaries through intricate and complex maneuvers, but in this particular case he should consider the strength of his opponent and simplify. After 22. . . . QxQ 23. NxQ BxB 24. KxB P–K4 25. N–N3 (if 25. N–B5 R–B7 26. R–Q8ch K–R2 27. R–KB8 RxP 28. RxP K–N3 and wins) 25. . . . R–B7 26. R–Q2 RxR 27. NxR K–B1 28. K–B3 K–K2, Black could hold his own.

23. N–K1	Q–K7
24. BxB	RxB
25. Q–Q2	QxQ
26. RxQ	. . .

Black was not able to avoid the Queen endgame anyway, and now White's Rook enjoys greater potential than Black's. The endgame is more difficult for Black than it would have been after the Queen exchange on move 22. White's QNP is relatively safe because it is not so far advanced as Black's and is therefore easier to defend if attacked.

26. . . .	**R–R8**
27. K–B1	**R–N8**
28. K–K2	**N–Q4**

If 28. . . . N–K5 29. R–Q8ch K–R2 30. N–Q3 followed by R–QN8, winning the pawn.

29. N–Q3 . . .

Bad is 29. P–K4 N–N3 30. N–Q3 P–N6 (threatening 31. . . . N–B5), and if 31. N–K5 P–B3, etc.

29. . . . **R–KR8**

29. . . . P–N6 loses to 30. R–Q1 (not 30. N–B5 N–N3 31. NxNP N–B5 and draws) 30. . . . RxR 31. KxR N–B3 32. P–B3 N–Q2 33. K–Q2 winning the pawn and the game. Recognizing this, Korchnoi decides to look for counterplay by exerting pressure against White's Kingside pawns.

30. P–R4 . . .

Both sides have isolated QNPs. White, however, is much better off because his King is closer to the pawns. Consequently, Black is at a distinct disadvantage because he is compelled to avoid an exchange of Rooks, for he would then lose his QNP through the combined attack on it by King and Knight. If Black's QNP were not so far advanced, he would be able to defend it with his King.

30. . . .	**P–B4**
31. R–Q1	**R–R7**
32. N–K5!	. . .

A clever move, preventing 32. . . . P–N4 by threatening to win a pawn with 33. N–B3. If 32. . . . K–B1 33. N–B3 R–R6 34. R–KN1 followed by 35. K–B1 and 36. K–N2, trapping the Rook.

32. . . .	**N–B3**
33. N–B3	**R–R6**
34. R–Q8ch	. . .

Against 34. R–KN1, Black has 34. . . . N–N5 35. K–B1 N–R7ch. Black even has the possibility of 34. . . . N–N5 35. K–B1 P–K4

36. K–N2 P–K5 37. KxR PxN with drawing chances because White's King is stuck in the corner.

| 34. . . . | K–B2 |

Unavailing is 34. . . . K–R2 on account of 35. R–Q4 N–Q4 36. P–K4 PxP 37. RxKP R–R8 38. N–K1 with an easy win.

35. N–K5ch	K–K2
36. N–B6ch	K–B2
37. NxP	. . .

At last White has something to show for his effort, but scoring the point is still not an easy task. The following technical part of the game is very instructive.

37. . . .	N–K5
38. N–Q3	P–N4
39. PxP	PxP
40. R–B8	P–N5

40. . . . R–R7 would be satisfactorily met by 41. P–KN4 PxP 42. N–K5ch K–K2 43. NxP R–R8 44. R–B4 N–Q3 45. R–B7ch, etc. Black now seriously threatens 41. . . . R–R7 and thus prompts White's reply.

41. N–B5	NxN
42. RxN	R–R8
43. R–B2	. . .

If he places the Rook in front of the pawn with 43. R–N5, then after . . . R–QN8 44. P–N4 R–N7ch White could make no progress.

| 43. . . . | K–K2 |

14   *The Art of Positional Play*

44. P–K4!	R–R8
45. K–Q3	K–Q3
46. PxP	PxP
47. K–B4	K–B3
48. K–Q4ch	K–Q3

Obviously Black has to keep his King where it can guard his remaining pawns. It is interesting to see how Smyslov finally compels Black's monarch to abandon them.

| 49. P–N3 | R–K8 |
| 50. K–B4 | K–B3 |

If 50. . . . R–K1 (50. . . . R–K5ch 51. K–N5 R–K1 52. R–Q2ch K–B2 53. K–B5, and if 53. . . . R–K4ch 54. R–Q5) 51. R–R2! followed by R–R6ch.

| 51. K–Q3ch | K–Q4 |

If 51. . . . K–N4 52. R–K2 R–Q8ch 53. K–K3 followed by K–B4. Note how White alternates threats to advance his passed pawn with threats to attack Black's pawns. Sooner or later, Black will be unable to defend against everything.

| 52. P–N4 | R–QN8 |
| 53. K–B3 | K–B3 |

Unavailing is 53. . . . R–KB8 54. P–N5 K–B4 (54. . . . R–QN8 55. R–N2) 55. K–Q3ch KxP 56. K–K3 and K–B4 and wins.

54. K–Q4ch	K–Q3
55. K–B4	K–B3
56. R–K2	R–B8ch
57. K–Q4	K–Q3
58. R–N2	R–QR8
59. P–N5	R–R5ch
60. K–K3	K–B2
61. P–N6ch	K–N2
62. R–N5	R–K5ch

62. . . . P–B5ch fails: 63. PxP R–R6ch 64. K–K4 R–R7 65. K–B5.

63. K–Q3	R–K1
64. RxP	KxP
65. R–N5	R–Q1ch

66. K–K4	R–K1ch
67. K–B5	R–B1ch
68. K–K6	. . .

To cut off the King.

68. . . .	RxP
69. RxP	R–K7ch
70. K–B5	K–B4
71. R–K4	R–B7ch
72. R–B4	R–Q7

If 72. . . . R–KN7 73. P–N4 K–Q3 74. K–B6 K–Q2 75. R–K4
R–B7ch 76. K–N6 R–B1 77. K–N7 followed by P–N5, etc.

73. P–N4	R–Q4ch
74. K–N6	Resigns

The pawn cannot be stopped. A very instructive endgame.

Game 3

Bad Pawns, Bad Pieces

Black incurs a couple of weak, isolated pawns as the result of an
opening novelty by Tal. Such a purely defensive task is surely not
what Black hopes for in the Sicilian Defense; but if Najdorf had
chosen to avoid those weak pawns, he would have had a lifeless,
passive position, and for Najdorf that is intolerable.

USSR vs. the Rest of the World
Belgrade, 1970

SICILIAN DEFENSE

M. Tal	M. Najdorf
1. P–K4	P–QB4
2. N–KB3	N–QB3

Not the Najdorf Variation! That line has developed to such an
extent that it bears little resemblance to the system popularized
by Najdorf so long ago. Perhaps it no longer suits his style?!

3. P–Q4	PxP
4. NxP	P–K3
5. N–QB3	Q–B2
6. P–KN3	P–QR3
7. B–N2	N–B3
8. 0–0	P–Q3
9. R–K1	B–Q2
10. NxN!	PxN

If 10. . . . . BxN 11. N–Q5 Q–Q1 12. B–N5 with pressure. The weakening of Black's Queenside pawns has begun.

| 11. N–R4 | P–K4 |
| 12. P–QB4 | . . . |

White's plan is clear: to further weaken Black's pawn structure on the Queenside and, via the open files, to attack the pawns directly.

| 12. . . . | B–K2 |

To be considered is 12. . . . . P–B4 13. B–N5 B–K2 14. N–B3 B–B3 with a scarcely perceptible advantage for White, but not a hint of play for Black.

| 13. P–B5! | 0–0 |

Since 13. . . . . PxP does not win a pawn, that move would simply lose tempo.

| 14. PxP | BxP |

Black's two weak pawns, particularly the QBP, stifle his pieces. No great subtlety is needed here: the pawns are clearly vulnerable targets for which Black has no discernible compensation. However, Najdorf is always dangerous, and so Tal sees no reason to complicate matters.

| 15. B–N5 | B–K2 |

15. . . . . B–QN5 can be satisfactorily met by 16. R–K3 N–N5 17. R–Q3 B–K3 18. P–KR3, etc.

16. Q–B2	P–R3
17. B–K3	QR–N1
18. QR–B1	KR–Q1
19. P–KR3	N–R2
20. B–B5	B–K1

Because he has to tend his weak pawns, Black cannot become active. Little by little, White's pieces occupy better positions and Black's become more passive.

21. KR–Q1	RxRch
22. RxR	N–N4
23. BxB	QxB
24. N–B5	N–K3
25. NxN	. . .

Better than 25. NxP R–N3 26. B–B1 N–Q5 with sufficient play for the pawn.

25. . . .	QxN
26. P–N3	Q–K2
27. Q–B3	. . .

Putting pressure on the KP with the intention of following up with B–B1 attacking the QRP. Black's defensive problem is very difficult.

27. . . .	R–N5

Tying the White Bishop to the protection of the KP.

28. P–KR4	. . .

To be in a position to activate the Bishop via KR3 when the opportunity arises.

28. . . .	P–B3
29. R–Q3	. . .

Intending to continue with Q–Q2 and to invade Black's territory with the Rook.

29. . . .	K–R2

Unsatisfactory is 29. . . . P–QB4 on account of 30. R–Q5 P–B5 31. PxP B–B2 32. P–B5! R–N8ch 33. K–R2 BxR 34. PxB, and the two passed pawns would win easily.

30. B–R3	B–N3
31. R–Q7	. . .

Obviously White's pieces are better placed. He has a Rook on the seventh rank, Black's Queen is tied to the defense of the King, and Black's Bishop is a defensive piece only. Meanwhile, Black's weak pawns are about to fall.

31. . . .	Q–B1

32. QxBP	RxKP

If 32. . . . BxP 33. QxRP Q–B4 34. QxP Q–B8ch 35. B–B1 and wins.

33. QxRP	R–K8ch
34. K–R2	P–B4

No relief is offered by 34. . . . B–K5 35. B–N2 BxB 36. KxB Q–N5 37. QxP Q–K5ch 38. P–B3 Q–B7ch 39. K–R3 R–R8ch 40. K–N4 and wins.

35. R–Q6	B–R4

A better try is 35. . . . Q–B2, but after 36. Q–Q3 (threatening P–R5) P–K5 37. Q–Q2, White's task would be easy.

36. Q–Q3	P–K5
37. Q–Q5	B–N5
38. R–Q8	Q–B3
39. Q–N8ch	K–N3
40. Q–K8ch	K–R2
41. BxB	PxB
42. Q–N8ch	K–N3
43. R–B8	Q–K2 and Resigns

After 44. R–K8, Black's position is hopeless.

Game 4

Unsupported Pawn Chain

In many variations of the King's Indian Defense (and in other openings), White strives for space-gaining maneuvers on the

Queenside, usually including P–QN4, because his advanced QBP and QP have already given him an edge in space on that wing. Black's typical reaction is to try for counterplay by a pawn advance on the Kingside, often including . . . P–KB4. In addition to his strategic goal of weakening White's QP (on Q5) by attacking the KP, he hopes to create complications and to distract White from his grand design. However, Black's pawn advances are bound up with certain risks because he exposes his King. If his pawns should advance too far or become weakened, his King would be in direct danger.

White's play must be flexible and undogmatic. If he stubbornly insists on his Queenside advance and underestimates Black's threats, his own King could be in trouble.

The present game illustrates the risks for Black. As soon as Black plays . . . P–KB4, White abandons the Queenside and takes aim at Black's KBP, which supports the imposing KP. In his writings Nimzovich emphasized the importance of attacking the base of a pawn chain. That strategy works here almost to perfection.

Interzonal Tournament

Sousse, 1967

KING'S INDIAN DEFENSE

S. Reshevsky	H. Mecking
1. P–Q4	N–KB3
2. P–QB4	P–Q3
3. N–QB3	P–KN3
4. P–K4	B–N2
5. B–K2	0–0
6. N–B3	P–K4
7. 0–0	QN–Q2
8. R–K1	P–QR4
9. B–B1	P–B3
10. R–N1	R–K1
11. P–Q5	. . .

To be considered is 11. P–QN3. If then 11. . . . Q–N3 12. P–Q5 and Black's Queen would be misplaced. If 11. . . . PxP 12. NxP N–B4 13. P–B3 with a solid center.

11. . . .	**N–B4**
12. P–QN3	. . .

Planning to continue with 13. P–QR3 and 14. P–QN4. If White plays 12. P–QR3 instead of the text, Black can foil White's plan by playing 12. . . . P–R5 13. B–K3 KN–Q2.

12. . . .	**N–R3**
13. P–QR3	**P–B4**

With his last two moves Black has made White's Queenside advance more difficult; in fact, White never does play P–QN4.

14. B–Q2	**R–B1**

Now he prepares counterplay via . . . P–KB4 with the support of this Rook, which also allows the King Knight to get out of the way to K1.

15. P–N3	. . .

Better is 15. P–R3, preventing Black's next move.

15. . . .	**B–N5!**

Forcing White to play P–R3 (to release the pin) and foiling White's plan, which was, after . . . P–B4, to exchange pawns and follow with B–R3 and N–KR4, exerting pressure on the KBP.

16. P–R3	**B–Q2**
17. B–N5	. . .

Since there is no reasonable way to prevent Black from carrying out his planned . . . P–B4, at least I can provoke a weakness in Black's camp.

17. . . .	**P–R3**

Otherwise Black cannot carry out his plan; for if 17. . . . Q–B1 18. K–R2 N–K1? 19. B–K7.

18. B–K3	**N–K1**
19. Q–Q2	**K–R2**
20. N–KR4	**P–B4**
21. PxP	**PxP**
22. P–B4	. . .

Fixing Black's KBP so that it can be attacked.

22. . . .	**P–K5**

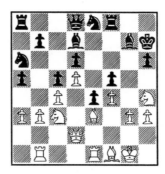

This type of position has arisen in numerous games. Black enjoys temporary control of the center and has a passed pawn, but the latter can become vulnerable, as this game illustrates. White's chances are better.

From Black's standpoint, however, he has forced White to play on the Kingside and to abandon his calm Queenside expansion. Whether or not this is a gain for Black remains to be seen, but at least he is in an active fight.

23. B–B2		N–B3
24. N–Q1		. . .

The Knight is headed for K3, where it will bear down on the KBP and blockade the passed pawn.

24. . . .		N–KN1
25. N–K3		Q–B3
26. B–N2		QR–K1

All of Black's pieces, except his Queen Knight, are well posted. As has been known for a century, even one badly placed piece (other things being equal) can be a serious disadvantage.

27. Q–K2		. . .

I discarded 27. QxP on account of 27. . . . R–R1 28. Q–Q2 N–B2 which offers Black counterplay; for if 29. P–R4 N–R3, heading for QN5, and if 29. R–R1 P–N4.

27. . . .		N–K2
28. P–KN4		. . .

An indirect strike against the KP, and the only way White can hope to make progress. In fact, this move is thematic proof of the instability of Black's KB4–K5 pawn chain: the concept of attacking the base of a pawn chain (in this case, the KBP) is well-known theory.

28. . . .   **K–N1**

Mecking is in serious time pressure. Better is 28. . . . PxP, but after 29. NxP QxP 30. BxPch K–N1 31. N–N2 Q–B2 32. B–N3, Black's problems would not be solved.

29. **B–N3**   **PxP**
30. **PxP**   . . .

Black's once-proud KP is no longer so secure.

30. . . .   **N–N3**
31. **N/4–B5**   . . .

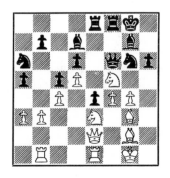

31. . . .   **B–R1?**

A blunder, losing a pawn. Correct is 31. . . . N–B2.

32. **NxPch**   **K–R2**
33. **N/6–B5**   . . .

33. P–N5 fails because of 33. . . . NxP 34. PxQ (if 34. BxN QxB 35. Q–R5 K–N2) 34. . . . NxQch 35. RxN KxN 36. BxQP RxP with equality.

33. . . .   **K–N1**
34. **N–R6ch**   **K–R2**
35. **R–KB1**   . . .

This move appears sound, since it threatens P–N5 followed by Q–R5. I played too quickly, however, having underestimated my young adversary's ingenuity. 35. N/6–B5 K–N1 36. P–N5 QxN 37. NxQ BxN did not appeal to me since Black's KP would become too powerful.

| 35. . . . | Q–B6! |

A fine move, bidding for counterplay. If 36. P–N5 B–Q5 37. QR–K1 Q–Q6 38. P–B5 N–K4 with complications.

| 36. N/3–B5 | B–N2 |

So that if 37. NxB KxN/2, which leaves two White pieces hanging.

| 37. QR–B1 | QxNP |

Black has little play after 37. . . . Q–Q6 38. QxQ PxQ 39. NxB KxN 40. P–N5.

38. R–N1	QxRP
39. RxP	N–N1
40. NxB	QxB
41. NxR	NxP

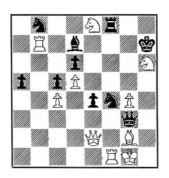

Despite being a Rook to the good, White still has problems. The game was adjourned here. Many pieces are en prise!

| 42. RxN/4 | . . . |

Forced if White wishes to play for a win, for if 42. QxPch KxN with the strong threat of 43. . . . N–R6ch.

| 42. . . . | QxR |
| 43. NxP | . . . |

After 43. QxPch QxQ 44. BxQch KxN 45. NxP K–N4 with good drawing prospects.

| 43. . . . | KxN |

Unpromising for Black is 43. . . . Q–QB8ch 44. B–B1 KxN 45. NxP Q–B5 46. P–N5ch K–N3 47. R–N6ch K–N2 48. Q–N2ch and wins. Also, after 43. . . . QxN (Q3) 44. N–B5 Q–B5 45. BxP Black's position would be untenable.

44. NxP	**BxP**
45. R–N6ch	**K–R4**

Forced, for if 45. . . . K–N2 46. Q–N2ch K–N1 47. R–N6ch, etc.; if 45. . . . K–R2 46. N–B6ch! RxN 47. Q–K7ch R–B2 (if 47. . . . K–N3 48. B–K4ch K–N4 49. Q–N7ch) 48. B–K4ch K–R1 (if 48. . . . K–N1 49. R–N6ch K–R1 50. Q–R4ch R–R2 51. Q–Q8ch, etc.) 49. Q–Q8ch R–B1 50. Q–R4ch followed by mate.

46. Q–K1	**N–Q2!**

The best try. A courageous and fearless young man!

47. N–N3ch	**K–R5**
48. Q–K7ch	. . .

If 48. N–K2ch Q–B7ch!, leading to equality.

48. . . .	**R–B3**

Not 48. . . . N–B3 49. QxR KxN 50. R–N3ch, etc.

49. Q–R7ch	. . .

After 49. N–K4, Black has a perpetual check with 49. . . . Q–QB8ch.

49. . . .	**K–N4**
50. N–K4ch	**QxN**
51. QxQ	**RxR**
52. Q–K3ch	**K–N3**
53. B–R3	. . .

Better is 53. B–K4ch K–B2 (53. . . . B–B4 54. BxBch KxB 55. Q–R3ch) 54. Q–B4ch N–B3 55. Q–B2, winning the important QBP.

53. . . .	**BxB**
54. QxB	**N–K4**
55. Q–K3	**K–B4**
56. QxP	**R–N8ch**
57. K–N2	**R–N7ch**
58. K–B1	**P–R5**
59. P–Q6	**R–Q7**
60. K–K1	. . .

If 60. Q–B8ch K–B5 61. P–B5 N–B6, and the threat of . . .

N–R7ch would have given me some trouble. The text avoids the perpetual check.

60. . . .	R–Q5
61. K–K2	K–K5
62. Q–R3	R–Q6

If 62. . . . RxBP 63. P–Q7 R–Q5 64. Q–K3ch, followed by QxR. If 62. . . . NxP 63. Q–B3ch K–K4 64. P–Q7 RxP 65. Q–N3ch, winning a piece on the next check.

63. Q–N4	. . .

63. QxRch NxQ 64. P–Q7 doesn't win because of 64. . . . N–B5ch 65. K–Q2 N–K3 66. P–B5 K–Q4 (or 66. K–B3 K–K4).

63. . . .	P–R6
64. P–B5ch	K–B4
65. Q–QR4	K–K3
66. Q–R8!	. . .

The winning move, which threatens 67. P–B6 KxP 68. Q–N8ch.

66. . . .	R–QN6

If 66. . . . R–Q4 67. Q–N8ch. If 66. . . . K–Q2 67. P–B6ch.

67. Q–N8ch	N–B2
68. Q–N6ch	K–K4
69. QxN	P–R7
70. Q–QR7	R–KR6
71. P–Q7	Resigns

Chapter 2

Passed Pawns

The great chess theorist Aron Nimzovich illustrated the power of the passed pawn by this brilliant metaphor: "The passed pawn is a criminal, who should be kept under lock and key." He wrote also of the passed pawn's "lust to expand."

Why should a mere pawn—the unit lowest in rank and most limited in mobility—inspire such figurative language in Nimzovich and (as we saw in the last chapter) Philidor? The reason is this: a Queen will always be a Queen, a Rook never more than a Rook, a Bishop and a Knight always the same, but a pawn alone has the power of promotion. This is a crucial property, for most won games are decided by a pawn that cannot be prevented from becoming a Queen.

A single weak pawn can lead to loss of the game (as we saw in Chapter 1), and so can a single pawn be strong enough to win. So potent is a passed pawn that entire opening systems are strongly influenced by the idea of creating a majority of pawns on one wing; from this majority a passed pawn will eventually emerge, if all goes well. For example, in the Exchange Variation of the Caro-Kann Defense (1. P–K4 P–QB3 2. P–Q4 P–Q4 3. PxP PxP) White has already obtained a pawn majority of four against three on the Queenside. In the Exchange Variation of the Ruy Lopez (1. P–K4 P–K4 2. N–KB3 N–QB3 3. B–N5 P–QR3 4. BxN QPxB 5. P–Q4 PxP 6. QxP) Black's Queenside pawn majority is crippled due to the doubled pawns, whereas White's Kingside majority is healthy and mobile. In a main line of the Gruenfeld Defense (1. P–Q4 N–KB3 2. P–QB4 P–KN3 3. N–QB3 P–Q4 4. PxP NxP 5. P–K4 NxN 6. PxN), after Black's eventual . . . P–QB4 and . . . PxQP he will have a two-to-one pawn majority on the Queenside.

A pawn majority does not guarantee, however, that a passed pawn will emerge, nor does it promise, even if a passed pawn is created, that it will inevitably be promoted to a Queen. Chess is not so simple. Certain other conditions must be present, the most important and obvious of which is mobility. A pawn that cannot advance is weaker than one that can; a passed pawn that cannot be pushed may as well not be passed. Therefore, the player who has an incipient passed pawn must bend every effort to see that the pawn will be able to advance once it becomes passed.

Game 5 demonstrates the proper technique for converting a pawn majority to a passed pawn. White's error is instructive: his 22nd move actually blocks his own pawn majority and hinders his creation of a passed pawn.

Game 6 is an excellent example of correct counterplay against a passed pawn: another passed pawn. Black's mistake near the end is also instructive: he fails to break White's blockade when he has the chance.

Game 7 illustrates correct blockading strategy. Because he has the means available for a successful blockade White permits Black to obtain a protected passed pawn early in the game; by sacrificing that small battle White wins the war, for the effort Black expends on his passed pawn is too costly.

Not all passed pawns are destined for Queenhood, but the very existence of that long-range possibility casts a special light over the board. In game 8, for example, White's passed pawn cannot be maintained, but it serves nobly while it lives.

Because pawns can only advance along a file (except when capturing), a single passed pawn is best supported by a piece that thrives on open files, the Rook. It cannot be said too often: Rooks Belong Behind Passed Pawns. See game 9.

If one passed pawn is strong, several must be overwhelming.

Game 10 illustrates this perfectly: connected passed pawns, when they cannot be stopped, are worth more than several pieces.

Game 5

Converting a Pawn Majority

The opening of this game gives each side a local pawn majority. Conversion of a majority to a living, breathing passed pawn is one of the techniques that must be mastered if regular success is desired; but this is not easy to do. A close study of Korchnoi's technique in this game, and a full understanding of Ivkov's error, are valuable to the student.

This game also illustrates the difference between a pawn majority on the Queenside and one on the Kingside. A passed pawn on the Queenside—often called an outside passed pawn— is not in direct danger of blockade or attack by the enemy King. Passed pawns in the center or the Kingside do not have this advantage (but other factors are usually involved). Furthermore, a typical strategy when one player has or will soon have an outside passed pawn is to combine threats to advance the pawn with threats against the King; usually, both threats cannot be satisfactorily met.

In this game note especially how Korchnoi advances his Queenside majority while keeping White's King busy on the other side.

Wijk aan Zee, 1968

QUEEN'S INDIAN DEFENSE

B. Ivkov	V. Korchnoi
1. P–Q4	P–K3
2. P–QB4	. . .

What, no French Defense? Ivkov, who often uses that opening, is evidently not anxious for a fight, particularly in one of Korchnoi's favorite defenses, and prefers a quiet game leading, he hopes, to a peaceful draw. Such an attitude is often costly.

2. . . .	N–KB3
3. N–KB3	P–QN3
4. P–KN3	B–N2
5. B–N2	B–K2
6. 0–0	0–0
7. N–B3	N–K5
8. Q–B2	NxN
9. QxN	Q–B1

The text is as satisfactory as 9. . . . P–KB4 10. P–N3 B–KB3 11. B–N2 P–Q3 or 11. . . . N–B3.

10. R–Q1	P–Q4
11. PxP	BxP

Better than 11. . . . PxP when the QB becomes inactive. The text also creates an imbalance in the pawn structure which offers both players scope for imaginative play in search of winning chances. That is precisely Korchnoi's forte.

12. N–K5	. . .

More natural is 12. B–B4 P–QB4 13. QR–B1.

12. . . .	BxB
13. KxB	Q–N2ch

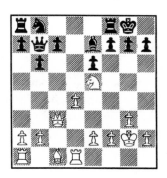

Black has a potential Queenside pawn majority; if he can somehow remove White's QP his majority will become mobile.

14. Q–B3	. . .

White's efforts to simplify will cause him trouble. Wiser is 14. K–N1, and if 14. . . . P–QB4 15. PxP BxP 16. P–QN4 B–K2 17.

B–N2 B–B3 18. QR–B1. In this line, if 17. . . . R–B1? 18. N–B6!
B–B3 19. N–K7ch and wins.

14. . . .	**QxQch**
15. KxQ	**P–KB3**
16. N–Q3	**N–B3**
17. N–B4?	**. . .**

This allows Black to obtain a majority of pawns on the Queenside which will advance faster than White's majority on the
Kingside. Correct, therefore, is 17. B–K3, and if 17. . . . P–K4
18. PxP PxPch 19. K–K4, with advantage because of White's
favorable King position and Black's isolated KP. If 17. . . . KR–Q1
18. QR–B1 NxPch 19. BxN RxB 20. RxP, with advantage. Black's
best, therefore, would be 17. . . . B–Q3 18. QR–B1 N–K2 19.
N–B4 K–B2 (19. . . . P–K4 20. N–K6 KR–B1 21. PxP BxP 22.
R–Q7) 20. P–Q5 with some initiative, for if 20. . . . BxN 21.
PxPch, etc., and if 20. . . . P–K4 21. N–K6 KR–B1 22. NxBP BxN
23. P–Q6.

17. . . .	**P–K4**
18. N–K6	**NxPch**

Thus White's QP leaves the board and Black's Queenside pawn
majority becomes a crucial factor.

19. NxN	**PxN**
20. RxP	**KR–Q1**
21. RxRch	**RxR**
22. B–K3?	**. . .**

In order to counteract Black's pawn majority on the Queenside,
White has to mobilize his own majority. The text blocks the KP,
slowing down the achievement of this objective. Imperative is 22.
B–B4 P–QB4 23. P–K4 K–B2 24. K–K2, followed by B–K3 and
P–B4.

22. . . .	**K–B2**
23. P–QR4	**. . .**

This only expedites Black's objective of establishing a passed
pawn. More prudent is 23. R–QB1 P–QB4 24. R–B3 (intending
to fight for control of the Q-file with R–Q3), and if 24. . . . R–Q8
25. R–R3 P–QR4 26. R–N3 R–Q3 or 26. . . . B–Q1 27. R–Q3.

Black's control of the Q-file keeps the White King from reaching the Queenside, where it is needed to aid in the blockade of Black's potential passed pawn.

In general, avoid moving pawns on the side of your opponent's pawn majority, for this can hasten pawn exchanges and simplify the creation of a passed pawn.

23. . . .	K–K3
24. P–KN4	R–Q4
25. R–QB1	P–QB4
26. P–N3	B–Q3
27. P–R3	P–N3
28. K–K4	B–K4
29. R–B4	. . .

Preferable is 29. P–B4 P–B4ch 30. PxPch PxPch 31. K–B3 B–B3 32. P–R5. Or 29. . . . B–Q5 30. P–B5ch PxPch 31. PxPch RxP 32. BxB PxB 33. R–B6ch K–Q2 34. KxR KxR 35. KxP K–Q4 36. K–B5 with equality.

29. . . .	R–Q8
30. R–B1	P–B4ch
31. PxPch	PxPch
32. K–B3	RxR
33. BxR	K–Q4

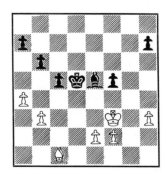

White's trouble stems from his inability to bring his King to the Queenside where it could stop the advance of Black's potential passed pawn. For instance, 34. K–K3 P–B5 35. P–N4 (if 35. PxP KxP, and Black gets two connected passed pawns by winning the QRP, whereas White is without any rapid counterplay with his center pawns) 35. . . . P–B5ch 36. K–Q2 (36. K–B3 P–B6, and the Black King walks in unhindered) 36. . . . B–Q5 37. P–K3 PxP 38. PxP B–K4, and Black has little difficulty in making progress.

> **34. B–N5**   . . .

Unplayable is 34. B–B4 (in order to continue, after 34. . . . B–B3, with 35. B–N8 P–QR3 36. K–B4 K–K3 37. P–K4 PxP 38. KxP P–N4 39. PxP PxP 40. P–B4 with an easy draw) because of 34. . . . P–QR3 35. BxB KxB 36. K–K3 P–N4 37. PxP (37. P–R5 P–B5ch 38. K–Q3 K–B4 and wins) 37. . . . PxP 38. K–Q3 K–B5 39. K–B3 K–N4–R5, etc.

> **34. . . .**   **P–QR3**

The immediate 34. . . . P–QB5 does not suffice for the win on account of 35. PxPch KxP 36. P-K4 PxPch 37. KxP B–Q3 38. P–B4, and this pawn, supported by the King and Bishop, will travel fast.

> **35. B–Q8**   **P–N4**
> **36. PxP**   **PxP**
> **37. B–R5**   **P–QB5**
> **38. PxPch**   **KxP**

Not 38. . . . PxP 39. K–K3 P–B5ch 40. K–Q2, holding the position easily.

> **39. P–K4**   . . .

A little too late. Futile is 39. K–K3 because of 39. . . . B–B6 followed by . . . P–N5, etc.

> **39. . . .**   **PxPch**
> **40. KxP**   **B–B6**

Black has a won position because his passed pawn, aided by the King and Bishop, cannot be stopped from queening—White's King is too far away.

> **41. B–Q8**   **P–N5**
> **42. B–K7**   **P–N6**
> **43. B–R3**   **B–N2**

44. P–B4	K–B6
45. P–B5	. . .

The position is untenable. The only other try is 45. K–Q5, but it would also fail: 45. . . . K–B7 46. K–B4 B–B1 47. B–B1 B–K2 48. P–B5 B–B3 with White in zugzwang.

45. . . .	K–B7
46. K–Q5	B–B1
47. BxB	P–N7
48. K–K6	P–N8=Q
49. P–B6	Q–N6ch
50. K–K7	QxP

And now Black's last pawn, untouched since the game began, begins to play a surprising backstage role. Without it Black cannot win!

51. P–B7	Q–R6ch
52. K–K8	Q–R5ch
53. K–K7	Q–N5ch
54. K–K8	Q–N1ch
55. K–K7	Q–K4ch
56. K–Q7	Q–B3
57. K–K8	Q–B3ch
58. K–K7	Q–KN3
59. K–K8	. . .

For if 59. B–R6 QxB 60. P–B8=Q QxQch 61. KxQ P–R4, etc. The purpose of Black's 50. . . . QxP now becomes clear: his is a passed pawn!

59. . . .	K–N6
60. B–K7	. . .

If 60. B–B5 Q–B3ch followed by . . . QxB.

60. . . .	K–B5

Resigns

If 61. K–B8 K–Q4–K3. If 61. B–R3 Q–B3ch 62. K–K7 Q–N2ch 63. K–B6 (63. K–K8 Q–R1ch followed by . . . QxB) 63. . . . Q–R3ch followed by . . . QxB.

A fine performance by Korchnoi, displaying his excellent endgame technique.

Game 6

Passed Pawn versus Passed Pawn

This game, between two of the strongest players of our time, demonstrates perfectly—up to a point—correct play and counterplay involving passed pawns. White obtains a strong passed pawn in the center, but Black, undismayed, properly goes about mobilizing his Queenside majority while blockading White's pawn. Portisch maintains the initiative and brings his King to an advanced, active position; nevertheless, Spassky is able to make progress with his majority until, probably in time pressure, he errs in failing to break White's blockade at a critical moment.

Match: USSR vs. Hungary

Budapest, 1968

QUEEN'S GAMBIT DECLINED

L. Portisch	B. Spassky
1. P–Q4	P–Q4
2. P–QB4	P–K3
3. N–QB3	B–K2
4. N–B3	N–KB3
5. B–N5	0–0
6. P–K3	P–KR3
7. B–R4	P–QN3

Both Spassky and Petrosian prefer this continuation in this opening, convinced that Black can obtain full equality. Tournament experience has confirmed this opinion.

8. R–B1	B–N2
9. B–Q3	PxP

Unsatisfactory is 9. . . . QN–Q2 because of 10. PxP which forces 10. . . . PxP (if 10. . . . NxP 11. NxN BxN 12. BxB QxB 13. RxP BxP 14. Q–R4 and wins) 11. 0–0 with the better game because of the restricted mobility of Black's QB.

The exchange of pawns gives White a central pawn majority,

which Portisch is not long in exploiting to create a passed pawn. The exchange has also provided Black with a pawn majority on the Queenside. Because White has the initiative, he is the first to obtain a passed pawn.

10. BxP	**QN–Q2**
11. 0–0	**P–B4**
12. Q–K2	**N–K5**
13. NxN	**BxN**

13. . . . BxB is not attractive; White could continue with 14. N–Q6 B–QB3 (if 14. . . . BxN 15. QxB with the potential threat of NxP) 15. KR–Q1 with advantage.

14. B–KN3 . . .

Better than 14. BxB QxB, simplifying Black's defensive task.

14. . . . **P–QR4**

This curious-looking move is necessary. Black is trying to develop his Queen, and the logical square is QN2. This cannot be accomplished without the text move, for if 14. . . . Q–B1 15. KR–Q1 Q–N2 16. B–R6 Q–B3 17. B–N5 Q–N2 18. BxN QxB 19. PxP, etc. The text move prevents B–R6.

15. KR–Q1	**Q–B1**
16. B–N5	**R–Q1**
17. N–K1	**Q–N2**
18. P–B3	**B–QB3**

After 18. . . . B–R2, White could also continue 19. P–K4 and obtain a passed QP. For if 19. . . . N–B3 20. B–B2 PxP 21. B–B6.

19. BxB	**QxB**
20. P–K4	**B–N4**

White is assured of a passed pawn; for if Black tries to prevent it by 20. . . . N–B3, then 21. P–Q5 PxP 22. PxP NxP 23. RxN QxR 24. QxB Q–Q7 (if 24. . . . R–K1 25. Q–Q6) 25. R–B2 and wins.

21. R–B2	**P–R5**
22. P–B4	**B–K2**
23. P–Q5	. . .

From here on, only White has winning prospects because of his passed QP, which can be protected by the Rooks.

23. . . .	**PxP**
24. PxP	**Q–B3**

25. N–B3		**Q–B4**

Better than 25. . . . B–Q3 (in an attempt to block the pawn)
26. N–K5 Q–B4 27. N–B4 B–B1 28. P–Q6 with great advantage.

26. P–Q6		**B–B3**
27. R/2–Q2		**Q–K3**
28. QxQ		. . .

White is compelled to exchange Queens, for if 28. N–K5,
Black could continue safely with 28. . . . QxRP, and if 29. Q–N5
or 29. Q–N4 BxN 30. PxB Q–K3, and White has insufficient
compensation for the sacrificed pawn.

28. . . .		**PxQ**
29. R–K2		**K–B2**
30. B–R4!		. . .

The object of this move is to induce Black to exchange Bishops,
in which case White would be in a position to post his Knight
at K5. If Black then exchanges Knights, White's passed pawn
would be protected by a pawn, which is extremely advantageous.

30. . . .		**R–K1**

Spassky refuses to oblige. If White exchanges Bishops now,
Black would recapture with the pawn, preventing N–K5.

31. P–KN4		**P–R6**
32. P–N3		**P–QN4**
33. B–N3		. . .

White changes his plan. Interesting is 33. P–N5 PxP 34. PxP
B–B6 35. P–N6ch KxP 36. B–K7 B–B3 37. RxP K–B2 38. R/1–K1
with the threat of BxB followed by R–K7ch.

33. . . .		**QR–B1**

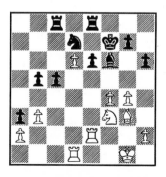

Black is now poised to create a passed pawn of his own. White has to come up with diversionary action quickly. This is a crucial stage of the game.

34. R/1–K1	**B–B6**

To be considered is 34. . . . P–B5 35. PxP RxP (35. . . . PxP 36. N–K5ch BxN 37. PxB with advantage because Black's passed pawn and his QRP would be subject to attack. White would also soon have the benefit of controlling the KB-file.) 36. P–B5 (36. P–N5 B–B6 37. P–N6ch K–B3 38. B–R4ch K–B4 with complications) 36. . . . P–K4 with even chances.

35. R–KB1	**R–B3**
36. N–K5ch	**BxN**

After 36. . . . NxN 37. PxNch K–N1 38. B–R4 P–N4 39. B–K1 B–Q5ch (after the exchange of Bishops, White's passed pawn would be decisive) 40. K–N2 with the threats of B–R5 and R–B6.

37. PxBch	**K–N1**
38. R/2–KB2	**R–KB1**

38. . . . P–B5 would be met by 39. PxP PxP 40. R–B7 R–Q1 41. R–K7 P–B6 42. RxP P–B7 43. R–B1 and wins.

39. RxRch	**NxR**
40. R–B1	**N–Q2**
41. K–B2	**K–B2**
42. K–K3	**N–N3**
43. K–K4	**N–Q4**
44. B–K1	**K–K1**
45. B–Q2	**R–B1**

Black bides his time. He dares not advance his QBP because it would easily become subject to attack by the King.

46. P–R4	**K–Q2**
47. P–R5	**K–K1**
48. R–B2	**K–Q2**
49. B–B1	**P–B5**

Insufficient is 49. . . . P–N5 because of 50. K–Q3 K–K1 51. K–B4 K–Q2 52. R–B2 K–K1 53. B–Q2 N–N3ch 54. K–N5 N–Q4 (if 54. . . . N–Q2 55. B–B4 R–N1ch 56. K–B6 R–B1ch 57. K–N7 R–N1ch 58. K–B7 R–R1 59. P–N5 PxP 60. BxP followed by B–B4 and R–KN2, etc. If 60. . . . NxP 61. R–K2 and wins.) 55. R–B3, and Black would find himself in zugswang.

50. BxQRP	R–KB1
51. K–Q4	. . .

If 51. PxP R–B5ch 52. K–Q3 PxPch 53. K–Q2 (53. RxP R–B6ch winning the Bishop) 53. . . . P–B6ch, with counterplay.

51. . . .	P–B6
52. K–B5	P–N5
53. B–B1	R–B8
54. P–R3	. . .

54. . . .	R–K8??

Spassky has been defending himself exceptionally well, but here he throws away the draw. Perhaps he was pressed for time just before the time control. Black could draw as follows: 54. . . . PxP 55. BxQRP R–QN8! 56. P–N4 (if 56. R–B2 RxP 57. R–B7ch K–Q1 58. B–B1 R–N8 59. K–B6 N–N5ch, etc.; if 59. P–Q7 K–B2) 56. . . . R–N6 57. R–QR2 P–B7 58. B–B1 R–N8 59. RxP NxP 60. R–B3 N–R7, etc.

55. R–B2	RxB
56. R–B7ch	K–K1
57. P–Q7ch	KxR

Forced, for if 57. . . . K–Q1 58. K–Q6 followed by mate.

58. P–Q8=Q	PxP

Or 58. . . . P–B7 59. P–N5 (threatening P–N6 mate) PxP 60. QxP R–QR8 61. Q–N6ch K–B1 62. QxBP PxP 63. K–Q6 and wins.

59. P–N5	PxP
60. QxP	R–KR8
61. Q–N6ch	K–B1
62. QxP	N–K2

62. . . . P–B7 would be met by 63. Q–B5ch followed by QxP, and 62. . . . P–R7 is also unsatisfactory because of 63. Q–B8ch K–K2 64. Q–N7ch K–B1 65. P–K6 K–N1 (if 65. . . . R–KB8 66. Q–B8ch K–K2 67. Q–Q7ch K–B1 68. Q–Q8 mate) 66. Q–R8ch followed by QxP. The Queen is just too powerful.

| 63. Q–QR6 | RxP |

63. . . . P–B7 64. Q–R8ch followed by QxR.

64. K–Q6	N–B4ch
65. K–Q7	P–N3
66. QxNP	P–B7
67. P–K6	Resigns

Mate is unavoidable. A very interesting game, replete with tactical maneuvers.

Game 7

Blockade versus Breakthrough

Considering the well-known potential of a passed pawn, why does White start an action on the Queenside that practically forces Black to create a passed QBP? The reason is this: White recognizes that he has the resources to maintain a virtually permanent blockade on QB3, and since the rest of the Queenside is locked, Black's single means of obtaining counterplay is impeded. A passed pawn that cannot advance is not dangerous. In the meantime, White prepares a breakthrough in the center and creates a passed pawn which Black, deficient in maneuvering space—a defect inherent in many systems of the King's Indian type (which includes the Benoni)—lacks the resources to blockade.

Inaccurate play on my part at a later stage prolongs the game unnecessarily. But from a strategic standpoint White's method of handling the opening is quite effective. After the game, in fact, my opponent had the idea that the Benoni Defense was

refuted! This was not a realistic assessment, of course: Black
could have played better.

Buenos Aires, 1971

BENONI DEFENSE

S. Reshevsky	R. Garcia
1. P–Q4	N–KB3
2. P–QB4	P–B4
3. P–Q5	P–Q3
4. N–QB3	P–KN3
5. P–K4	B–N2
6. N–B3	0–0
7. B–K2	P–K3
8. 0–0	PxP
9. BPxP	. . .

After 9. KPxP R–K1 10. B–Q3 (otherwise . . . N–K5, and Black
has no problems) 10. . . . N–R4, to be followed by . . . N–Q2–K4
with equality. Black now has a potent Queenside majority, but
he also has to prevent White's P–K5 breakthrough, which will
give White a passed QP as well as possibilities for attack against
the Black King.

9. . . .	R–K1

An alternative is 9. . . . B–N5 10. P–KR3 BxN 11. BxB P–QR3
12. P–QR4 QN–Q2 followed by an eventual . . . Q–B2 and . . .
P–QB5.

10. N–Q2	N–R3
11. P–B3	N–B2
12. P–QR4	P–N3
13. N–B4	B–QR3
14. B–N5	. . .

14. B–B4 can be met by 14. . . . N–R4 15. B–Q2 (if 15. B–K3
P–B4, and if 15. BxP? QBxN 16. BxN BxB 17. BxQ BxQ, winding
up a piece ahead) 15. . . . P–B4 16. PxP Q–R5 with complications.

14. . . .	P–R3?

This permits White to gain a valuable tempo. Wiser is 14. . . . BxN, intending eventually to effect . . . P–QN4.

15. B–K3	BxN
16. BxB	P–R3
17. Q–Q2	K–R2

Black's King move contributes nothing to his overall plan, whereas White's Queen move protects the Queen Knight, a perfect blockading piece on QB3. The fact that the Knight is protected also facilitates White's important advance P–QN4, which is a step toward immobilizing Black's Queenside.

18. QR–N1	Q–Q2
19. P–QN4	. . .

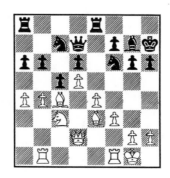

19. . . .   P–QN4

If White's Queen were now at Q1 where it would not protect the Queen Knight, Black would have the strong reply 19. . . . N–KN5, attacking the Queen Bishop and the Queen Knight.

20. B–K2   . . .

Better than 20. B–R2 BPxP 21. RxP P–QR4 22. R–N1 (22. RxP? NxR 23. NxN or 23. PxN is speculative) 22. . . . P–N5 with a fair position.

20. . . .   P–B5

Inadvisable, of course, is 20. . . . BPxP 21. RxP P–QR4? (21. . . . PxP 22. NxP with the strong threat of N–N6; if 21. . . . QR–N1 22. PxP PxP 23. KR–N1 winning the NP) 22. RxP NxR 23. BxN, etc.

21. P–R5!   . . .

Closing the Queenside and depriving Black of any counter-action on that wing. Since Black's passed pawn is solidly blocked, it poses no serious problem for White, who can now turn his attention to the opposite side. From here on, Black is reduced to virtual passivity.

21. . . .	Q–K2
22. B–Q4	. . .

I spent some time considering the advisability of posting a Knight at Q4 but found the maneuver too difficult to carry out effectively. For instance, if 22. B–Q1 N–Q2 (insufficient is 22. . . . Q–K4 23. N–K2 N/2xP 24. B–Q4 and wins) 23. N–K2 N–K4 24. N–Q4 N–Q6 with good play.

22. . . .	Q–B1
23. B–Q1	. . .

In order to activate the Bishop at QB2 and clear the King file for action by the Rooks.

23. . . .	N–Q2
24. BxB	QxB
25. B–B2	R–K2
26. QR–K1	N–K1
27. P–B4	. . .

White clearly cannot make progress unless he advances this pawn, for then with P–K5 he can look to eliminating Black's QP and to opening the KB- or K-file. Black must thwart this plan if he can.

27. . . .	N/1–B3
28. R–K2	K–R1
29. R/1–K1	. . .

Preparing for a breakthrough with P–K5. P–B5 is unwise since it allows Black an excellent post for his Knights at K4.

29. . . .	N–KN1

Faulty is 29. . . . QR–K1 on account of 30. P–K5 PxP 31.
P–Q6 R–K3 32. P–B5 PxP 33. BxP winning the Exchange. The
text move provides the square KB3 for the Rook from K3.

30. P–K5!   . . .

A planned advance which could certainly have been no surprise to my opponent. Timing is important, naturally. White
sacrifices a pawn in order to divert Black's QP, to obtain a passed
pawn, and to acquire new squares for his forces.

30. . . .   PxP
31. P–Q6   . . .

This passed pawn, so far advanced, clears a path for White to
make inroads into Black's position. For instance, it enables White's
Queen to reach the important Q5 square, if so desired, and for
White's Knight to operate more efficiently.

31. . . .   R–K3

31. . . . R/2–K1 is no more promising because of 32. N–Q5
with the menacing threat of N–B7. Now, of course, 32. N–Q5?
is answered by 32. . . . RxP.

32. P–B5!   . . .

The point of White's tactics: he opens the B-file, which en-
hances his chances for successful action.

32. . . .   R–B3
33. PxP   . . .

I discarded 33. N–K4 because of 33. . . . PxP (not 33. . . . RxP
34. N–B5 NxN 35. PxN and wins because if 35. . . . R–B5 36.
RxP, etc.) 34. NxR QxN, and Black could offer some resistance,
although White would eventually win.

33. . . .	PxP
34. N–K4	. . .

34. . . .	R–K1

Black is unable to save the Exchange. If 34. . . . R-B2 35. N–B5
N/1–B3 36. N–K6 Q–R2 37. N–B7 R–R2 38. Q–K3 R–QN2 39.
NxRP, and with the capture of this pawn Black's defense collapses
immediately. If 34. . . . R–B5 35. P–N3 (not 35. N–B5 because of
35. . . . R–Q5) 35. . . . R/5–B1 36. N–B5 and wins.

35. NxR	N/1xN
36. R–K3	R–K3
37. R–KN3?	. . .

A hasty move which gives me difficulty. Correct is 37. R–KR3
N–R4 (if 37. . . . P–N4 38. B–B5 R–K1 39. R/3–K3, and Black
would be in virtual zugzwang) 38. P–N3 with the unpleasant
threat of B–Q1.

37. . . .	N–R4

In time trouble, Garcia misses the correct reply.

38. R–KB3	N/4–B3
39. R–KN3?	. . .

I repeated moves because I wanted to reach the time control,
but I did not see Black's rejoinder.

39. . . .	N–K1!

Winning the once-powerful QP by force. Now, if I expected
to win I would have my work cut out for me.

40. R–Q1	RxP

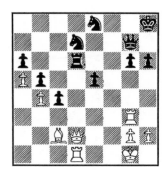

41. Q–K1   . . .

The sealed move. I spent approximately fifteen minutes on the
tempting 41. QxR NxQ 42. RxP Q–K2 43. RxPch K–N1 44.
R–N6ch K–B2 45. R/1xN N–B1, with an unclear position.

        41. . . .   **N–B1**

Better than 41. . . . RxR 42. QxR N–B1 43. Q–Q8 Q–R2ch 44.
K–B1 Q–B2ch 45. R–B3 and wins.

        42. RxR   **NxR**

        43. Q–Q2   . . .

Preventing Q–Q8.

        43. . . .   **N–B2**

        44. Q–Q5!   **P–K5**

Black is compelled to give up this pawn; otherwise his pieces
would become completely immobilized: 44. . . . P–R4 45. B–K4
N–R3 46. Q–Q6, etc.

        45. P–R3   . . .

Superior to 45. BxP Q–R8ch 46. K–B2 N–N4 with some counterplay. Also inadvisable is 45. P–R4 P–R4 46. BxP N–R3–N5 with
some play.

        45. . . .   **Q–R8ch**

        46. K–R2   **K–N2**

        47. BxP   **Q–N7**

        48. R–KB3   . . .

48. Q–N7 can be met by 48. . . . Q–K4 49. B–Q5 N–K3 50. Q–Q7 N–Q1!

        48. . . .   **Q–K4ch**

Forced, for if 48. . . . N–K4 49. R–B1 N/1–Q2 50. Q–K6 (but not 50. BxP N–KB3!) QxP 51. BxP with the threat of R–B7ch!.

        49. K–N1!   **. . .**

Gaining an important tempo. The King is needed on the Queenside.

        49. . . .   **QxQ**

If 49. . . . N–K3? 50. RxNch.

        50. BxQ   **N–Q3**

Preventing B–N7.

        51. K–B2   **N–Q2**

        52. R–K3   **. . .**

Preventing . . . N–K4. Adding to Black's troubles is the fact that his King is out of action.

        52. . . .   **N–KB4**

        53. R–K1   **N–B3**

        54. B–N7   **N–Q5**

        55. BxP   **N–Q4**

        56. B–N7   **. . .**

Black was hoping for 56. R–Q1 P–B6 57. RxN P–B7!.

        56. . . .   **NxP**

        57. P–R6   **Resigns**

For if 57. . . . N–Q6ch 58. K–B1 NxR 59. KxN, etc. If 57. . . . N/N–B3 58. BxN NxB 59. P–R7 and wins. Notice that Black's passed pawn hasn't moved since the 20th move!

Game 8

Passed Pawn in the Middlegame

After one of Geller's rare opening lapses, a White passed pawn suddenly appears in the middle of the board. So profound is the effect of this pawn that both players direct all their efforts either to preserve and advance it (White) or to restrain and capture it (Black). As it turns out, the pawn is finally lost, but not before White has exacted his price for it: a pawn-up endgame.

The endgame is not at all easy, for Geller is one of the toughest competitors in the world. In fact, at the second adjournment the Russian team of analysts proclaimed that Geller could draw! But what his team claimed they could do in the analysis room Geller could not do over the board. This was his only loss in this very strong tournament.

Interzonal Tournament

Sousse, 1967

KING'S INDIAN DEFENSE

S. Reshevsky	Y. Geller
1. P–Q4	N–KB3
2. P–QB4	P–KN3
3. N–QB3	B–N2
4. P–K4	P–Q3
5. B–K2	0–0
6. N–B3	P–K4
7. B–K3	P–B3
8. Q–Q2	QN–Q2
9. 0–0	Q–K2?

Correct is 9. . . . R–K1, threatening to win White's KP after . . . PxP and forcing White either to protect his pawn or play P–Q5, leading to an equal position.

10. B–N5! . . .

This not only protects the KP by pinning the Knight but also constricts the mobility of Black's forces. After 9. . . . R–K1, 10. B–N5 could be met by simply moving the Queen out of the pin, whereas now 10. . . . Q–K1 is bad because of 11. PxP PxP (11. . . . N/2xP 12. NxN) 12. Q–Q6 with enormous pressure (12. . . . N–Q2 13. B–K7).

10. . . .	PxP
11. NxP	R–K1
12. P–B3	N–N3
13. QR–Q1	P–Q4

Black is practically forced to give up a pawn. His QP is subject to immediate attack. For example, if 13. . . . B–Q2 (13. . . . B–K3 14. NxB followed by QxP) 14. N–B2 B–K3 15. QxP QxQ 16. RxQ, and the QBP is immune because the KN is unprotected.

14. BPxP	PxP
15. PxP	B–Q2
16. K–R1	. . .

To avoid any checks by the Queen at QB4.

16. . . .	Q–B1
17. N/Q–N5	BxN
18. BxB	KR–Q1
19. P–Q6	P–QR3
20. B–K2	N–B1
21. B–KB4	. . .

With such a Queen pawn, I must confess that I became complacent, not fully realizing how foxy my adversary was. The point of the text is that Black is unable to continue with 21. . . . N–R4 on account of the crushing 22. P–Q7 N–N3 23. B–Q6 and wins.

| 21. . . . | P–QN4 |

The only chance for some counterplay. Black hopes to get his Knight to QB5.

| 22. N–K4 | . . . |

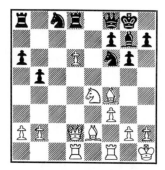

More precise is 22. P–QR4 P–N5 (if 22. . . . PxP 23. NxP, denying Black's QN development) 23. N–K4 with a greater edge than in the actual game because the QNP would be attacked.

22. . . .	**N–N3**
23. R–B1	. . .

More forceful is 23. B–N5 N/N–Q2 (not 23. . . . . NxN 24. PxN R–Q2 25. B–K7 Q–K1 26. B–N4, etc.) 24. R–B1.

23. . . .	**QR–N1**
24. R–B6	. . .

More prudent is 24. Q–R5, and if 24. . . . N/N–Q4 25. B–N3 or 24. . . . NxN 25. PxN BxP 26. R–QB2. In either case, White's task would be simplified.

24. . . .	**Q–K1!**

At this point, I began to feel a little disappointed and discouraged because I was unable to find a clearly promising continuation.

25. NxNch	. . .

Insufficient is 25. P–Q7 on account of 25. . . . . RxP 26. Q–B1 (if 26. Q-R5 NxN 27. BxR N–Q7) NxN 27. BxR N–Q7 28. RxN NxR 29. BxN (29. QxN R–K2) Q–Q1 with multiple threats.

25. . . .	**BxN**
26. KR–B1	. . .

26. P–Q7 would be met by 26. . . . . RxP 27. Q–B2 N–Q4 or 27. . . . B–K4.

26. . . .	**N–B5**
27. BxN	**PxB**
28. R/6xBP	**RxNP**

29. R/4–B2	RxR
30. QxR	P–KR4
31. Q–B6	Q–K3
32. QxP	P–N4
33. B–N3	P–R5
34. R–K1	Q–Q4
35. P–Q7	. . .

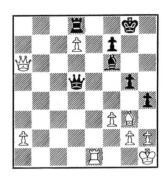

35. . . .	B–B6?

Geller was in severe time trouble. Correct is 35. . . . K–N2, although White can maintain some advantage with 36. Q–Q6 QxQ 37. BxQ RxP 38. B–N4.

36. Q–B8	QxQP
37. QxB	PxB
38. PxP	Q–Q3
39. P–N4	Q–R3ch
40. K–N1	. . .

Two pawns down and his King exposed, Black has only limited counterplay, and so I felt I should encounter very little opposition.

40. . . .	R–R1
41. Q–Q4	. . .

Prevents any checks and protects the pawn indirectly; for if 41. . . . RxP 42. R–K8ch K–R2 43. Q–R8ch or 43. R–R8ch, etc.

41. . . .	Q–QB3
42. R–K5	P–B3
43. R–K7?	. . .

A bad move: this gives Black the opportunity to exchange Rooks, which makes White's task tougher because of the increased possibility of perpetual check. Correct is 43. R–K2, after which there are many ways of making progress. One plan is to advance the QRP and another to effect an eventual P–B4.

43. . . .	R–K1!
44. RxRch	. . .

I had thought I would be able a play 45. R–Q7 but overlooked that Black could force a draw with 45. . . . Q–B8ch 46. K–R2 Q–K8!.

44. . . .	QxR
45. K–B2	Q–B3
46. P–B4	. . .

A safer plan is 46. P–R4 K–B2 (46. . . . Q–B7ch 47. K–N3 Q–B2ch 48. P–B4 PxPch 49. QxP Q–B6ch 50. K–R2, etc.) 47. Q–R1 K–N2 (47. . . . Q–B4ch 48. K–B1 Q–B5ch 49. K–N1 Q–B4ch 50. K–R1) 48. P–R5 Q–R3 49. Q–R2 K–N3 50. P–N3 K–N2 51. K–N2 K–N3 52. Q–Q2 K–N2 53. P–B4 with little resistance left for Black.

46. . . .	PxP
47. P–R4	Q–B8
48. P–R5	Q–R6
49. QxP/4	QxP
50. QxP	. . .

50. . . .	Q–Q7ch
51. K–N3	Q–K8ch
52. K–R2	K–R2
53. P–N3	K–N1
54. Q–Q8ch	K–N2
55. Q–Q7ch	K–N1
56. Q–Q5ch	K–N2
57. K–R3	Q–K7
58. Q–Q7ch	K–N3
59. Q–Q6ch	K–N2

The second adjourned position. At this point, the Soviet analysts claimed that Geller would probably draw the game. I felt that if I could advance the pawn to N5, I would win, but this is difficult to effect because of Black's constant threat of perpetual check, 59. . . . K–N4 loses: 60. Q–Q8ch K–N3 61. Q–N8ch K–B3 (if 61. . . . K–R3 62. P–N5ch K–R4 63. Q–R7ch KxP 64. Q–R4ch K–B4 65. Q–B4ch K–N3 66. Q–N4ch and wins) 62. P–N5ch K–K2 (if 62. . . . K–B4 63. Q–B7ch KxP 64. Q–B4ch K–R4 65. Q–R4ch K–N3 66. Q–N4ch) 63. Q–N7ch K–K1 64. Q–N6ch K–K2 65. Q–B6ch K–K1 66. P–N4, and Black has no perpetual.

60. K–R4	Q–K5
61. Q–Q7ch	K–R3
62. Q–Q2ch	K–R2
63. Q–B1!	Q–Q4

If 63. . . . Q–K7 64. Q–B7ch K–N3 (if 64. . . . K–N1 65. K–R5) 65. Q–B6ch K–N2 66. P–N5 Q–R7ch 67. K–N4 Q–K7ch 68. Q–B3 Q–K3ch 69. K–R4, etc.

| 64. P–N5 | . . . |

At last! From here on, Black's position becomes untenable.

64. . . .	Q–K5ch
65. Q–B4	Q–R8ch
66. K–N4	Q–Q8ch
67. Q–B3	Q–R5ch
68. K–R5	Q–K1ch
69. K–R4	K–N1
70. P–N6	Q–K2ch

Not 70. . . . QxP 71. Q–N4 and wins.

71. K–N4	Q–K3ch
72. Q–B5	Q–K7ch
73. K–R3	Resigns

For if 73. . . . Q–K2 74. Q–B7ch QxQ 75. PxQch KxP 76. K–R4 K–B3 77. K–R5, etc. An interesting and theoretical endgame.

Game 9

Rook behind Passed Pawn

Black has an extra pawn in the position below, and White has no real compensation. Black's QP, the support of his passed pawn, can be a problem because it is itself unsupported and is exposed on an open file, but Black has the resources to solve this problem.

How to make progress, however, is a more difficult problem for Black. The activity of White's Queen, if properly exploited, can prevent Black's Rook from stationing itself behind the passed pawn, where it belongs, and thus Black could not advance the pawn safely. White, however, misplays it and allows Black to set up his Rook advantageously. The rest is relatively easy.

Hastings, 1967/68

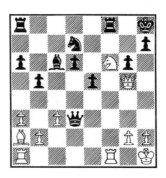

White to play

| A. Lombard | Nicolai |
| 24. K–N1 | . . . |

In order to answer 24. . . . Q–K7 with 25. R–B2 and to protect the Rook so that the Knight can move. In addition, Black has to contend with the threat of 25. QR–Q1.

24. . . .	NxN
25. RxN	B–Q4!
26. QR–KB1	. . .

Faulty is 26. RxQP on account of 26. . . . Q–K7 (threatening 27. . . . Q–B7ch followed by 28. . . . Q–B8ch), and if 27. R–KB6 BxB 28. RxB Q–K8ch. And 26. B–N1? loses after 26. . . . Q–Q8ch 27. K–B2 RxRch 28. QxRch K–N1, threatening, among other things, . . . R–KB1; and if 29. BxP Q–Q7ch, etc.

26. . . .	RxR
27. QxRch	K–N1
28. BxBch	. . .

28. QxQP? Q–K6ch.

| 28. . . . | QxB |
| 29. P–KR4? | . . . |

The losing move. After 29. Q–K7 Black would be unable to make progress for the important reason that his Rook would be kept out of play; if he proceeds with 29. . . . P–K5, the pawn would be indefensible after 30. R–K1.

| 29. . . . | R–K1 |

Now . . . P–K5 is possible and productive. Rooks belong behind passed pawns!

30. P–R5	Q–K3
31. PxP	PxP
32. Q–N5	K–N2
33. R–B3	Q–K2

Preventing 34. R–R3 followed by 35. Q–R6ch.

| 34. QxQch | . . . |

Unavailing is 34. Q–N4 P–K5 35. R–N3 Q–K3.

| 34. . . . | RxQ |
| 35. R–Q3 | R–Q2 |

Bad is 35. . . . R–K3: there would follow 36. R-Q5 K–B3 37. P–QN4 K–K2 38. P–R4 PxP 39. R–R5 and draws.

| 36. P–R4 | . . . |

Now if 36. R–Q5 K–B3 37. P–R5 K–K3.

36. . . .	P–Q4
37. PxP	PxP
38. K–B2	R–Q3

Unnecessary. 38. . . . K–B3 is more precise.

| 39. R–Q1 | . . . |

Trying to get the Rook behind the Black pawns. Each Black pawn advance further limits White's Rook and increases the scope of Black's.

39. . . .	K–B3
40. R–QR1	P–N5!
41. K–K3	. . .

If 41. PxP R–N3 42. R–R4 K–B4, etc.

41. . . .	PxP
42. PxP	R–B3
43. K–Q3	. . .

43. R–R3 RxPch.

| 43. . . . | K–B4 |
| 44. R–R5 | . . . |

If 44. R–B1ch K–K3 45. R–K1 P–K5ch 46. K–Q2 K–K4. But neither does the text move stop the relentless advance of King and pawns.

44. . . .	R–Q3
45. R–R4	P–K5ch
46. K–Q4	K–B5
47. R–R2	P–K6
48. R–K2	R–K3
49. KxP	R–K1

Since White's Rook is tied down, Black can afford to give up the pawn and lure the White King away from the queening square. White is lost.

50. P–B4	R–Q1ch
51. K–K6	R–Q7
52. R–K1	RxP
53. R–QB1	. . .

If 53. P–B5 R–QB7 54. K–Q6 P–K7 55. P–B6 K–B6 and wins.

| 53. . . . | R–Q7 |
| 54. P–B5 | P–K7 |

55.	P–B6	R–Q8
56.	R–B4ch	K–B6
57.	R–B3ch	K–B7
58.	R–B2	K–B8
	Resigns	

Game 10

Pieces against Pawns

A piece sacrifice in the endgame mobilizes a mass of pawns and decides the game. The minor pieces' inability to stop the passed pawns is instructive: at the time of the sacrifice the pieces are on the other side of the board; by the time they get to where the action is, the pawns have advanced too far to be stopped.

U.S. Championship
New York, 1968

KING'S INDIAN DEFENSE

S. Reshevsky		H. Seidman
1.	P–Q4	N–KB3
2.	P–QB4	P–KN3
3.	N–QB3	P–Q4
4.	N–B3	B–N2
5.	B–B4	0–0
6.	R–B1	. . .

This setup against the Gruenfeld Defense was popularized by the gifted Hungarian grandmaster Lajos Portisch, who has scored numerous victories with it. In theory, however, White gets no more than a minimal opening advantage.

6.	. . .	P–B4
7.	QPxP	B–K3
8.	P–K3	Q–R4

8. . . . N–B3 9. N–Q4 Q–R4 leads to the same position as in the game.

9. N–Q4	N–B3
10. NxB	. . .

The only try to procure any semblance of an opening advantage. Against 10. B–K2, Black has 10. . . . KR–Q1 11. NxB PxN 12. Q–N3 P–Q5 13. PxP NxP, and if 14. QxP NxB 15. KxN QxBP with advantage.

10. . . .	PxN
11. Q–R4	. . .

Other moves are inadequate. If 11. B–K2 P–K4 12. B–N5? P–Q5 winning a piece. On 11. B–K2 P–K4, and if 12. PxP PxB 13. PxN NPxP 14. PxP QR–N1 with counterchances. On 15. Q–R4 Black could continue 15. . . . QxP 16. Q–B4ch QxQ 17. BxQch K–R1 18. B–N3 N–Q2.

11. . . .	QxP
12. Q–N5	QxQ
13. PxQ	N–N1

Seidman prefers to give this Knight an opportunity to reach QN3 via Q2. Also possible is 13. . . . N–QR4 where the Knight is quite safe. 14. B–B7 could be satisfactorily met by 14. . . . P–N3, and if 14. P–QN4 N–B5 15. BxN PxB with the serious threat of . . . N–Q4. After 16. N–K2 N–Q4 17. RxP QR–B1 18. RxR (18. R–K4 R–B7!) RxR 19. 0–0 R–B7 with the brighter prospects.

14. B–Q3! . . .

Superior to 14. B–K2 QN–Q2 15. 0–0 QR–B1 16. N–R4 N–K5 to be followed by . . . N/2–B4 forcing an exchange of Knights and thereby reducing activity substantially. 17. B–N4 would be innocuous because of 17. . . . K–B2. I decided that my King would be needed in the middle of the board for the anticipated endgame.

14. . . .	QN–Q2
15. K–K2	P–K4

Seidman had rather undertake aggressive action than play defensively and make waiting moves. But the latter course is more prudent. I was intending to continue with 16. B–N1 to be followed by R–B2 and KR–QB1 in an attempt to gain control of the QB-file.

16. B–N3	P–K5
17. B–N1	. . .

Unproductive is 17. B–B2 P–K3 18. B–Q6 KR–B1 19. P–B3 PxPch 20. PxP N–K1 21. B–N4 B–B1 with equality.

17. . . .	QR–B1
18. N–R4	. . .

I discarded the idea of P–QR4 followed by B–R2 because Black could easily defend the QP with . . . P–K3, and moving the Bishop from its present diagonal would allow a Black Knight to occupy White's strategically important Q3.

18. . . .	N–N5

Black wants to get a Knight to K4 and keep an eye on Q6 as well as QB5, but White's well-placed Bishop on N3 makes this difficult. White initiates a series of forced moves which, thanks to the position of Black's Knight on N5, leads to the destruction of Black's pawn center.

19. KR–Q1	P–K3

20. RxR	RxR
21. P–B3	. . .

Not 21. BxP? on account of 21. . . . R–B5 winning a piece. Unproductive is 21. P–KR3 N–R3 to be followed by either . . . N–B4 or . . . B–K4, in either case with a comfortable position for Black.

21. . . .	PxPch
22. PxP	N/5–K4
23. P–K4!	. . .

Now the purpose of White's 20th move becomes apparent. By forcing the following exchange of pawns, White is able to activate his Rook and QB. Black's formidable-looking central pawn majority has vanished, and his remaining majority, which includes the crippled KP, is anything but dangerous. The pressure exerted by White's pieces against the Queenside will soon bear fruit.

23. . . .	PxP
24. BxP	P–N3
25. R–Q6	. . .

It annoys me that 25. P–B4, the obvious move, is insufficient. There would follow 25. . . . N–KB3 26. B–N7 R–B7ch 27. R–Q2 RxRch 28. KxR N/4–Q2 with equality even though White would have the two Bishops.

25. . . .	N–B1

Best. I was hoping for the normal-looking reply 25. . . . K–B2, in which case I intended 26. P–B4 R–B5 (if 26. . . . N–KB3 27. B–N7 R–B7ch 28. K–Q1 and wins. I had this variation in mind when I made my 25th move.) 27. N–B3 N–KB3 28. B–QB2 (28. PxN NxB 29. R–Q7ch K–B1 30. K–Q3 N–B4ch; if instead in this line 30. R–Q8ch K–K2 31. B–R4ch P–N4) 28. . . . N/4–Q2 29. B–N3 R–N5 30. P–B5! PxP 31. BxPch K–K2 32. BxP RxPch 33. K–B3 N–B4 34. R–B6 with a strategically won position.

26. P–N3	P–N4

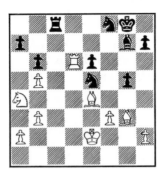

Suddenly Black's position becomes critical, but this is not immediately apparent. It seems, at first glance, that Black has nothing to be seriously concerned about; but White does have the advantage of the Bishops, and Black is saddled with an isolated KP.

27. NxP!   . . .

A bolt out of the clear sky! After this sound sacrifice, Black's game becomes untenable. I get only two pawns for the piece, but the passed pawns with the aid of the Rook and the two Bishops are not to be stopped by Black's forces.

27. . . .	PxN
28. RxNP	P–R4
29. R–R6	. . .

Stronger is 29. P–QR4.

29. . . .	P–R5
30. B–KB2	N/4–N3
31. R–R8	. . .

Much stronger is 31. R–B6 cutting off Black's Rook.

31. . . .	RxR?

A much better try, which would make the win more difficult, is 31. . . . N–B5ch 32. K–Q2 (32. K–B1 is faulty on account of 32. . . . R–B8ch 33. B–K1 B–B6. Also unsatisfactory is 32. K–K1 RxR 33. BxR N–Q6ch 34. K–B1 NxB 35. KxN N–Q2 36. P–QR4 B–B6, etc.) 32. . . . RxR 33. BxR N–R6 34. B–R7 B–K4 35. K–K2 BxP 36. K–B1, and White's passed pawns would prevail but not without a struggle. Black's minor pieces are unable to organize an effective blockade now.

32. BxR	B–K4
33. B–N1	N–B5ch
34. K–B1	N–Q2

Futile is 34. . . . N–R6 35. B–R7, and the RP is immune to capture because of K–N2 winning a piece.

35. P–R4	B–B2
36. B–B6	N–N1
37. B–K4	. . .

And now White is ready to advance his pawns with P–N6 and P–R5. Black must parry this threat.

| 37. . . . | N–Q4 |

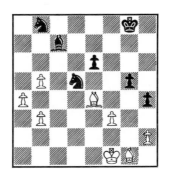

Black seems to have stopped the onrushing pawns, and indeed he might have if his King had been closer to the Queenside.

| 38. BxN! | PxB |
| 39. P–N4 | . . . |

The winning move. Insufficient is 39. P–N6 B–Q3 40. P–R5 K–B2 41. P–N7 K–K3 42. B–R7 K–Q2 43. P–N4 K–B3, and the pawns are stopped. It is imperative to advance the RP, and in order to effect this advance White's QNP has to remain at QN5.

| 39. . . . | K–B2 |

If 39. . . . B–Q3 40. P–R5 (even 40. B–B5 suffices) BxNP 41. P–R6 and queens.

| 40. P–R5 | N–Q2 |

So that if 41. P–R6 N–N3 42. P–R7 N–R1, and the pawns are stopped.

41. P–N6	B–Q1

Against either 41. . . . NxP or 41. . . . BxP, White wins easily with 42. BxN or BxB.

42. P–N7	N–N1
43. B–R7	B–B2
44. P–N5	N–Q2

Hoping for 45. P–N6 B–N1 46. BxB NxB, but even in this White could win with 46. P–R6 BxP 47. P–N8=Q.

45. P–R6	BxP
46. P–N8=Q	Resigns

Chapter 3

King Position

King safety is a fundamental element of chess, like piece development, material, pawn structure, and center control. An insufficiently protected King, unlike a weak square or a weak pawn,
can result in an immediate and violent loss of the game. Therefore, adequate protection for the King is necessary at every stage.

The castling move is a convenient method of securing the King
in a safe corner, but castling alone should never be considered
sufficient. The pawns in front of the castled King should not be
touched unless absolutely necessary, and at least one piece
should remain on guard (when castled on the Kingside, for
example, a Knight at KB3 serves well). A player who unnecessarily moves the pawns in front of his King, or who leaves
no piece to defend it, or who is so engaged elsewhere that he
does not castle in time is just begging for trouble. Because an
attack on the King results in an immediate win if successful, it is
extremely dangerous; that is why the experienced player takes
great care to safeguard his King's position in an effort to dissuade
his opponent from considering any such assault.

It is your task to find some way to weaken the enemy King's
position. Two such methods appear in games 11 and 12. In the
first, Black sacrifices in the center in order to create mating
threats which force White to expose his own King. After that,
nature takes its course. In the second, Black uses his pawns as
battering rams to destroy the White King's shelter.

Some openings, like the King's Gambit, call for the early advance of the KBP even though White will castle on the Kingside. The intention of such openings is aggressive, however; White moves so quickly that Black has no time even to consider taking advantage of the slight exposure created by White's second move. But what if your idea fails to work or you make some kind of error or lose time? Then it may be too late to think of King safety. See game 13.

As for that Knight at KB3: what if it gets pinned? Surely such pins should be prevented, if possible, for the consequences can only be bad. Sometimes the pinned piece is simply lost; at other times—see game 14—the King's cover is blown.

And then there are opening systems that call for development of the King Bishop to N2. Of course, you must first play P–KN3, which weakens the squares KB3 and KR3. Those squares will be defended, however, by the Bishop on N2, which also operates very effectively on the long diagonal. But if that fianchettoed Bishop is exchanged or transferred to a distant battlefield, those weak squares so near the King can be disastrous. Mating attacks based on the weakness of those squares are common; two examples are games 15 and 16.

A weak King position is not necessarily decisive in itself; there may be compensating advantages, such as material or initiative, or the position may be such that the opponent cannot exploit the situation. Game 17 is an excellent example of play by both sides against insecure Kings. Black's King is worse off in this respect, but Black has a material advantage. As soon as White weakens his own King in attempting to avoid simplification, his opponent has the extra edge he needs to win.

Often a player will create a weakness near his King while carrying out aggressive operations in the middlegame. What happens when those operations turn out to be mere dreams is beautifully demonstrated in game 18. Another version of this sad tale is game 19: Portisch seems to want to use his Kingside pawns for attack and begins to advance them. Then, indecisive, he switches strategy and abandons the attack. This gives Black the opportunity to capitalize on White's breach of security.

The King left too long in his castle is another danger. In game 20, an endgame in Black's favor is in the making, but he misjudges his chances and leaves his King behind, with disastrous consequences. Alone, the King is weak; with his army, especially in the endgame, the King is a strong fighting piece.

Sometimes a player will castle thinking more to mobilize his Rooks than secure his King. He should not be too surprised, then, when he must greet the enemy forces at the castle gate. Larsen explains in game 21.

There is such a thing as a false sense of security. In game 22, White believes that Black's King position is weak and that his own is leakproof. In fact, all of Black's sensitive spots are covered, but White, seeing all those advanced Black pawns and all that air around the Black King, refuses to believe it: he disdains the possibility of Black threats and blithely proceeds to set up his "winning" formation. A psychological pitfall.

Game 11

Breaking and Entering

After about two hours of play it became clear that I had to win, since my main rival in the tournament was winning his game. Positional jockeying would have been too slow (and the outcome not at all certain), so direct attack had to be considered. The conditions were right: White's King was not protected by his pieces, and Black had certain positional advantages, including an advanced pawn near the enemy King and the more active pieces. The solution was a positional sacrifice to force White to open the gate to his King's fortress; the ensuing attack resulted in a won endgame for Black.

The type of sacrifice that occurs in this game does not require calculation down to the last move. An insufficiently protected King, even though the pawn cover has not been disturbed, is itself an invitation for the opponent to look for combinations or direct attack. In this case it was enough to see that White would have to weaken his King's position and that Black's very active pieces would gain control of vital squares near White's King.

U.S. Championship
New York, 1970

QUEEN'S INDIAN DEFENSE

L. Evans	S. Reshevsky
1. P–Q4	N–KB3
2. P–QB4	P–K3
3. N–KB3	P–QN3

The Queen's Indian Defense, one of the safest setups against the QP opening. While it does not offer Black winning chances, it should suffice for a draw.

4. N–B3	B–N2
5. P–QR3	P–Q4

Best. Against 5. . . . B–K2, White has the restricting 6. P–Q5.

6. B–N5	B–K2

6. . . . PxP? 7. P–K4 B–K2 8. BxN BxB 9. P–K5 B–K2 10. BxP with advantage.

7. R–B1	0–0
8. P–K3	N–K5

Also possible is 8. . . . QN–Q2 9. PxP PxP, but not 9. . . . NxP 10. NxN BxN 11. BxB QxB 12. RxP. I prefer the text simplification, however.

9. BxB	QxB
10. PxP	PxP
11. NxN	PxN
12. N–Q2	. . .

Against 12. N–K5, Black has to be careful. Not 12. . . . P–KB3? 13. B–B4ch K–R1 14. N–N6ch! PxN 15. Q–N4 R–B2 16. QxNP K–N1 (16. . . . R–B1 17. Q–R5 mate) 17. BxRch QxB 18. QxQch KxQ 19. RxPch and wins. A perfect demonstration of the dire consequences of exposing one's own King! The correct plan, after 12. N–K5, is 12. . . . P–QB4 13. B–B4 PxP 14. QxP N–B3 15. NxN BxN, and now 16. BxPch fails because of 16. . . . QxB 17. RxB QxPch.

12. . . .	R–B1

The correct move, permitting Black to develop his Knight at Q2 instead of at QB3. At Q2, the Knight is more useful: it can

24. . . .	NxBch
25. RxN	BxP
26. R–QB1	R–K1

Of course not 26. . . . RxR? 27. QxR BxR 28. Q–B8 and mate. The text move suffices for the win, however. Black's passed pawn plus his threats of mate are more than adequate compensation for the Exchange.

27. R/2–K1   . . .

Unavailing is 27. R/2–QB2 because of 27. . . . P–K7 28. R–B3 (28. K–B2 Q–K6ch 29. K–K1 Q–N8ch 30. K–Q2 QxPch 31. K–K1 Q–N8ch 32. K–Q2 R–Q1ch 33. K–B3 Q–Q5ch 34. K–N3 B–Q4ch, etc.) 28. . . . Q–Q7 29. R–K1 QxPch followed by mate.

27. . . .   B–N2

I considered 27. . . . B–R1 but discarded it on account of 28. Q–R2 (to meet . . . Q–Q4), and I would not have been able to attempt to get my Queen to the QR1–KR8 diagonal: 28. . . . Q–KR4? 29. RxP RxR? 30. R–B8 mate. The text move guards QB1 and prevents the above saving resource.

White's position is untenable. The immediate threat is 28. . . . Q–Q4 with the possibility of mate with . . . Q–R8 or . . . Q–N7. White is the Exchange ahead, but his King position is wide open; moreover, Black's passed pawn is dangerously advanced, tying down White's Rooks.

28. R–B7   . . .

There is no alternative but to return the Exchange. If 28. Q–R2 Q–KR4 29. R–B1 (29. R–B7 Q–B6, or even better 29. . . . B–Q4, followed by . . . Q–B6) 29. . . . P–K6 30. KR–K1 Q–B6.

| 28. . . . | Q–Q4 |
| 29. RxB | QxR |

Since Black's extra pawn is very far advanced, White has little hope of saving himself. It is in just such positions that the player with the advantage is often tempted to relax, but he must be careful not to let the win slip from his hands. Experience teaches composure. The game is not over until the opponent resigns.

| 30. Q–Q3 | Q–K5 |

Superior to 30. . . . Q–B6 31. R–K2 (31. . . . R–QB1? 32. QxP) followed by the advance of the QP. Allowing White to keep his Queen gives him opportunities for counterplay.

| 31. QxQ | . . . |

White cannot avoid the exchange of Queens. If 31. Q–Q1 P–KR4 32. P–Q5 P–R5 33. P–Q6 P–R6 34. R–K2 R–Q1 followed by . . . Q–B3.

| 31. . . . | RxQ |
| 32. K–N2 | P–B4! |

After 32. . . . RxP 33. RxP K–B1 34. P–QN4, Black has only minimal chances of winning.

| 33. K–B3 | K–B2 |

Black gives up the pawn, but White cannot hold the resulting endgame. The principle involved in this type of King-and-pawn endgame is that the outside passed pawn (in this case Black's potential passed pawn on the Kingside) is stronger than a passed pawn in the center. The reason is that White's King will eventually have to move from the center and abandon his passed pawn in order to stop Black's; then Black's King will be in a position to move to the other side and win White's Queenside pawns before White's King can get back to defend them.

34. RxP	. . .

No relief is offered by 34. P–KR4. There would follow 34. . . . P–N3 35. RxP RxRch 36. KxR P–KR3 37. K–B4 (37. P–Q5 P–KN4 38. K–Q4 K–B3, and Black wins the QP) 37. . . . K–B3 followed by . . . P–KN4 with the same result as in the game.

34. . . .	**RxRch**
35. KxR	**P–KN4!**

Assuring Black a passed pawn and tying White's King down to the Kingside.

36. P–KR4	**P–KR3**
37. P–Q5	**K–K2**
38. K–Q4	**K–Q3**
39. PxP	**PxP**
40. P–R4	**P–R4**
41. P–N3	. . .

If 41. K–B4 K–K4 42. K–N5 KxP 43. KxP P–B5 and wins.

41. . . .	**P–N5!**
42. K–K3	. . .

If 42. K–B4 P–B5 wins.

42. . . .	**KxP**
43. K–Q3	**K–B4**

Also sufficient is 43. . . . K–K4 44. K–K3 P–B5ch 45. PxPch K–B4, etc.

44. K–K3	**K–N5**
45. K–B4	**KxP**
46. KxP	**KxP**
47. KxP	**K–N5**
Resigns	

Game 12

Shattered Pawn Cover

As we saw in the previous game, a weak King cannot contend with active forces. The present game provides further evidence. Black has the initiative and the better-placed pieces, but his opponent's King is not vulnerable. Taimanov knows what to do—expose White's King.

This was the second of a four-game match, part of the famous confrontation between ten-member teams from the Soviet Union and the combined rest of the world. Taimanov, as White, had defeated Uhlmann in the first game, and the East German grandmaster, understandably seeking revenge and not a draw, avoids simplification at several points and pursues, perhaps too energetically, aggressive continuations.

USSR vs. the Rest of the World
Belgrade, 1970

QUEEN'S INDIAN DEFENSE

W. Uhlmann	M. Taimanov
1. P–Q4	N–KB3
2. P–QB4	P–K3
3. N–KB3	P–QN3
4. P–KN3	B–N2
5. B–N2	B–K2
6. 0–0	0–0
7. P–Q5?	. . .

An attempt to veer from the trodden path, but, as this game demonstrates, the text is no improvement over the more usual moves.

7. . . .	PxP
8. N–Q4	N–B3
9. PxP	NxN
10. QxN	P–B4!

11.	Q–Q3	P–Q3
12.	N–B3	P–QR3
13.	B–B4	. . .

13. P–QR4 looks better (in order to stop . . . P–QN4), but after
13. . . . Q–B2 14. P–N3 N–Q2 15. B–B4 B–KB3 16. N–K4 B–K4,
Black stands well.

13.	. . .	P–QN4
14.	P–QR4	P–N5

Not 14. . . . P–B5 15. Q–Q4 Q–Q2 16. PxP PxP 17. Q–N6!.

15.	N–Q1	P–QR4
16.	P–N3	. . .

Better is 16. N–K3 B–R3 17. N–B4.

16.	. . .	B–R3
17.	Q–B2	N–Q2
18.	B–K4	P–N3
19.	B–Q3	N–N3

20. B–R6 . . .

White, wishing to play N–K3, feared . . . P–KN4, which traps
his Bishop. But correct is 20. BxB RxB 21. P–K4 followed by
N–N2.

Through a number of inaccuracies, White has relinquished the
initiative. Black now begins to accumulate positional advantages.

20.	. . .	R–K1
21.	N–K3	B–B3
22.	QR–Q1	Q–B1

23. K–N2		BxB
24. RxB		R–R2
25. N–B4		NxN
26. QxN		R/2–K2
27. R–KB3?		. . .

In trying to obtain counterplay, White begins to go astray and gradually drifts into an untenable position. Indispensable is 27. R–K3, in order to exchange one Rook and simplify the position.

27. . . .		R–K5
28. Q–N5		Q–Q1

Everything is protected, and White's Queen remains out of play.

29. B–K3		. . .

Still preferable is 29. R–K3.

29. . . .		B–Q5
30. BxB		RxB
31. R–Q3		R/5–K5

Taimanov wisely avoids the exchange of one of his Rooks.

32. P–K3		P–R4
33. P–R4		K–N2
34. R–B1		. . .

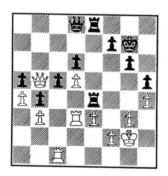

34. . . .		P–N4!

The two Kings are identically situated, neither being particularly exposed. But Black's control of the K-file and his much more active Queen are the important factors now. Knowing how lethal the initiative is in the presence of an exposed King, Black proceeds to rip open the pawn cover protecting White's King.

| 35. PxP | P–R5 |
| 36. R–B4 | . . . |

Forcing an exchange of Rooks, but too late!

36. . . .	QxP
37. RxR	RxR
38. Q–Q7	Q–N3

Threatening 39. . . . PxP 40. PxP R–N5, etc.

39. R–Q1	PxP
40. R–KN1	R–R5
Resigns	

If 41. PxP Q–K5ch 42. K–B1 R–R7 and wins. If 41. K–B1 Q–N8ch 42. K–N2 R–R7ch 43. K–B3 RxPch 44. K–N4 Q–N3ch 45. K–R3 R–R7 mate.

Game 13

The Pawn Roller

Beware of hasty judgments. The fact that White advances his KBP on the second move and is later crushed by a Kingside pawn roller does not really mean that the King's Gambit is unplayable for White. But it can be risky, especially in those variations where Black has a Kingside pawn majority, as in the present case. White's trouble stems from two sources: the weakness of his Kingside castled position and a loss of time (moves 14 and 16) that allows Black to take the initiative. Again, the weak King cannot hope to survive when the enemy has the initiative. To prove this, look at the position after Black's 22nd move; Black's King is in fact more exposed than White's, but with inactive and uncoordinated pieces White can do nothing about it. "Exposed" is not always synonymous with "weak." Black's King is exposed but White's is weak, indefensibly so given the force of Black's pawn roller.

Amsterdam, 1969

KING'S GAMBIT

F. Gheorghiu	L. Portisch
1. P–K4	P–K4
2. P–KB4	PxP
3. B–B4	N–KB3
4. Q–K2	P–Q4

The correct continuation. Black gives back the pawn for rapid development; otherwise, White gets the upper hand.

5. PxPch	B–K2
6. N–KB3	0–0
7. 0–0	. . .

Or 7. P–Q4 R–K1 8. 0–0 NxP 9. BxN QxB 10. BxP N–B3 with a good position.

7. . . .	P–B3

White's QP at Q5 restricts the mobility of Black's forces and must be liquidated. The text move is therefore preferable to the natural development 7. . . . QN–Q2 8. N–B3 N–N3 9. B–N3 B–KN5 10. P–Q4 B–Q3 11. B–Q2 R–K1 12. Q–B2 Q–Q2 13. QR–K1 with the strong possibility of an eventual N–K5.

8. PxP	NxP
9. P–B3	B–Q3
10. P–Q4	B–KN5
11. QN–Q2	R–K1
12. Q–B2	B–R4!

A strong move which accomplishes several things. It protects Black's KBP and, with the threat of . . . N–KN5, forces a further weakening in the White King's camp by P–KR3. With White's KBP already absent (see his second move!), this can be serious.

13. P–KR3	P–KR3

Preparing to advance the KNP. Black's four-to-two pawn majority on the Kingside is a potent force, considering White's weakened King.

14. B–N5?	. . .

A costly loss of time, which causes White serious trouble.

Mandatory is 14. B–Q3 followed by either 15. N–B4 or 15. N–N3, freeing the QB and advancing the Knight toward the center.

14. . . .	B–B2
15. R–K1	. . .

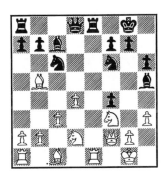

Unplayable is 15. BxN PxB 16. N–K5 BxN 17. PxB RxP 18. QxBP R–K7 with Black's advantage or 15. BxN PxB 16. N–B4 N–K5 17. Q–R4 (17. Q–B2 N–N6 18. R–B2 BxN followed by . . . R–K8ch) 17. . . . QxQ 18. NxQ N–N6 19. R–B2 R–K8ch and wins.

15. . . .	Q–Q4
16. B–Q3	. . .

An admission that this 14th move was wasteful (or had Gheorghiu made some miscalculation?). Of no value is 16. P–B4 Q–KB4 17. N–R4 Q–Q6! with a bind. If in this line 17. P–Q5? NxP 18. PxN B–QN3. The beautifully centralized Black pieces now go to work.

| 16. . . . | B–KN3! |

Disposing of White's active Bishop.

17. BxB	PxB
18. P–QN3	P–KN3

Taking immediate advantage of his pawn majority on the Kingside.

19. B–N2	P–N5
20. PxP	NxNP
21. Q–B1	. . .

To be considered is 21. Q–R4 N–K6 22. N–B1.

21. . . .   N–K6
22. Q–B2   . . .

If 22. Q–Q3 N–K4 23. Q–K2 N/4–N5 24. Q–Q3 Q–KR4 25.
P–B4 N–B4! 26. N–B1 N–N6 27. NxN PxN and wins because of
the strong threat of . . . N–B7 and . . . Q–R8 mate.

22. . . .   P–KN4

Posing the problem of how to stop the pawn roller. The exposure of Black's King is not dangerous because of the restricted
activity of White's forces. Note how Black methodically strips
the White King of defenders to simplify the final assault.

23. P–B4   Q–B4
24. N–B1   P–N5

Now the two pawns (the potentially passed KBP and the
KNP), together with the Queen, pose a serious threat to the
White monarch's exposed position.

25. N–K5   N/6xN

Not 25. . . . N–B7? because of 26. N–N3 Q–R2 27. QxP.

26. RxN   . . .

26. . . .   NxN
27. PxN   Q–R4

Best. After 27. . . . BxP (27. . . . P–N6? 28. Q–Pch) 28. BxB
RxB 29. QxBP, Black would have nothing. Unsound is 27. . . .
RxP 28. BxR BxB 29. QR–Q1 B–B2 30. R–Q5 with nothing to fear.

28. QxBP   B–N3ch
29. B–Q4?   . . .

Loses immediately. White could offer some resistance with 29.
P–B5 (making Q–QB4ch possible) BxPch 30. R–B2 BxRch 31.
QxB with some play because of Black's exposed King.

29. . . .	R–KB1
30. Q–K3	BxB
31. QxB	P–N6
32. R–B6	QR–Q1
33. Q–B4	Q–R7ch

This wins, of course, but a quicker finish is possible by 33. . . .
RxR 34. PxR R–Q8ch 35. RxR QxRch 36. Q–B1 Q–Q5ch 37.
K–R1 Q–R5ch 38. K–N1 Q–R7 mate.

34. K–B1	RxR
35. PxR	Q–R8ch
36. K–K2	QxPch
Forfeited	

White lost on time, but his position is hopeless anyway. If
37. K–K1 R–K1ch 38. K–Q1 Q–K7ch 39. K–B1 R–K6 and wins
because Black's King can avoid a perpetual check. But not 39.
. . . Q–K8ch because of 40. K–B2 R–K7ch 41. K–Q3, etc.

Game 14

The Mighty Pin

The late I. A. Horowitz used to quip: "The pin is mightier than
the sword." Indeed, sometimes a pin is so dangerous that the
temptation to get rid of it, even at the cost of serious weakening,
may be irresistible. That's one of the reasons pins are so
dangerous.

In this game White pins Black's King Knight in order to gain
control of White's Q5, which Black's Knight watches. Recognizing
that to allow the pin to remain would lead to a solid positional
advantage for White, Polugaevsky decides to break the pin by
advancing the pawns in front of his castled King. You know the
rest.

Interzonal Tournament
Palma de Majorca, 1970

ENGLISH OPENING

S. Reshevsky	L. Polugaevsky
1. P–Q4	N–KB3
2. P–QB4	P–B4
3. N–KB3	. . .

I refused the Benoni, which would have been reached by 3. P–Q5. I was not in the mood for that type of game.

3. . . .	PxP
4. NxP	P–K3
5. N–QB3	B–N5
6. N–N5	. . .

The only try to obtain an opening advantage.

6. . . .	0–0

Preferable is 6. . . . P–Q4 after which it is difficult for White to get an advantage.

7. P–QR3	BxNch
8. NxB	P–Q4
9. B–N5!	. . .

Challenging Black to get out of the pin by weakening his Kingside. Polugaevsky accepts the challenge.

9. . . .	P–KR3
10. B–R4	. . .

It is unwise for White to win a pawn: 10. BxN QxB 11. PxP PxP 12. QxP R–Q1 13. Q–N3 leaves Black too far ahead in development.

10. . . .	P–KN4?

Wiser is 10. . . . N–B3 (if 10. . . . PxP 11. QxQ RxQ 12. N–K4 QN–Q2 13. 0–0–0 with advantage) 11. PxP PxP 12. P–K3 B–K3 with only a slight advantage for White.

Black will later be haunted for having exposed his King.

11. B–N3	P–Q5
12. N–N5	N–B3
13. P–K3	PxP

Unsatisfactory is 13. . . . P–K4 14. PxP PxP (14. . . . P–R3 15. PxP) 15. B–Q3 R–K1ch 16. K–B1 with promising play. The threats of N–B7 and P–KR4 would be unpleasant for Black.

14. PxP	**P–K4**
15. B–Q3	**B–N5**
16. Q–B2	**P–K5**
17. B–K2	. . .

17. BxP R–K1.

17. . . .	**Q–R4ch**

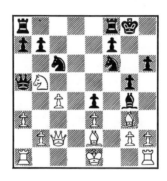

18. K–B2!	. . .

The only way to enliven the game. It is usually risky to forego castling and this is no exception, but I felt that my King would be fairly safe since Black's forces are not coordinated. I was also encouraged because my adversary's King position was not too healthy. I expected to launch a vigorous and rapid attack.

Not 18. N–B3 N–N5, and if 18. Q–B3 QxQch 19. NxQ BxB 20. KxB N–QR4 with equality.

18. . . .	**BxB**
19. KxB	. . .

Better than 19. QxB. The King is quite safe at K2, and the Queen can also maintain its pressure on the KP.

19. . . .	**QR–B1**

Although this turns out badly, there is no better move (the threat is 20. . . . QxN). If 19. . . . Q–Q1 20. QR–Q1, and the Queen has no good square.

20.	**N–Q6**	**R–R1**

Bad is 20. . . . R–B2 on account of 21. P–N4.

21.	**QR–Q1**	**N–R4**
22.	**B–K1**	**. . .**

22. QxP or 22. R–Q5 is also good, but I was looking for bigger gains.

22.	**. . .**	**Q–N3**

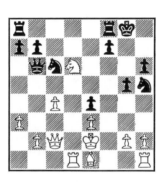

23.	**P–KN4!**	**. . .**

The winning move.

23.	**. . .**	**N–B3**
24.	**B–B3**	**NxP**

From here on, Black's moves are forced.

25.	**QxP**	**P–B4**

If 25. . . . P–KR4 26. R–Q5.

26.	**Q–K6ch**	**K–R2**
27.	**NxBP**	**N/3–K4**
28.	**R–Q7ch!**	**NxR**
29.	**QxNch**	**K–N3**
30.	**P–KR4!**	**P–KR4**

If 30. . . . PxP 31. NxPch N–K4 32. Q–Q5ch. And if 30. . . . RxN 31. Q–N7ch.

31.	**N–K7ch**	**K–R3**
32.	**PxPch**	**KxP**
33.	**Q–Q5ch**	**Resigns**

Game 15

The Danger of the Fianchetto

The flank development (fianchetto) of a Bishop incurs both risks and advantages. The fianchettoed Bishop plays an enormous part in modern opening systems; the Indian defenses, the Gruenfeld, the Sicilian Dragon, the Pirc, the Reti Opening, the Classical Queen's Gambit, and many variations of the English Opening are but a few examples.

To fianchetto a Bishop you have to play P–N3; but when the King is castled on the Kingside and the KB fianchettoed, there is danger inherent due to the potential weakness of KB3 and KR3. If the fianchettoed Bishop is exchanged, the weakness of those squares can be disastrous because of their proximity to the King. The following game is an example.

Palma de Majorca, 1971

BENONI DEFENSE

S. Reshevsky	B. Larsen
1. P–Q4	P–QB4
2. P–Q5	. . .

If White is in a conservative mood, he can continue 2. N–KB3 or even 2. P–K3.

2. . . .	P–Q3
3. P–K4	. . .

3. P–QB4 leads to better-known lines.

3. . . .	N–KB3
4. N–QB3	P–KN3
5. N–B3	B–N2
6. B–K2	0–0
7. 0–0	N–R3
8. N–Q2	N–B2

Obviously preparing for an advance of the Queenside pawns. Herein lies one of the main strengths of the fianchettoed Bishop when White's QP advances beyond Q4 and no longer influences that important square. The Bishop's open diagonal is very threatening to White's Queenside pawns, especially in conjunction with Black's advancing pawns on that flank. In view of this, one of White's objectives is to exchange Black's fianchettoed Bishop, which would simultaneously safeguard his own Queenside and weaken Black's KB3 and KR3 squares.

9. P–QR4		P–QR3
10. P–B3		. . .

Unnecessary. Wiser is 10. N–B4 R–N1 11. B–B4, and Black would have to take measures to prevent P–K5.

10. . . .		B–Q2
11. N–B4		P–QN4

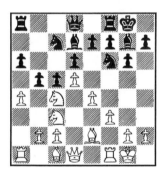

12. N–N6		R–N1
13. P–R5		. . .

Temporarily anchoring the Knight on a favorable square. White should keep the Queenside closed as long as he can, at the same time trying to build an initiative in the center and on the Kingside.

13. . . .		B–K1

Preparing to dislodge the Knight with . . . N–Q2.

14. B–K3		N–Q2
15. NxN		BxN
16. Q–Q2		P–N5
17. N–Q1		. . .

I did not object to my Knight's being driven away since I wanted to relocate it anyway.

17. . . .		B–N4
18. BxB		. . .

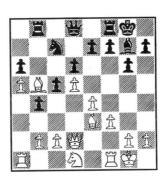

18. . . .		PxB?!

This move came as a great surprise to me. I expected the natural 18. . . . NxB, attempting to post the Knight at Q5, or even 18. . . . RxB, applying pressure against my QRP. The text move is intended to win the QRP by lining up Black's Rooks and Queen in direct attack on it. I believe that Larsen also wanted to upset my equilibrium by making an unpredictable move.

19. R–R2		. . .

In order to protect the QNP and thereby free my Knight for immediate action on the Kingside.

19. . . .		R–R1
20. N–B2		P–K3

Larsen sees that the only way I can proceed with the attack is to begin weakening the Black King's position, but after the text move 21. B–R6 loses a pawn by 21. . . . BxB 22. QxB PxP. Pointless is 21. N–N4 on account of 21. . . . P–R4 22. N–R6ch K–R2 with no plausible continuation for White.

21. PxP		. . .

The only logical move.

21. . . .		NxP

Gaining time by attacking my QRP with his Queen. But . . .

    22. P–KB4!   **. . .**

White's plan becomes clear. The KBP is to play a significant role in the contemplated attack. Black's commitment to his Queenside operation, for which he has weakened his Queenside pawns and given White a pawn majority on the Kingside, must be carried through; otherwise all his preparations will have been in vain. Perhaps he failed to appreciate the strength of White's imminent breakthrough.

    22. . . .   **RxP**

Larsen has accomplished his mission of winning the pawn, but will he get away with it?

    23. RxR   **QxR**

    24. P–B5!   **. . .**

I considered 24. QxQP and saw that it would be to my advantage after 24. . . . R–Q1 25. Q–K7 BxP 26. N–N4 with an irresistible attack because of the double threat of P–B5 and N–R6ch. However, after 24. QxQP, I saw that Black could continue 24. . . . Q–Q1! 25. Q–B6 (25. QxQ RxQ 26. P–B5 N–Q4 and Black gets the better of it) 25. . . . B–Q5 26. R–Q1 (26. BxB QxB favors Black) Q–K1 27. QxQ RxQ 28. BxB NxQ with equality.

    24. . . .   **N–Q5**

    25. B–R6!   **. . .**

With the serious threat of 26. BxB followed by 27. N–N4 and 28. Q–R6ch. Larsen suddenly realizes the seriousness of the situation and that immediate stringent measures are necessary.

    25. . . .   **Q–Q1**

The only defense. The Queen has to be recalled to the defense of the King.

    26. N–N4   **Q–R5**

Preventing White's Queen from reaching White's KR6. It appears that Black has solved his problem, but . . .

    27. BxB   **KxB**

    28. P–R3   **. . .**

A quiet but effective move! The simple threats now are P–B3 and, after the Knight moves, QxQP with Black in a completely hopeless position.

28. . . .   **R–K1**

To no avail is 28. . . . R–Q1 because of 29. P–B3 PxP 30. PxP N–B3 31. Q–Q5 N–R4 32. P–K5 with a winning position; for if 32. . . . QPxP 33. P–B6ch wins, and if 32. . . . NPxP 33. N–K3! PxP 34. NxPch K–N1 35. QxKP and wins. Another possibility is 28. . . . PxP 29. PxP R–K1 30. R–B2 (preventing . . . N–K7ch and . . . R–K7); however Black would still be faced with the problem of how to parry the threat of P–B3 which wins the QP. Black's best try would be 30. . . . Q–R4, attacking the KBP. White could press his advantage with 31. P–B6ch K–N1 32. P–B3 PxP 33. PxP N–B4 34. Q–B4 (but not 34. Q–Q5? R–K8ch 35. K–R2 R–R8ch 36. KxR N–N6ch, winning the Queen).

Now the weakened squares near Black's King are at White's mercy.

29. P–B6ch   **K–R1**

Bad is 29. K–N1 on account of 30. P–B3 PxP 31. PxP N–K3 32. N–R6ch K–B1 33. QxPch.

30. P–B3	PxP
31. PxP	N–K3
32. QxP	Q–N4
33. N–K5	K–N1?

The only try is 33. . . . N–Q1!, but then 34. N–B3 (34. QxN? Q–K6ch) Q–K6ch 35. K–R2 QxBP (35. . . . QxKP? 36. R–K1) 36. Q–K7! R–N1 37. R–Q1 wins.

34. Q–Q7	R–KB1
35. NxBP	Q–K6ch

After 35. . . . RxN 36. QxN followed by R–R1, Black's position is hopelessly lost.

36. K–R1	QxKP
37. N–N5!	Resigns

I was awarded the prize "best attacking game" for this contest.

Game 16

A Strong Diagonal

To become a target for the enemy forces a King does not have to be wide open and defenseless. A single weak square is often enough. Although the present game is virtually decided in the early middlegame, it is in the concluding phase, when White's fianchettoed Bishop leaves the scene, that the defensive value of that piece is clearly demonstrated—in abstentia.

It is also interesting that, early in the game, Black's fianchettoed Bishop plays a powerful role in dislocating White's minor pieces, which in turn forces White to part with his KB, leading to the final phase.

U.S. Championship
New York, 1972

SICILIAN DEFENSE

I. A. Horowitz	S. Reshevsky
1. P–K4	P–QB4
2. N–KB3	P–Q3
3. P–KN3	. . .

One of the less-used variations. Horowitz, who is out of practice, attempts to veer away from the more analyzed lines. The text move poses no problems for Black to achieve equality.

3. . . .	N–KB3
4. N–B3	. . .

Against 4. P–K5 Black can obtain a free game with 4. . . . PxP 5. NxP Q–Q4 6. N–KB3 B–N5.

4. . . .	**N–B3**
5. P–Q4	**PxP**
6. NxP	**P–KN3**

6. . . . B–N5 7. P–B3 NxN 8. PxB offers interesting possibilities for White; or 6. . . . B–N5 7. Q–Q2 NxN 8. QxN B–B6 9. R–N1, and it is questionable whether White's loss of Kingside castling is sufficient compensation for Black's loss of time. Playable is 6. . . . P–K3 followed by . . . B–K2 and . . . 0–0.

7. B–N2	**B–Q2**

Necessary, for if 7. . . . B–N2 8. NxN PxN 9. P–K5.

8. 0–0	**B–N2**
9. QN–K2	**. . .**

Intending to set up the well-known Maroczy Bind with P–QB4. The plan is not sufficiently active, however, and allows Black to establish an aggressive position.

9. . . .	**Q–N3!**

This move prevents White from carrying out his plan, for if 10. B–K3 N–KN5! 11. N–K6. NxB 12. NxBch K–B1 13. PxN QxPch 14. K–R1 KxN with a won position.

10. N–N3	**. . .**

The Knight here prevents White's P–N3 and thus allows Black's Knight to aim for QB5. But Black was beginning to threaten White's KP, and 10. NxN BxN is clearly bad for White. His 9th move is already giving him problems.

10. . . .	**0–0**
11. B–K3	**. . .**

If 11. P–QB4 Black could choose between 11. . . . Q–N5, which practically forces 12. N–Q2, and 11. . . . N–K4 12. B–K3 Q–N5 13. P–B5 NxKP 14. P–QR3 Q–R5.

11. . . .	**Q–R3**
12. P–KR3	**N–K4**

QB5 is usually an advantageous post for a Knight.

13. B–Q4	**N–B5**
14. R–K1	**. . .**

Offering the possibility of B–KB1.

14.	. . .	B–B3
15.	N/2–B1	P–K4
16.	B–QB3	. . .

16.	. . .	P–Q4!

Opens the Q-file, bringing Black's Rooks into active play. By seizing control of the center, Black has gained the initiative. From here on, White remains on the defensive.

17.	N–Q3	. . .

Interesting but unsound is 17. PxP QR–Q1, and if 18. BxP? NxB 19. RxN NxP! 20. RxN (if 20. R–K1 N–K6, etc.) BxR 21. BxB Q–N4 22. P–QB4 QxP 23. BxQ RxQch 24. K–N2 (if 24. B–B1 BxP 25. R–N1 B–R6 26. K–N2 R–B1 27. B–K2 R–K8, etc.) 24. . . . BxP 25. R–N1 BxN 26. NxB R–B1, etc.

17.	. . .	NxP
18.	BxN	. . .

Black's Knight on K5 is intolerable!

18.	. . .	PxB
19.	N/Q–B5	Q–N3
20.	NxKP	QR–Q1

Without a Bishop at KN2, the White King is in a perilous situation. Black's Queen and QB can be posted in various ways to menace the White King. Black's control of the QR1–KR8 diagonal contributes heavily to White's eventual downfall.

21.	Q–K2	B–Q4!

A strong move, which enables ... Q–QB3 with threats to annoy White along the QB3–KR8 diagonal. Notice how soon after White's KB disappears the Black initiative increases in tempo.

22. QR–Q1	Q–QB3
23. N–R5	. . .

Gets rid of the strongly posted Knight, but Black now has a strongly posted Bishop.

23. . . .	NxN
24. BxN	P–N3
25. B–N4	KR–K1
26. Q–K3	. . .

26. . . .	P–B4

Not 26. . . . QxP 27. N–Q6.

27. N–Q6	R–K3

Of course not 27. . . . RxN 28. BxR QxB 29. P–QB4.

28. R–Q2	. . .

28. P–QB4 would be met by 28. . . . B–R8. A good example of the weakness of White's King position caused by the hole at KN2. White has no way to protect his light squares.

28. . . .	P–QR4
29. B–R3	R/3xN
30. BxR	RxB
31. KR–Q1	B–R8
32. P–KB3	RxR
33. QxR	. . .

A better try is 33. RxR, but Black could continue 33. . . . QxKBP
34. QxNP QxPch 35. K–B1 (35. KxB Q–K8ch) P–R4, etc.

33. . . .	BxP
34. Q–Q8ch	B–B1
35. R–Q3	Q–K5
Resigns	

Game 17

Both Kings Exposed

In this game Black's King is less sheltered than White's; yet Black
wins. Why? During the middlegame complications Black wins a
piece. True, for many moves thereafter his extra piece plays
almost no role in the game, and his King must be constantly alert
to threats from all sides. But White's problem is that he cannot
afford to simplify the position, for then Black's extra piece would
win. In the continuing complications White has to expose his own
King, and that means the end. Finally it is the weakness of
White's King, not Black's, that decides the game.

This game is instructive in many ways, but the reader will
profit most of all from careful study of the mutual tactical
threats against the Kings. The position after White's 31st move
and Black's solution are particularly intriguing.

36th Soviet Championship

Alma-Ata, 1969

SICILIAN DEFENSE

M. Tal	I. Platonov
1. P–K4	P–QB4
2. N–KB3	P–Q3
3. P–Q4	PxP
4. NxP	N–KB3
5. N–QB3	P–QR3
6. B–N5	P–K3
7. Q–B3	. . .

More usual is 7. P–B4 which leads to almost unfathomable complications. The text move is less difficult for Black to handle and has not produced satisfactory results for White in serious competition.

7. . . .	**P–R3**
8. **B–R4**	. . .

8. BxN QxB 9. QxQ PxQ 10. 0–0–0, handing Black a weak pawn structure for the endgame, is preferable. Also 8. B–K3 is to be considered.

8. . . .	**QN–Q2**
9. **0–0–0**	**Q–B2**
10. **B–K2**	**B–K2**
11. **KR–K1**	**P–KN4**
12. **B–N3**	**N–K4**
13. **Q–K3**	**P–N4**
14. **P–QR3?**	. . .

Giving Black the opportunity to open the QN-file with attacking possibilities later. Preferable is either 14. P–B3 or 14. P–KR4.

14. . . .	**QR–N1**
15. **P–B3**	**KN–Q2**

More exact is 15. . . . N–R4 preventing P–B4.

16. **P–B4**	**PxP**
17. **BxBP**	**P–N5**
18. **PxP**	**RxP**
19. **R–B1**	. . .

White rejects 19. BxKRP on account of 19. . . . N–QN3 with the annoying threat of . . . N–B5. If 20. P–QN3? RxB 21. QxR QxN.

19. . . .	**Q–N3**

20. P–QN3? . . .

Correct is 20. N–N3 in order to exchange Queens or, if Black avoids that, to attempt the exchange of Rooks with R–Q4, in either case relieving the pressure exerted by Black's pieces.

20. . . . **N–N3!**

21. B–R5? . . .

The text move hands over the initiative to his opponent. Imperative is 21. N–B3, but Tal dislikes simplification.

21. . . . **RxN!**

Bad is 21. . . . P–K4 22. N–Q5 PxB (22. . . . PxN 23. Q–Q2 winning the exchange) 23. BxN PxQ (23. . . . PxB 24. QxP with the threat of Q–B7ch) 24. BxPch followed by 25. N–K6 mate.

22. RxR **NxB**

Again best, for if 22. . . . P–K4 23. R–B4 and wins.

23. RxN **B–N4**

The most advisable. If 23. . . . P–K4 24. RxBP B–N4 (24. . . . PxR 25. R–R7ch K–Q1 26. RxRch N–B1 27. QxRP and wins) 25. R–R7ch K–B1 26. RxRch K–N2 27. QxBch PxQ 28. RxB with chances for a draw.

24. BxPch **K–Q1**

Not 24. . . . K–K2? 25. BxP KxB 26. Q–R3ch K–K4 27. R–Q5ch KxR 28. Q–B3 mate. Black now seriously threatens . . . PK4.

25. P–K5 . . .

A good try but still insufficient to save the game.

| 25. . . . | R–B1 |

A strong reply, winning a piece. Not 25. . . . PxP because of 26. RxNch, winning the Queen, nor 25. . . . NxP because of 26. QxN.

| 26. N–K2 | . . . |

The only defense. If 26. PxP RxB 27. QxP RxR, and if 26. P–R4 BxR 27. QxB PxP and wins.

26. . . .	RxB
27. P–R4	BxR
28. NxB	P–Q4

This locks in the Bishop but is unavoidable. 28. . . . PxP is still out because of RxNch, and 28. . . . NxP still loses to QxN. Although White has only one pawn for the piece, he still has some tactical chances because of the immobility of Black's pieces.

29. P–KN4	R–N2
30. P–N5	PxP
31. PxP	. . .

31. . . .   **K–K1!**

Black's task of making progress is difficult because his pieces are out of play. 31. . . . RxP is out of the question because of 32. NxPch; 31. . . . N–B1 is bad because of 32. RxPch; 31. . . . N–B4 throws away the win because of 32. NxP PxN 33. RxPch, etc.; and finally 31. . . . K–K2 32. P–N6 N–B1 33. Q–QB3 NxP (33. . . . B–Q2 34. RxP Q–N8ch 35. R–Q1, or 33. . . . B–N2 34. R–N4) 34. QxB QxR 35. Q–B7ch K–K1 (35. . . . K–B1 36. NxPch) 36. Q–B8ch and draws.

32. N–R5   **R–R2**

Bad is 32. . . . RxP 33. QxR QxR 34. Q–N8ch K–K2 (34. . . . N–B1 35. N–B6ch K–K2 36. Q–N7ch) 35. Q–N5ch (not 35. QxB QxP trapping the Knight) with a perpetual check.

33. N–B6ch   **. . .**

33. P–N6 simply fails to 33. . . . RxN 34. P–N7 K–B2.

33. . . .   **NxN**
34. KPxN   **R–R8ch**
35. K–N2   **R–R5!**
36. P–B3   **. . .**

Black has succeeded in weakening the position of White's King. Unavailing is 36. P–B7ch K–B1.

36. . . .   **R–R7ch**

Not 36. . . . RxR 37. PxR K–B2 38. Q–R3 QxPch 39. K–R2 Q–K5 40. Q–R8, compelling Black to resort to perpetual check.

37. K–R3   **R–QB7**

Because White's King is exposed, Black is able to set up various threats for White to parry. This prevents White from advancing his passed pawns—his only chance to survive.

    38. Q–R3   . . .

White is unable to advance the passed pawns because of the immediate threat of . . . Q–B4ch.

38. . . .	**Q–R4ch**
39. R–R4	**Q–B4ch**
40. R–N4	**P–R4**

Inadvisable is 40. . . . QxP 41. QxQ RxQ 42. R–KR4 R–N6 43. R–R8ch K–B2 44. R–R7ch (not 44. RxB RxP with good chances to win) 44. . . . K–N1 45. R–N7ch K–B1 46. P–N6 P–K4 47. R–B7ch K–N1 48. R–N7ch, etc.

41. Q–R8ch	**K–Q2**
42. Q–R7ch	**K–B3**
43. QxR	**PxRch**
44. K–R2	**PxP**
45. P–N6	**P–K4**

At last, the Bishop is getting active.

46. P–B7	**B–K3**
47. Q–Q3	. . .

If 47. QxP QxQ 48. P–B8=Q Q–B7ch followed by 49. . . . QxKNP and wins.

    47. . . .   **Q–B7ch!**

Black could go wrong here with 47. . . . P–B7 48. Q–R6ch K–B2 49. P–B8=Q QxQ 50. Q–R7ch K–B3 51. Q–R6ch K–Q2 (51. . . . K–B4 52. Q–R7ch K–N5 53. Q–R3ch) 52. Q–N7ch K–K1 53. Q–N8ch K–K2 54. Q–N4ch K–Q2 55. Q–N7ch K–Q1 56. Q–N6ch and draws by perpetual check.

48. K–R3	**Q–R2ch**
49. K–N4	**Q–B4ch**
50. K–R4	**P–B7**
51. P–B8=Q	**Q–R2ch**

Black can also win with 51. . . . QxQ 52. QxBPch K–N3 53. P–N4 Q–R1ch 54. K–N3 P–Q5ch 55. K–N2 Q–R7ch, etc.

52. K–N4	**Q–N2ch**
53. K–R4	**P–B8=Q**

54. Q(B8)–B1	QxQ
55. QxQ	Q–R2ch
56. K–N4	Q–B4ch
57. K–R4	K–N3
Resigns	

If 58. P–N4 Q–B7ch 59. K–R3 P–Q5 with mate to follow. A fine game by Platonov.

Game 18

Quick Punishment

I suspect that Larsen made some kind of miscalculation on his 15th turn—how else can voluntary exposure of his own King be explained? This game tells us nothing new about such situations, but it is a model demonstration of the harsh punishment for violating a basic principle.

Of course, Larsen knows the principles better than most; his frequent experiments to challenge blandly accepted theories are part of his style and are to some extent designed to have a psychological effect. I believe that in this case he expected to defeat Donner with relative ease and thought he could get away with "anything." Such an attitude often leads to error. The lesson Donner gives him should not be lost on the reader.

Leiden, 1970

BENONI DEFENSE

J. H. Donner	**B. Larsen**
1. P–Q4	P–QB4
2. P–Q5	P–Q3
3. P–K4	N–KB3
4. B–Q3	P–KN3
5. N–K2	B–N2
6. 0–0	0–0

To be considered is 6. . . . P–B5 7. BxP NxP.

| 7. P–QB4 | P–K3 |
| 8. N/2–B3 | . . . |

White's Knight maneuver at first seems cumbersome, but after closer inspection the setup proves justifiable. The QN will be developed via Q2.

8. . . .	PxP
9. BPxP	QN–Q2
10. N–Q2	P–QR3
11. P–QR4	N–R4
12. P–B4	. . .

Preventing . . . N–B5.

| 12. . . . | B–Q5ch |

Larsen is pressing hard, counting on weak resistance by his opponent, but he is in for a surprise.

| 13. K–R1 | QN–B3 |

Faulty is 13. . . . Q–R5 because of 14. N–K2 (not 14. Q–B3 on account of 14. . . . N–K4 15. PxN B–N5 trapping the Queen) followed by N–KB3.

| 14. N–B3 | . . . |

Black's KB is now in trouble.

| 14. . . . | R–K1 |

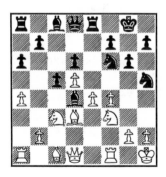

15. P–B5!   . . .

White is unconcerned about losing a pawn. If 15. . . . BxN 16. PxB NxKP 17. BxN RxB N–N5 with excellent attacking possibilities; for instance, 18. . . . R–K2 19. P–B4 BxP 20. RxB PxR

21. B–N2 (21. QxN?? R–K8 mate) N–N2 22. Q–B3 with the
serious threats of 23. Q–B3 and 23. Q–KR3.

       15. . . .   **PxP?**

Not the best defense. Correct is 15. . . . B–Q2, and if 16. B–KN5
Q–R4 with counterplay. The text move exposes the King, and
after the capture of Black's vital KB he cannot hope to defend
successfully.

        16. PxP   **K–R1**
        17. NxB   **PxN**

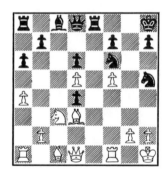

        18. N–K4!   **. . .**
With the strong threat of B–KN5.

        18. . . .   **NxN**
        19. QxN   **. . .**
And now Black's exposed and undefended King is subjected
to an irresistible onslaught.

        19. . . .   **Q–B3**
        20. B–R6   **B–Q2**
        21. R–B4   **N–B4**
        22. B–KN5   **Q–K4**
If 22. . . . Q–N2 23. P–B6 Q–N1 24. B–R6 and wins.
        23. Q–R6   **Resigns**

Game 19

No Time to Hesitate

One cannot always conduct a successful attack with pieces only; the pawns are needed to breach the defenses and to support the pieces. When both sides castle on the same wing, however, for one side to advance his pawns in attacking the enemy King is to weaken his own King's defenses. Therefore, such positions contain some risk for the attacking side, particularly when the defender is as difficult to beat as Yugoslavia's Borislav Ivkov. Portisch, aware both of his positional advantage and of Ivkov's skill in defense, seems unable to decide whether to attack directly or to increase the positional pressure against Ivkov's QP. The result is that he gradually exposes his King's position and, not following through with an attack, succumbs to Ivkov's counterplay based precisely on the exposed White King.

Raach, 1969

KING'S FIANCHETTO OPENING

L. Portisch	B. Ivkov
1. N–KB3	N–KB3
2. P–KN3	P–Q3
3. P–Q4	B–N5

A favorite defense of Ivkov's. Black is willing to give up this Bishop, solving the problem of how to develop it.

4. B–N2	QN–Q2
5. P–KR3	BxN
6. BxB	P–B3
7. P–K4	P–K4
8. 0–0	B–K2
9. B–K3	0–0
10. P–QR4	P–QR4
11. N–B3	Q–B2
12. Q–Q2	QR–Q1

12. . . . KR–Q1 appears more logical since Black's best chance for action is on the Queenside where he needs the QR.

13. QR–Q1	KR–K1
14. B–N2	N–B1

Both sides have now completed their development. White's position is preferable because of his greater control of space and greater freedom for his forces. But he has to adopt a promising plan. The most obvious and plausible idea is the advance of his KBP.

15. Q–K2	PxP

Against 15. . . . N–K3, White could continue 16. P–Q5 N–B4 (16. . . . PxP gives White's Knight a strong post at his QN5) 17. BxN PxB 18. N–N1, followed by N–R3–B4 with a strong position.

16. BxP	N–K3
17. B–K3	N–Q2

18. Q–Q2	. . .

Getting the Queen out of the way of Black's KR, but this is not the best square for it. Better is 18. P–B4 followed by 19. Q–B2, where the Queen is more comfortably placed.

18. . . .	N/2–B4

Black is not in a position to undertake anything. His respect for White's two Bishops is well founded, and he wisely avoids any risky action that would open the position. His pawns on QB3 and K3 are keeping the White pieces at bay, and Black does not want to move them. He is correct to adopt a waiting strategy, ready to respond to White's lead.

| 19. KR–K1 | . . . |

Giving additional protection to the KP.

19. . . .	B–B3
20. P–N3	N–B1
21. P–B3	N–R3
22. B–B2	. . .

Unnecessary. White should play 22. P–B4; his failure to undertake aggressive action is difficult to understand. He can't seem to decide whether to play for a Kingside attack or to attempt operations against Black's QP. However, he has loosened his King's position, which, though not dangerous at present, is perhaps one reason he hesitates to initiate a risky attack. If the attack failed, his King would then be at the mercy of the enemy pieces.

| 22. . . . | N–K3 |
| 23. P–B4 | . . . |

Finally! White seems to have all the play, but he is up against a great defender with a fighting heart.

| 23. . . . | N/K–B4 |
| 24. R–K2 | . . . |

Timidly played. Correct and logical is 24. P–KN4.

| 24. . . . | N–N5 |
| 25. Q–K1 | . . . |

Threatening 26. P–K5.

25. . . .	N–K3
26. P–R4	N–B1
27. N–N1?	. . .

A sign of indecision and lack of confidence. Why not 27. P–KN4–5?

27. . . .	B–K2
28. K–R1	N–Q2
29. Q–B1	B–B1
30. R/2–Q2	N–R3
31. B–B3	N/3–B4
32. Q–N2	N–B3

33. N–B3	Q–N3
34. B–Q4	N/3–Q2
35. N–N1	Q–B2
36. B–N2	B–K2
37. B–B3	P–QN4

White's meaningless maneuvering has allowed his opponent to effect this significant advance.

        38. R–Q4   . . .

Unwise is 38. PxP PxP 39. P–QN4 on account of the strong rejoinder 39. . . . N–R5. The text move is pointless since Black could force a repetition of moves with 38. . . . N–K3, but it is apparently made to gain time until adjournment.

38. . . .	P–N5
39. B–K1	B–B1
40. B–B2	N–B3

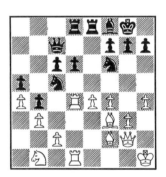

        41. N–Q2   . . .

The sealed move but not the best. As will soon become evident, correct is 41. B–N1. Note that 41. R–B4 fails to 41. . . . P–Q4! 42. RxN (42. PxP PxP 43. BxP R–K7, threatening to win material) 42. . . . PxP 43. B–K2 RxRch 44. BxR P–K6, and if 45. RxBP PxB 46. RxQ R–K8ch, etc.

41. . . .	P–Q4
42. PxP	. . .

42. P–K5 N/3–Q2 43. N–B1 is preferable.

42. . . .	PxP
43. BxP	. . .

White has no other plausible move. 43. P–N4 loses to 43. . . . N–K3, and 43. N–B1 is unappetizing on account of 43. . . . N/4–K5 44. N–K3 NxBch 45. QxN B–B4, etc.

| 43. . . . | NxB |
| 44. RxN | R–K7! |

This strong reply would not be available to Black if White had played 41. B–N1. The insecurity of White's King is becoming a factor, since it is clearly a target for Black's counterplay.

| 45. K–N1 | . . . |

The only move. If 45. N–B4 RxR 46. RxR RxP with an easily won position.

| 45. . . . | NxRP! |
| 46. N–B4 | . . . |

Not 46. PxN RxR 47. QxR QxQBP with great advantage.

| 46. . . . | RxR |
| 47. QxR | . . . |

Best, for if 47. RxR N–B6 48. R–Q2 [if 48. RxP RxP (not 48. . . . N–K5 49. Q–B3 RxB 50. QxN and wins; or 48. . . . N–Q8 49. Q–B1 RxB 50. QxN and wins) followed by . . . Q–Q2 with strong pressure] 48. . . . P–R5 with advantage.

| 47. . . . | N–B6 |
| 48. Q–Q8 | Q–B3 |

Stronger is 48. . . . Q–N2 with the powerful threat of 49. . . . Q–B6. The text move permits White an important tempo.

49. N–K5	RxN
50. PxR	NxR
51. QxN	Q–QB6
52. Q–K2	. . .

Insufficient is 52. Q–Q5 QxBP 53. P–K6 Q–B2 54. PxPch QxP 55. QxP QxP and wins.

| 52. . . . | B–B4 |
| 53. BxB | QxBch |

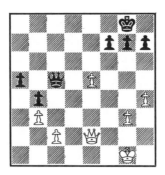

54. K–N2??   . . .

The losing move and an unbelievable blunder. With 54. K–R2, Portisch could draw: if 54. . . . P–R4 (after 54. K–R2) 55. P–K6 draws; or if 54. . . . K–B1 55. P–R5, and Black could not make any progress.

54. . . .   **P–R4!**

The winning move because Black is now in a position to win the KP without losing any of his own.

55. Q–K4   . . .

Unfortunately White is unable to play 55. P–K6 because of 55. . . . Q–Q4ch. An exposed King, particularly with Queens still on the board, always makes possible such tactical twists because of checks.

55. . . .   **K–B1**

Thanks to White's weak 54th move, his isolated KP has become vulnerable and indefensible.

56. K–B3	**K–K2**
57. P–N4	**PxPch**
58. KxP	**P–N3**
59. K–N5	**K–K3**
60. K–B4	**Q–B7ch**
61. K–N4	**Q–N8ch**
62. K–B3	. . .

If 62. K–B4 Q–R7ch.

62. . . .	**Q–R8ch**
63. K–B4	. . .

If 63. K–K3 Q–R6ch 64. K–Q4 (64. K–K2 Q–R7ch winning the KP) 64. . . . Q–B6 mate.

      63. . . .   **QxPch**

      Resigns

Game 20

Left in the Lurch

In this game extract, Portisch can retain a positional advantage by advancing his King toward the center, bringing it under the protection of his pieces, and at the same time preparing it for a role in the game. Instead, his premature pawn break allows White to activate his pieces, and a later error gives White the key to Black's fortress. Black's lagging King suffers the consequences despite his gaining a new consort in the far reaches of his kingdom—a clear case of too little too late.

2nd Match Game

Porec, 1968

Black to play

B. Larsen   **L. Portisch**

28. . . .   **P–B5?**

Portisch has a perfectly satisfactory position. Overrating it, he embarks on an aggressive plan which proves unsound. After 28.

. . . K–N2 followed by . . . K–B3 he would enjoy a slight positional advantage, with his King more secure and ready to participate in further operations.

29. PxP   R–Q7

Portisch must have been relying on 30. R–Q1 R–B7, winning the RP, but Larsen has different intentions.

30. R–K1!   . . .

Beginning an indirect attack against the QP.

30. . . .   B–B2

30. . . . K–B2 fails to 31. N–N5 with the threat of 32. N–B7.

31. N–N5   P–R3?

Unavailing is 31. . . . RxRP on account of 32. R–K7 which wins the RP because of the threat of 33. N–Q6. Best is 31. . . . K–B1, for if 32. NxP RxQP with the superior position for Black, but 32. P–R3 gives White the better chances. The text move allows White's Rook to penetrate.

32. N–Q6   RxQP
33. R–QN1   . . .

Now the inferiority of Black's 31st move becomes evident. It enabled White's Rook to seize the seventh rank, and this, as we shall see, is more dangerous for Black than Black's QBP is for White. Black's King is in peril.

33. . . .   N–Q2

Unfortunately for Portisch, 33. . . . P–B6 does not suffice: 33. . . . P–B6 34. NxB KxN (34. . . . P–B7 35. NxPch K–N2 36. R–QB1) 35. RxN P–B7 36. R–B6 R–B5 37. BxPch.

34. R–N7   . . .

White has achieved favorable placement of his Rook and Knight, causing trouble for Black's minor pieces, especially for the miserably placed Bishop. Of course, Black's King is not too happy. Portisch certainly underestimated White's potential.

34. . . .   P–B6

A good try but insufficient. The trap is 35. RxN P–B7 36. R–B7 R–B5, and Black queens under favorable conditions.

35. R–B7   RxP

Against 35. . . . B–K3, White has 36. P–B5, winning a piece. 35. . . . R–B5 does not work now.

| 36. NxB | R–B5 |
| 37. RxN! | . . . |

Allowing Black to queen, but charging quite a price for it!

| 37. . . . | P–B7 |
| 38. N–K5 | P–B8=Q |

If 38. . . . R–B6 (38. . . . R–B4 39. N–Q3) 39. BxPch K–B1 40. NxPch K–K1 41. R–K7ch K–Q1 42. R–K1 P–B8=Q 43. RxQ and wins.

| 39. BxPch | K–B1 |
| 40. BxR | Q–K8? |

Another mistake, losing the new Queen. But the position is hopeless for Black in any case.

| 41. NxPch | Resigns |

Game 21

Castling Wrong

Castling is supposed to bring the King to safety, not danger. Spanish International Master Medina, however, gets the idea that he can launch a successful Kingside attack against Larsen and castles long. Indeed, the attack succeeds—Larsen's, not Medina's.

White's King is unsafe on the Queenside for several reasons, principal among them that he cannot avoid the opening of lines in that sector. He should have realized that before castling there.

Palma de Majorca, 1969

KING'S FIANCHETTO OPENING

A. Medina	B. Larsen
1. P–K4	P–KN3
2. N–QB3	B–N2
3. P–KN3	P–K4
4. B–N2	P–Q3
5. P–Q3	B–K3
6. P–KR4	. . .

White wants to avoid the exchange of his King Bishop; if 6. N–B3 Q–B1 7. 0–0 (if 7. N–KN5 B–Q2 followed by . . . P–KR3 and . . . B–R6) 7. . . . B–R6, but it is questionable whether that is enough to justify the text move.

6. . . .	N–KB3
7. N–R3	N–B3
8. N–Q5	BxN
9. PxB	N–K2
10. P–QB3	. . .

So that if 10. . . . N/2xP or 10. . . . N/3xP 11. Q–N3, regaining the pawn favorably.

10. . . .	P–KR3
11. Q–N3	Q–B1
12. B–K3	0–0
13. 0–0–0?	. . .

Underestimating Black's attacking potential. Relatively better is 13. P–QB4 followed by 14. 0–0. Even so, Black has good chances because of the awkward position of White's Knight.

13. . . .	P–QR4

Already this means trouble for White.

14. P–R4	P–B3
15. PxP	PxP

Now Black has an open file for attack.

16. Q–R3	N–B4
17. B–Q2	R–N1
18. P–R5	P–N4
19. N–N1	P–B4
20. Q–R2	. . .

White has no promising continuation. Although he has the two Bishops, his pieces are miserably placed, and he hasn't the least prospect of counterplay against Black's forthcoming on-slaught. Larsen's tactical play is an artful lesson in conducting an attack against the King.

20. . . .	Q–R3

Target: White's weak QP.

21. K–B2	KR–B1
22. N–K2?	. . .

Expediting Black's attack. The only try is 22. B–Q5 R–B2 23.
N–B3.

    22. . . .   **P–K5!**

Larsen was planning this sooner or later to activate his KB.
Thanks to White's last move, this move is now quite strong.

    23. B–QB1   . . .

23. PxP QxN 24. PxN QxBP is in Black's favor; 23. BxKP NxB
24. PxN QxN 25. PxN QxBP 26. KR–B1 QxP 27. P–B6 is an
improvement for White; but after 23. BxKP NxB 24. PxN N–Q5ch
25. NxN PxN, Black's attack is difficult to parry.

    23. . . .   **P–Q4**
    24. KR–K1   . . .

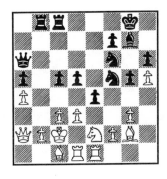

    24. . . .   **N–Q5ch!**

The beginning of the end. The sacrifice is justified by the many
sensitive points around White's King.

    25. PxN   . . .

If 25. K–N1 NxN 26. RxN PxP, etc.

    25. . . .   **KPxPch**
    26. RxP   **PxPch**
    27. K–Q2   **N–K5ch**
    28. BxN   **PxB**
    29. R–R3   . . .

29. R–N3 Q–B5 30. RxR Q–B7 mate.

    29. . . .   **Q–QB3**
    30. Q–N1   **P–Q6**
    31. N–N1   . . .

31. N–B3 BxNch 32. RxB QxRch, etc.

31. . . .	Q–B4

Threatening 32. . . . QxR.

32. R–R1	QxPch
33. K–Q1	B–B6
34. PxB	RxQ
35. RxR	Q–B7 mate

Game 22

"Skim Milk Masquerades as Cream"

"Things are seldom what they seem," begins the famous couplet from Gilbert & Sullivan's *H.M.S. Pinafore*. In chess terms, this can be applied to the perception of weakness where none exists.

Look at the position after Black's 19th move and compare the Kings' relative situations. Black's certainly appears to be in trouble, since White's Rooks are ready to occupy the KB-file and his Knight the Q5 outpost, all bearing down on Black's KBP. In addition, the pawns in front of Black's King have been advanced. White's King, however, seems to have his personal security well in hand, and Black appears to have no offensive punch in that area.

But appearances are deceiving. This is the psychological pitfall Medina tumbles into: believing Black's position to be vulnerable, he pays too little attention to the opportunities at his opponent's disposal. By continuing correctly, White would have only a slight disadvantage in view of Black's growing menace on the Queenside, but instead he blunders and goes home early.

Palma de Majorca, 1971

SICILIAN DEFENSE

A. Medina	S. Reshevsky
1. P–K4	P–QB4
2. N–QB3	P–Q3
3. P–KN3	N–QB3
4. B–N2	P–KN3

5. P–Q3	B–N2
6. P–B4	. . .

The usual 6. N–B3 P–K3 (or 6. . . . P–K4) 7. 0–0 KN–K2 leads to well-known lines. The text move is more aggressive and is intended to prepare for a quick Kingside build-up.

6. . . .	P–K4
7. N–R3	. . .

7. N–B3 looks more natural, but the text move is not so silly as it may appear. Its purpose is to activate White's KR immediately (after castling) on the KB-file.

7. . . .	PxP

The most precise move. If 7. . . . KN–K2 8. 0–0 0–0? 9. P–B5, and White's opening strategy will succeed, for if 9. . . . PxP 10. PxP BxP 11. RxB! NxR 12. B–K4 KN–K2 13. BxPch KxB 14. Q–R5ch K–N1 15. N–KN5 with a winning attack.

8. BxP	N–B3
9. Q–Q2	N–KN5
10. N–B2	N/5–K4

To be considered is 10. . . . NxN 11. QxN 0–0 with fewer complications.

11. B–R6	0–0
12. 0–0–0	. . .

It appears now that White will be able to make progress with P–KR4–5. I knew that I would have to offer stiff resistance.

12. . . .	B–K3
13. P–KR4	P–B3

14. B–R3	KBxB
15. QxB	Q–Q2

I would prefer to retain the Bishop, but if 15. . . . B–B2? 16. P–R5, and if 16. . . . P–KN4 17. B–B5 and wins.

16. BxBch	QxB
17. N–R3	. . .

17. P–R5? enables me to trap the Queen with 17. . . . P–KN4.

17. . . .	N–KN5
18. Q–Q2	P–KR4

Necessary; otherwise White would continue 19. P–R5 P–KN4, which weakens Black's KB4 square.

| 19. N–B4 | . . . |

The position is about even. White has no prospects for attack, but Medina dreams of it still. Black's King seems compromised but is quite safe given the absence of strong outposts for White's pieces and the freedom for Black's. The Q5-square, available to a White Knight, is less effective here than in some other positions because of White's lack of good targets. The seeming weakness of Black's King is, however, too tempting for an aggressive player like Medina. Insisting on his "attack," he is not alert to his opponent's threats.

20. QN–Q5	QR–K1
21. KR–B1	K–R2

Protecting the KNP and enabling the Queen to reach a more active square.

22. K–N1	Q–Q2
23. QR–K1	P–QN4

With everything safe on the Kingside, pawn action on the opposite wing is called for.

| 24. N–R3 | . . . |

Medina starts a faulty maneuver to double Rooks on the KB-file. Wiser is an attempt to simplify with an exchange of Knights by 24. N–K3, and if Black decides to avoid the exchange with 24. . . . N/5–K4 25. N/4–Q5 R–K3, then it would be useful to double Rooks on the KB-file with 26. R–B2, exerting pressure on the KBP.

| 24. . . . | P–N5 |

25. R–B4	K–N2
26. R/1–KB1	N–Q5
27. N–N1	P–R4

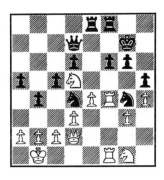

28. N–K2??	. . .

The losing move. This is not the kind of position Medina likes. Uninterested in patient maneuvering, which this position requires, he overlooks Black's simple reply and loses the Exchange. Correct is 28. N–K3 N–K3 29. R/4–B3 N–K4 30. R/3–B2 N–Q5 with only a small advantage for Black.

28. . . .	N–K3
29. N–N1	. . .

If 29. R/4–B3 N–R7.

29. . . .	NxR
30. PxN	P–B4

Destroying the remnants of any White hopes. White must submit to further exchanges, and his central pawns become weak and exposed.

31. R–K1	PxP
32. PxP	N–B3
33. NxN	RxN
34. N–B3	Q–N5

White's game now collapses quickly.

35. P–K5	RxBP
36. N–N5	R–Q5
37. Q–B2?	R–Q8ch
Resigns	

Chapter 4

Space

There are sixty-four squares on the chess board. Before the start of the game each side controls his own first three ranks, but as soon as White makes his first move—say 1. P–K4—his control of space increases dramatically: his pawn, his KB, and his Queen already strike at squares in Black's half of the board. As long as White makes no errors and loses no time, he should continue to command slightly more space than Black. That is why White wins most decisive games and why the first move is an advantage.

White's practical problem is to obtain a concrete advantage that can be counted on to deliver the win, for space alone is not enough except in a few cases. Often, White will be able to force Black to weaken his pawn structure, or he will be able to develop such a strong initiative that he may decide to launch a mating attack, or he may win material.

Black's problem is to limit White's spatial superiority while gaining his own foothold in critical areas. The usual methods are to fight directly for the same territory as White or to establish a second front where his own local advantage in space will counterbalance White's. The second is usually preferred today, for it offers better winning chances; merely to establish equality by neutralizing the opponent's threats is not enough for most players, particularly the younger, more ambitious ones.

However, for Black to recognize his problem and select the

method for meeting it is quite another thing from putting the method in practice, for White begins with an advantage. This is the most difficult problem in chess, as evidenced by the fact that White always wins more games than Black in all the major opening systems. The games in this chapter were chosen especially to point up Black's problems in meeting White's initial threat to obtain an advantage in space.

In game 23 Black decides to simplify by exchanging pieces, for an advantage in space is less meaningful when the forces are reduced. But his loss of time is too costly. In game 24 Black again loses time, in this case searching not for simplification but for complications. Both games demonstrate how an advantage in space leads almost of itself to one of time.

Some players take extreme methods to avoid cramp. In game 25 Black willingly accepts a couple of weaknesses, and in game 26 he even sacrifices material, but in both cases to no avail.

American Grandmaster Lubomir Kavalek shows in game 27 how a stubborn blockading strategy gives White the serious problem of converting his space advantage to something more concrete. One of the hazards of defending a cramped position, however, is that a single error can be fatal, and that is what happens here.

Game 28 again shows how a space advantage can be converted to a winning position, but so does it demonstrate White's need to follow through. In game 29 White makes it easy for Black: he is so awed by Black's great reputation as an opening theorist that he plays timidly and gives Black the space advantage. In the endgame White is reduced to zugzwang, a deficiency in space so extreme that any move loses.

Finally, a technical demonstration of the result of Black's failure to fight for space is seen in game 30: by not advancing either his KP or his QBP, two important pawns for controlling the vital center squares, he soon gets a terminally congested position.

Game 23

Loss of Time

Black experiments with a new idea in the opening and achieves a disaster. On his 11th turn, he begins a simplifying maneuver with his Knight which proves to be a serious loss of time and enables me to gain control of the center and thus deny him the chance to develop smoothly. Cramped for space, Black soon collapses.

72nd U.S. Open

Ventura, 1971

OLD INDIAN DEFENSE

S. Reshevsky	A. Karklins
1. N–KB3	N–KB3
2. P–KN3	P–Q3
3. P–Q4	QN–Q2
4. P–B4	P–K4
5. N–B3	P–B3
6. B–N2	B–K2
7. 0–0	0–0

This opening differs fundamentally from the King's Indian Defense in that here Black's King Bishop is developed at K2, where it protects the QP, instead of at KN2, as usual in the King's Indian. But at KN2 the Bishop can be more active, giving Black opportunities for aggressive play. At K2 the Bishop plays only a passive role, and this is a cause of Black's later problems.

| 8. P–K4 | P–QR3 |

Black evidently intends . . . P–QN4 in an attempt to gain space on the Queenside. White, however, refuses to allow it. Denying Black space soon proves to be significant.

| 9. P–QR4 | P–QR4 |

Otherwise, White can continue P–R5, cramping Black's position.

| 10. P–R3 | P–R3 |

A relatively untried idea, the purpose of which is to continue . . . N–R2–N4 and offer an exchange of Knights, but this maneuver proves to be a loss of valuable time, which would be better used to continue development. The thematic 10. . . . PxP 11. NxP N–B4, followed by . . . Q–N3, is more logical.

11. B–K3	N–R2?
12. K–R2	N–N4
13. N–R4	P–KN3

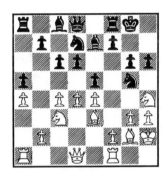

Forced in order to prevent N–B5, but now Black's Kingside is weakened.

14. P–B4! . . .

An enterprising move which announces White's serious intentions to work up an attack. From here on, Black confronts insurmountable problems, since he must try to defend against both an attack on his King and a breakthrough in the center. With such limited space, however, this proves to be too difficult.

14. . . . PxQP

The other possibility is 14. . . . PxBP (14. . . . N–R2 15. BPxP and 16. BxP and 14. . . . N–K3 are similar to the game). There would follow 15. PxP (also playable is 15. BxP) NxKP (15. . . . NxRP 16. NxP PxN 17. BxN with excellent chances) 16. NxN BxN 17. NxP with advantage.

15. BxP	N–K3
16. B–K3	BxN

120 *The Art of Positional Play*

This attempt to get rid of his weak QP turns out badly. Relatively better is 16. . . . N/3–B4 17. P–B5 P–KN4.

| 17. PxB | QxP |
| 18. P–KB5! | . . . |

An important move. If 18. QxP, N–B3 would give Black some breathing space; the double threat of 19. . . . N–N5ch and 19. . . . R–Q1 would be unpleasant.

| 18. . . . | N–N2 |
| 19. QxP | . . . |

It is now apparent that White enjoys greater space for his pieces, a result of Black's loss of time on moves 10 to 12. White has an active QB and complete control of the Q- and KB-files, whereas Black's QB is not developed and his Knights are clumsily placed. This greater mobility enables White to mass his forces for a quick breakthrough.

| 19. . . . | N–B3 |
| 20. R–B4 | . . . |

Another purpose of my 18th move now becomes clear: the threat of . . . N–N5ch is easily met, while an important tempo is won at the same time.

| 20. . . . | Q–N4 |
| 21. QR–KB1 | . . . |

Though disappointed to find that I could not trap my opponent's Queen, I *can* increase the pressure on the KB-file.

21. . . .	N/2–R4
22. R/4–B3	Q–R5
23. PxP	PxP

Unavailing is 23. . . . N–N5ch because of 24. K–N1 NxB 25. PxPch K–N2 26. Q–K5ch K–R2 27. RxN, etc.

24. K–N1! . . .

A quiet move, after which Black's defense crumbles The immediate threat is P–K5, which would have failed on the last move to 24. . . . N–N5ch 25. K–N1 RxR 26. QxPch N–N2 27. RxR Q–K8ch 28. B–B1 NxB, and if 29. R–B7 N–B4.

24. . . . **R–K1**

There is no better alternative. The lack of sufficient space for Black's pieces is the cause of his downfall.

25. RxN	NxR
26. RxN	Q–K8ch
27. K–R2	QxB

Black wins material but loses the game.

28. RxPch	K–R2
29. R–N3	Resigns

Game 24

Neglect of Development

Here Black wastes time in an effort not to simplify but to complicate. The result is the same as in the previous game: Black's laggard development and consequent lack of room to maneuver permit an uncomplicated attack.

Undeveloped pieces are not working pieces. To paraphrase a popular expression: if they're not part of the solution, they're part of the problem.

U.S. Championship
New York, 1970

NIMZO-INDIAN DEFENSE

S. Reshevsky	K. Burger
1. P–Q4	N–KB3
2. P–QB4	P–K3

3.	N–Q3	B–N5
4.	P–K3	O–O
5.	B–Q3	P–B4
6.	N–B3	P–Q4
7.	O–O	N–B3
8.	P–QR3	PxBP
9.	BxP	B–R4
10.	B–Q3	. . .

Steering away from the more popular 10. Q–Q3 P–QR3 11. R–Q1 P–QN4 12. B–R2 Q–K2 or 12. . . . B–N3.

10.	. . .	Q–K2
11.	N–K4	NxN
12.	BxN	B–N3

Preferable is 12. . . . R–Q1 with approximate equality. The text move permits White to gain a few tempos and expedite his development.

13.	PxP	QxP

To be considered is 13. . . . BxP 14. P–QN4 B–Q3 15. B–N2 B–Q2.

14.	P–QN4	Q–B5

Here Black embarks on a dangerous course in which his Queen becomes subject to attack. Again, the time wasted should have been used for development. Indicated is 14. . . . Q–KR4, where the Queen would not be so easily harassed.

15.	N–Q2	. . .

Better than 15. B–Q3 Q–B6 16. R–R2 N–K4 17. NxN QxN 18. B–N2 Q–Q4, and the Queen harassment is over.

15.	. . .	Q–B6
16.	R–R2	R–Q1
17.	R–B2	Q–K4
18.	B–N2	Q–KN4
19.	Q–K2	. . .

eventually falls to my concentrated pressure. In bad time trouble, Lombardy then overlooks a pin that costs him a piece.

U.S. Championship
New York, 1972

QUEEN'S INDIAN DEFENSE

S. Reshevsky	W. Lombardy
1. N–KB3	N–KB3
2. P–B4	P–K3
3. P–KN3	P–QN3
4. B–N2	B–N2
5. 0–0	B–K2
6. P–N3	0–0
7. B–N2	P–B4
8. P–Q4	. . .

A good alternative is 8. P–K3 followed by Q–K2 and P–Q3, an idea which former World Champion Botvinnik successfully experimented with.

8. . . .	PxP
9. QxP	. . .

Preferable to 9. NxP BxB 10. KxB P–Q4, leading to simplification and no hope of any advantage for White.

9. . . .	N–B3
10. Q–B4	Q–N1

This move is not new. It is designed to force the exchange of Queens and thus lead to an ending in which Black hopes to equalize easily. It is often true that, when Queens are off the board, the ensuing ending offers small hope for an advantage— but not always. In this particular position, White's pieces enjoy superior mobility. In addition, Black is temporarily saddled with a backward QP.

11. N–B3	. . .

The usual continuation here is 11. QxQ QRxQ 12. R–Q1 KR–Q1. My decision to allow Lombardy to make the exchange and double my pawns is quite deliberate. My idea is that the

pawn at KB4 will enable me to post a Knight at K5, where it
can exert considerable pressure on Black's QN and QP. This
advantage is worth enduring a doubled pawn.

11. . . .	**QxQ**
12. PxQ	**KR–Q1**
13. KR–Q1	**QR–N1**

Preparing for White's N–K5.

14. N–K5	**P–QR3**

Not to be recommended is 14. . . . NxN because of 15. PxN
N–K1 16. BxB RxB 17. N–K4 with a strong bind in which Black's
backward QP becomes really weak.

15. R–Q2	**N–R2**

Lombardy, feeling uncomfortably cramped in this position,
decides to try to exchange pieces.

16. QR–Q1	**. . .**

White gains valuable time by not exchanging Bishops himself,
forcing Black to do so instead.

16. . . .	**BxB**
17. KxB	**R–N2**
18. K–B3	**. . .**

White's greater control of space is obvious at this point. All of
White's pieces are well placed and ready for action. White
controls the important Queen file and is bearing down on the QP
with his Rooks, whereas Black's forces do not occupy space
beyond his third rank. White's pawn at KB4, although doubled,
helps anchor White's Knight at the important square K5.

18. . . .	**K–B1**

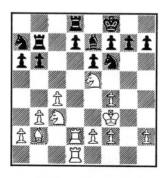

19. P–K4!   . . .

Preparing to immobilize my opponent's forces by posting a pawn at K5. There is no other way to make further progress. It is now up to Black to parry my threat.

19. . . .   **P–QN4**

Lombardy tries to obtain some counterplay on the Queenside. To continue defensively with 19. . . . P–Q3 20. N–Q3 R/2–Q2, which prevents the immediate advance of White's KP, is wiser.

20. PxP   **PxP**

After 20. . . . NxNP 21. N–B4 (21. NxN PxN is satisfactory for Black) 21. . . . NxN 22. BxN, White's position is strengthened. Black would not be able to continue 22. . . . P–Q4 because of 23. BxN followed by PxP, winding up with an extra pawn and with complete control of the vital Q6 square.

21. N–Q3   **P–Q4**

Black accomplishes one thing: his QP is no longer backward. But his QB3 square becomes accessible to White.

22. P–K5   **N–Q2**

23. N–K2   **P–N5?**

Overlooking White's plan; otherwise, he would play the correct 23. . . . P–N3.

24. P–B5!   . . .

A strong move. The opening of the position presents Black with problems of defense because of his weaknesses. And those weaknesses result from his attempts to free his cramped position.

24. . . .   **PxP**

Otherwise White would continue forcefully with 25. N/2–B4, exerting pressure on the KP.

25. N–Q4   **P–N3**

26. R–B2   . . .

Seizing control of the QB-file, which restricts Black's pieces. Black's extra pawn is of no significance. To add to Black's troubles, he is beginning to get into time trouble in a position that requires perfect defense, if that is possible.

26. . . .   **N–N4**

27. N–B6   **R–B1**

28. N/3xP   **BxN**

Forced. Not only is Black's QP attacked, but Black is being choked by White's Knights.

| 29. NxB | RxR |
| 30. NxR | . . . |

Critical features of this endgame are that Black's QP is isolated and subject to attack, that his doubled BPs are no asset to him; and that White has two connected passed pawns. It is superfluous to note that White stands better.

| 30. . . . | N-B2 |
| 31. N-K3 | R-R2 |

Black cannot protect his QP; if 31. . . . R-N4, White would strengthen his position with 32. B-R3ch K-K1 33. B-Q6 and would be able to win the QP at his pleasure. After 31. . . . N-N3 32. B-Q4, followed by P-QR4, Black would be in virtual zugzwang.

| 32. P-QR4 | . . . |

With one of Black's Knights tied down to the protection of the QP, White begins the advance of his two passed pawns. Black's pieces are unable to stem their progress.

| 32. . . . | R-N2 |

An indirect way of protecting the QP. 32. . . . R-R4 fails to 33. B-B3 R-B4 34. B-N4.

| 33. P-N4 | N-B4 |

If 33. . . . RxP? 34. B-R3.

| 34. P-R5? | . . . |

20. . . .   **R–B6!?**

This move looks terrific at first but is less attractive on closer examination. Questionable is 20. . . . NxP on account of 21. N–K2 with the menacing threat of 22. R–N3 (if 21. . . . B–K4, trying to prevent R–N3, then White could continue 22. N–B4! followed by an eventual R–N3). Black's best continuation is 20. . . . N–Q6 in order to cut off White's development. That, of course, would lead to another kind of game. The impetuous Ljubojevic cannot be expected to select a continuation which offers only distant and questionable promise. White's spatial advantage on the Queenside poses a long-range threat which Black feels compelled to counter by violent and immediate means. "The threat is stronger than its execution!"

21. N–K2!   . . .

21. . . . RxB was the immediate threat. If 21. K–R1 R–Q6 22. Q–K2 P–Q4 with pressure. The text move parries Black's threat of . . . RxB and, at the same time, threatens 22. N–B4, winning material.

21. . . .   **N–Q6**

To parry the threat of N–B4, but Black is only partially successful.

22. N–B4   . . .

This is necessary in order to dislodge Black's strongly posted Knight.

22. . . .   **RxN**
23. RxN   **PxR**
24. BxR   . . .

The air has been cleared. Black's possible attack has dissipated and White is a pawn ahead, but Black has some compensation in the passed QP, which can become dangerous if White ignores it.

24. . . .   **B–QB1!**

Well played! Black exchanges his inactive Bishop for White's active one.

25. BxB   **RxB**

26. R–K1   . . .

The position is tricky. The logical continuation, 26. Q–Q2 to
be followed by 27. R–Q1 in an attempt to win the pawn, would
fail: 26. Q–Q2 R–K1! 27. R–Q1 (if 27. B–K3 P–Q4 28. R–Q1
P–Q5 29. B–B4 R–K7) 27. . . . R–K7 with White in trouble
because of the mate if White captures the pawn. The text move
avoids that problem by preventing Black's Rook from controlling
the K-file; in addition, it threatens the passed pawn with R–K3.

      26. . . .   **R–B1**

Not 26. . . . B–Q5 because of 27. BxP, and if 27. . . . QxB 28.
Q–N4ch. Best under the circumstances is 26. . . . R–K1 27. RxRch
QxR 28. QxP (not 28. BxP Q–K7) Q–K8ch 29. Q–B1 QxP 30.
P–N3 with Black in a position to put up resistance.

      27. Q–Q2   **Q–B4**

Setting a trap. For if 28. BxP? B–B6! 29. QxB QxPch 30. K–R1
Q–B8ch followed by mate.

      28. P–N3   . . .

Now there is sufficient time to secure and consolidate my King
position, making possible a siege of Black's passed pawn.

      28. . . .   **P–Q4**
      29. P–B5   **P–KR4**
      30. P–KR4   . . .

Not permitting P–KR5–6, which would lock in my King.

      30. . . .   **B–Q5**
      31. K–N2   **R–B2**
      32. P–B3   . . .

In order to avoid . . . Q–K5ch after my Rook moves off the K-file.

32. . . .	K–R2
33. R–Q1	. . .

After my adequate preparation, the Black pawn is ready to be won.

33. . . .	B–K4
34. BxB	QxB
35. QxPch	K–N1
36. P–B4	Q–N7ch

A desperate attempt to snatch pawns, but Black's position is hopeless anyway.

37. R–Q2	QxNP
38. Q–N6ch	K–B1
39. Q–R6ch	R–N2
40. R–K2	QxQBP
41. Q–R8ch	K–B2
42. Q–K8ch	K–B3
43. Q–K6 mate	

Game 27

Sacrificial Breakthrough

As Black in a King's Indian Defense, my opponent makes an inferior 7th move, and I emerge from the opening with a decided advantage. Stiff defense thwarts all my attempts to turn this initial plus into a winning position, but on his 26th turn my opponent overlooks a possible sacrifice. (After the game, he told me that he saw it as soon as he had made his move.) Taking advantage of the chance, I give up a pawn to unblock the position and make an incursion with my pieces, after which Black's defense crumbles quickly.

Netanya, 1971

KING'S INDIAN DEFENSE

S. Reshevsky	L. Kavalek
1. P–Q4	N–KB3
2. P–QB4	P–KN3
3. N–QB3	B–N2
4. P–K4	P–Q3
5. B–K2	0–0
6. N–B3	P–K4
7. B–K3	R–K1?

Considered weak. After White's P–Q5, Black must strive for
. . . P–KB4 to get play on the Kingside, in which case the Rook
belongs on KB1. More usual is 7. . . . N–N5 or 7. . . . Q–K2.

8. P–Q5	N–N5
9. B–N5	P–KB3
10. B–R4	P–KR4
11. N–Q2	N–KR3
12. P–B3	. . .

To bring the QB to KB2 after . . . P–KN4.

12. . . .	N–Q2
13. 0–0	N–B2
14. P–QN4	. . .

White stands better: he enjoys good play on the Queenside,
whereas Black's counterchances on the opposite wing are not
promising. Note White's freedom to maneuver compared with
Black's relative lack of it. From here on Kavalek demonstrates
his resourcefulness at defensive tactics.

14. . . .	B–R3
15. N–N3	P–QB4

Necessary to prevent the strong P–QB5.

16. PxP e.p.	PxP
17. P–N5	. . .

In order to gain control of White's important square Q5.

17. . . .	B–QN2
18. P–R4	P–R4

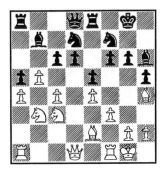

Otherwise White would continue forcefully with P–R5.

        19. Q–Q3?   . . .

Permitting Black to offer stronger resistance by closing the position. Correct is 19. PxP BxP 20. K–R1 followed by either 21. N–Q5 or 21. N–N5 with considerable advantage.

        19. . . .   **P–QB4**

Closing up the Queenside files and making it difficult for White to make any progress.

        20. N–Q5   **N–N4**

Intending to post this Knight at Black's Q5 with . . . N–K3–Q5.

        21. BxN   . . .

Though loathe to give up my Bishop for the Knight, I saw no better alternative.

        21. . . .   **PxB**

Weaker is 21. . . . BxB because of 22. P–N3 followed by P–B4 with good prospects.

        22. KR–Q1   **B–KB1**

        23. Q–K3   **BxN**

        24. BPxB   . . .

After 24. RxB the position remains blocked with little chance for White to make progress. 24. KPxB is to be considered, when White could place his Bishop at Q3 with Black's NP a possible target.

        24. . . .   **B–K2**

        25. Q–B3   **Q–N3**

        26. K–R1   **Q–R2?**

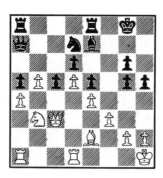

Although White enjoys a theoretical advantage, Black's stubborn defense has so far made it difficult for White to put his advantage to practical use. But here Black fails to appreciate the resources in White's position. Correct is 26. . . . KR–QB1 27. N–Q2 R–B2 28. N–B4 Q–R2, followed by . . . N–N3, maintaining the blockade of the Queenside.

27. P–N6!   . . .

The pawn sacrifice gives White complete control of the QN-file. Incredible though it may appear, Black's position is now untenable. Fortunately for me, Kavalek did not see this possibility until he had already played his 26th move.

27. . . .   QxP

If 27. . . . NxP 28. B–N5 R–KB1 29. B–B6 QR–N1 30. N–RP followed by B–N5 and N–B6, the RP advances unimpeded.

28. B–N5   KR–Q1
29. QR–N1   N–B3

Unable to stop or even slow down White's incursion on the Queenside, Black is compelled to undertake at all cost immediate counteraction on the Kingside.

30. N–Q2   Q–B2
31. N–B4   R–KB1
32. B–B6   R–R2

One of Black's problems is that his QR is tied down to the defense of his QRP. He cannot consider giving up the pawn because then White's passed RP would win the game, thanks to White's control of the Queenside.

33. R–N5   . . .

In addition to having complete control of the QN-file, White's pieces have access to practically the entire board; Black's pieces, on the other hand, are reduced to mere passivity.

33. . . .	B–Q1
34. KR–QN1	N–K1
35. R–N7	RxR
36. RxR	Q–B1

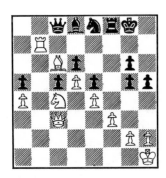

Black's extra pawn is meaningless given that all of Black's pieces are on the first rank.

      37. Q–N2   . . .

Protecting the Rook and threatening 38. BxN RxB 39. NxQP.

      37. . . .   **B–B2**

      38. R–R7   . . .

Preparing to make a decisive incursion to the seventh rank with the remaining pieces. I considered 38. N–N6 Q–Q1 (not 38. . . . BxN 39. QxB P–N5 40. B–Q7 PxP! 41. K–N1! Q–R1 42. R–N8, etc.) 39. N–Q7 R–B2, and Black could offer resistance. The text move threatens to win material immediately with 39. R–R8.

      38. . . .   **B–N1**

If 38. . . . Q–Q1 39. R–R8 Q–K2 40. Q–N7 P–N5 (if 40. . . . N–B3 41. NxRP) 41. RxN RxR 42. BxR Q–R5 43. P–N3 Q–R6 44. N–K3 and wins.

      39. B–Q7   . . .

Also good is 39. Q–N7 QxQ 40. RxQ N–B3 41. K–N1 followed by NxRP.

39. . . .	Q–Q1
40. B–K6ch	K–R1
41. R–Q7	Q–B3
42. QxB	Q–B5
43. Q–N2	N–B3
44. RxP	Resigns

Game 28

Four against Two

Throughout most of this game, Spassky enjoys twice as much maneuvering space as his opponent. Look at the position around move 30: Black is confined to his first two ranks only, having exhausted his play on the KB-file, and White has the use of his first four ranks. This is a large advantage, indeed; but thanks to Petrosian's skill in defense, White has difficulty finding the correct time and place for the decisive breakthrough. He finally does find the right spot, but he misses the right moment.

This game was played in the 1969 World Championship match. At this point in the match, Spassky was leading by two points, so both players wanted to win: Spassky to put the match out of reach with a three-point lead, Petrosian to stay within striking distance. This explains the tenseness of this game and the mistakes. Each player errs with his QR pawn, Petrosian by not advancing his far enough, Spassky by not advancing his at the right moment.

9th Match Game, 1969

BENONI DEFENSE

B. Spassky	T. Petrosian
1. P–Q4	N–KB3
2. P–QB4	P–B4

Not considered the safest defense for Black, but in view of his poor standing before this game, Petrosian is perhaps justified in choosing it.

3.	P–Q5	P–K4
4.	N–QB3	P–Q3
5.	P–K4	P–KN3
6.	B–Q3	N–R3

This setup leads to a cramped game for Black. Preferable is 6. . . . B–N2 7. KN–K2 0–0 8. P–KR3 N–K1, and if 9. P–KN4 Q–R5 followed by . . . B–KR3.

7.	KN–K2	N–QN5
8.	B–N1	B–N2
9.	P–KR3	B–Q2
10.	B–K3	0–0
11.	Q–Q2	N–R3

In order to bring this Knight to QB2 and effect an eventual . . . P–QN4.

12.	B–Q3	. . .

A psychological move, attempting to ascertain whether his opponent would be satisfied to repeat moves for a draw.

12.	. . .	N–QN5
13.	B–N1	N–R3
14.	P–R3	. . .

With a lead of two points and playing the White pieces, Spassky has no reason to concede a draw this early in the game. Petrosian probably did not really expect him to.

14.	. . .	N–B2
15.	B–Q3	R–N1
16.	P–QN4	. . .

Stopping Black's contemplated counteraction . . . P–QN4, but seeming to preclude White's Queenside castling.

16.	. . .	P–N3
17.	P–N4	. . .

With a disadvantage in space, Black has difficulty in maneuvering freely. White delays castling partly to deny Black a clear objective and partly in the hope that Black's position will offer White a clue as to the best location for his King.

17. . . .	**P–KR4**

An old refinement in the King's Indian. If 18. P–B3 N–R2 followed by . . . P–R5, depriving White of any action on that wing (19. PxP Q–R5ch followed by 20. . . . QxP).

18. P–KN5	**N–R2**
19. P–KR4	**P–B3**
20. 0–0–0!	**. . .**

Now that Black has made some committal moves on the Kingside, Spassky decides his King will be better off on the other side.

20. . . .	**PxKNP**
21. RPxP	**B–N5**
22. QR–N1	**Q–K1?**

Black has two continuations more promising than this: 22. . . . PxP 23. PxP Q–Q2, intending . . . P–N4, and 22. . . . R–B6 followed by 23. . . . RxB and . . . NxNP. Both offer Black good prospects. The text move prepares an action on the Queenside, but White is ready for it.

23. P–N5	**R–R1**
24. K–B2	**R–B6**
25. N–N3	**P–R3?**

Aiding White's possible action on the Queenside. Better is 25. . . . P–R4, and if 26. PxP e.p. RxRP with pressure against the QRP. Petrosian needs to win, however, and his anxiety may be affecting his usually excellent judgment.

| 26. P–R4 | PxP |
| 27. BPxP! | . . . |

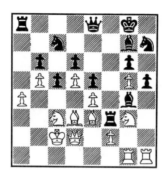

Making QB4 accessible to White's Knights and also enabling White to effect an eventual breakthrough with P–QR5. Petrosian probably underestimated the strength of this move; otherwise, he would have played 26. . . . P–R4.

| 27. . . . | Q–B2 |

Better is 27. . . . Q–KB1, and after 28. B–K2 R–B5 29. BxB PxB 30. BxR PxB 31. KN–K2 P–B6 with complications.

| 28. B–K2 | R–B5 |
| 29. P–B3! | . . . |

Forcing Black to give up the Exchange in a way favorable to White. Unplayable is 29. . . . BxP on account of 30. BxB RxB 31. NxP PxN 32. P–N6, etc. This would not have been available to White if Black had played 27. . . . Q–KB1. If 29. BxR? PxB and Black's KB enters the game.

Throughout most of the game, White has had far more maneuvering space than Black. This naturally offered him a greater choice of possible plans. With the end of Black's counterplay on the KB-file, White's advantage continues to grow. From now on White has four ranks on which to maneuver, whereas Black has only two.

29. . . .	RxBP
30. BxR	QxB
31. R–R2	Q–B1
32. R–B2	Q–B1

33. N–B1	R–R2
34. Q–Q3	Q–R1
35. Q–B4	Q–Q1
36. N–R2	B–Q2
37. N–B3	B–N5
38. Q–B1	B–Q2
39. K–N3	B–K1
40. N–Q2	. . .

White is finally accomplishing his goal of posting his Knight at QB4—an important step toward victory.

40. . . .	N–B1

The game was adjourned here and all the experts maintained that Spassky would score this point easily.

41. N–B4	N–R2
42. Q–N2	B–B1
43. R–R2	R–N2
44. K–B2	B–K2
45. R–N1	. . .

Spassky has built up a position in which he has a preponderance of material on the Queenside. Black is completely on the defensive. Spassky can easily open the QR-file and crush his adversary. His KNP cannot be safely captured.

45. . . .	Q–N1

46. R/2–N2?	. . .

White could win easily with 46. P–R5 PxP 47. NxRP R–N3 48. N–B6. After the game, Spassky declared that he did not know why he didn't follow this simple analysis done by his seconds during adjournment. The winning line is a perfect culmination of White's advantage in space.

| 46. . . . | N–R1 |
| 47. R–R2 | . . . |

47. P–R5 is still strong. If 47. . . . B–Q1 (if 47. . . . PxP 48. NxRP followed by N–B6) 48. PxP BxP/3 49. R–R2 B–Q1 50. R/1–QR1 and wins.

| 47. . . . | B–Q1 |
| 48. K–Q3 | . . . |

If now 48. P–R5, Black could hold the position with 48. . . . PxP 49. NxRP BxN 50. RxB N–B2.

48. . . .	B–Q2
49. R/1–QR1	N–B1
50. K–B2	B–K1
51. Q–K2	B–QB2
52. R–KB1	B–Q1
53. R/2–R1	N–R2
54. R–KN1	N–B1
55. B–Q2	N–R2
56. R–R3	N–B1
57. R/1–QR1	N–R2
58. P–R5	. . .

The breakthrough now leads to nothing. White could try action on the Kingside by placing both Rooks on the KB-file and his Knight on KR4 in an attempt to sacrifice the Knight at KB5 at the appropriate moment.

58. . . .	PxP
59. NxRP	BxN
60. RxB	N–B2
61. R–QN1	N–B1
62. B–K3	N–Q2
63. Q–B2	K–N2
64. K–Q3	K–N1
65. Q–KR2	

Draw

Game 29

Passive White Play

The amiable Czechoslovak (now living in West Germany) Grandmaster Ludek Pachman is well known as a strong competitor and an outstanding opening theoretician; he is not, however, famous as a specialist in endgame technique. Nevertheless, in this game he demonstrates keen understanding of an ending with Bishops of the same color. With material even and few pawns left on the board, Pachman makes full use of a weakness in his opponent's position. With precise play involving zugzwang, Pachman scores the point impressively. Zugzwang could be described as lack of space carried to its ultimate degree; that is, no move at all is safe.

Solingen, 1968

NIMZO-INDIAN DEFENSE

J. Nowak	L. Pachman
1. P–Q4	N–KB3
2. P–QB4	P–K3
3. N–QB3	B–N5
4. B–Q2	. . .

Infrequently seen. White obviously tries to steer away from the trodden path because of his adversary's reputation. This policy can be very risky.

4. . . .	0–0
5. N–B3	P–Q4

Black has a number of choices at his disposal: 5. . . . P–QN3, 5. . . . P–B4, and 5. . . . P–Q3, any of which is sufficient for equality, including the text move.

6. P–K3	QN–Q2
7. R–B1?	. . .

With this move White relinquishes all hope of an opening advantage. He could obtain a slightly better position with 7.

Q–N3 P–B4 8. QPxP BxN (if 8. . . . P–QR4 9. N–QR4 BxBch 10.
NxB Q–K2 11. N–N6 NxP 12. Q–R3) 9. BxB NxP 10. Q–R3.

7. . . .		**P–B3**
8. **B–Q3**		**PxP**
9. **BxP**		**B–Q3**

Black has steered the opening into the Semi-Slav Variation of
the Queen's Gambit, which means White lost an important tempo
when he played 7. R–B1. The misplaced Rook belongs on K1.

10. **Q–B2**	**P–K4**
11. **PxP**	. . .

This and the following exchange favor Black. Wiser is 11. 0–0
PxP (worse is 11. . . . R–K1 12. N–KN5 R–K2 13. N/3–K4 NxN
14. NxN B–B2 15. B–N4 with pressure; and if 11. . . . Q–K2 12.
N–K4 NxN 13. QxN N–B3 14. Q–R4) 12. NxP, and if 12. . . .
N–K4 13. B–K2. The suggested move would certainly bring about
more activity than the text.

11. . . .	**NxP**
12. **NxN**	**BxN**

13. **N–K2**	. . .

Having failed to obtain any opening advantage, White decides
on simplification by attempting to exchange black-squared
Bishops. There is little else for him to do.

13. . . .	**Q–K2**
14. **B–B3**	**P–B4**
15. **N–N3**	**P–QN3**

| 16. 0–0 | BxB |
| 17. QxB | B–N2 |

If Pachman were content to draw, he would attempt to simplify with 17. . . . B–K3. By posting the Bishop at QN2 he exerts pressure on White's KNP, hoping to provoke White to simplify by seeking exchanges. The endgame would favor Black because of his Queenside pawn majority.

18. KR–Q1?   . . .

Of course not 18. N–B5 because of 18. . . . Q–K5, but White misses an opportunity to put some life into the game by 18. P–K4!, which does not even cost the pawn: 18. . . . NxP 19. KR–K1 Q–R5 (19. . . . NxQ 20. RxQ, winning a piece) 20. QxPch (20. NxN BxN 21. P–KN3 Q–N5, and Black retains the pawn with impunity) 20. . . . KxQ 21. N–B5ch K–B3 22. NxQ QR–Q1 23. QR–Q1, with chances for both sides. If 18. . . . BxP 19. KR–K1 Q–N2 20. NxB NxN 21. Q–B3 QR–K1 22. QR–Q1, threatening 23. B–Q5. Black could decline the offer of the pawn: 18. . . . KR–K1 19. KR–K1 QR–Q1 20. P–K5 N–Q4 21. Q–B3 with a lively position. 18. KR–K1 is also preferable to the text move.

| 18. . . . | QR–Q1 |
| 19. B–K2 | . . . |

A better plan is 19. P–B3 N–Q4 20. N–B5 Q–N4 21. BxN BxB 22. P–K4 B–K3 (22. . . . BxRP 23. P–QN3, trapping the Bishop) 23. N–Q6 with an even position (not 23. P–KR4 Q–B3 24. QxQ PxQ giving Black the better endgame).

| 19. . . . | **P–N3!** |

This move serves a double purpose: it controls the important square KB4, denying White's Knight access to it, and it makes possible . . . P–KR4–5–6.

20. RxR	RxR
21. R–Q1	RxRch
22. BxR	N–K5!

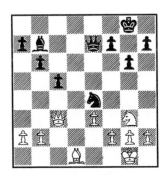

Pachman chooses the right course to give him winning chances. Black also had to consider . . . P–KR4–5–6. After 22. . . . P–KR4 White could not reply 23. P–KR3 on account of 23. . . . N–K5 24. Q–Q3 (not 24. NxN QxN 25. P–B3 Q–N8, winning a pawn) 24. . . . NxN 25. PxN with a bad position. But White can meet 22. . . . P–KR4 with 23. B–B3 BxB 24. PxB, and White's doubled pawns would not be enough for Black to win.

23. Q–Q3	NxN
24. RPxN	Q–K5
25. QxQ	BxQ

Black's chances of success in this endgame are based on his majority of pawns on the Queenside and on White's doubled pawns; moreover, the fact that White's KNP is attacked by Black's Bishop means that Black's King can reach the center whereas White's cannot. This can be translated as a lack of space for the White King, which is a decisive factor.

| 26. B–K2 | . . . |

Preferable is 26. P–KN4 followed by an eventual P–KN3. This would accomplish two things: relieve the pressure on the pawn at KN2 and prepare against the effective . . . P–B4.

26. . . .	K–B1
27. P–B3	B–Q4
28. P–R3	P–B4!

This ties up White's pawns on the Kingside, preventing any activity by White there. Having accomplished this, Black now proceeds to cash in his pawn majority on the other wing.

29. K–B2	K–K2
30. K–K1	K–Q3

31. K–Q2	P–QB5
32. K–B3	K–B4
33. B–Q1	. . .

Now White is reduced to complete passivity, which usually accompanies lack of space. Unproductive is 33. P–QR4 because of 33. . . . P–QR3 34. P–N4ch PxP e.p. 35. BxP P–N7 36. KxP (36. B–Q3 B–B5 37. B–B2 B–B8, etc.) 36. . . . K–N5 37. B–Q3 B–B5 and wins, for the King-and-pawn endgame after 38. BxB offers no hope.

33. . . .	P–QN4
34. B–K2	P–QR4
35. B–B1	P–N5ch
36. PxPch	PxPch
37. K–Q2	B–B3

38. B–K2	B–R5
39. B–B1	. . .

Black's control of the board reduces White's mobility almost entirely; White has only these Bishop moves at his disposal. 39. B–Q1 is, of course, out of the question: there would follow 39. . . . BxB 40. KxB P–B6, and the passed pawn would win easily. Also unsatisfactory is 39. P–K4 PxP 40. PxP K–Q5 41. B–B3 B–B3, etc. And 39. P–B4 would fail to 39. . . . B–B3 40. B–B3 P–R4 41. K–B2 B–K5ch 42. K–Q2 K–Q4 with White in zugzwang, which enables Black to advance his passed pawn.

39. . . .	P–N4
40. B–K2	P–R3
41. B–B1	B–B3
42. B–K2	B–R5
43. B–B1	B–N4

The beginning of a winning plan. Black now threatens . . . P–B6ch, which forces White to move his King and thereby relinquish protection of the KP. This fact plays an important role in the success of Black's ensuing strategy.

44. K–B2	P–R4
45. B–K2	P–R5

46. PxP	PxP
47. B–B1	P–B5

This pawn sacrifice makes it possible for Black's King to enter the Kingside and win the KNP, thus ensuring a passed KRP and the game. The rest is rudimentary. A very instructive contest, showing how the failure to neutralize a Queenside pawn majority by active play leads to defensive maneuvering in a constricted space.

48. PxP	B–Q2
49. K–Q2	K–Q5
50. B–K2	P–B6ch
51. PxP	PxPch
52. K–B1	B–B4
53. B–N5	K–K6
54. B–B6	K–B7
55. B–K4	BxB
56. PxB	KxP
Resigns	

Game 30

Bad Opening

White's advanced pawns on both wings severely restrict Black's activity. His efforts to simplify bring him no relief, however, and during most of the game his QR and QB remain undeveloped. Finally, on his 26th move, he gets his QB exchanged but this leaves his QR still out of play. When White threatens to open a file on the Kingside, Black's position becomes critical.

Black's experiment in the opening is the direct cause of his cramp, which leads to a steady worsening of his position. His failure to free himself by a timely . . . P–QB4 or . . . P–K4 allows the White pawns to take up dominating positions. Inexperienced players frequently overlook one of the primary functions of pawns: to create a safe outer perimeter behind which the pieces can maneuver freely. When and how far to advance the pawns are matters of judgment, of course, but, as this game shows, not to move them at all is not to get in the game.

72nd U.S. Open

Ventura, 1971

KING'S INDIAN DEFENSE

S. Reshevsky	D. Drapes
1. P–Q4	N–KB3
2. P–QB4	P–KN3
3. N–QB3	B–N2
4. P–K4	P–Q3
5. N–B3	0–0
6. B–K2	N–B3!?

An attempt to steer away from the usual continuations. I was not disturbed by the move since there are good reasons why rare continuations are so rare. Black's voluntary disdain for both . . . P–QB4 and . . . P–K4 give him a badly cramped position.

7. P–Q5	. . .

Possible is 7. 0–0 P–K4 8. P–Q5 N–K2, leading to familiar lines.

7. . . .	N–K4
8. NxN	. . .

A good alternative is 8. N–Q4 followed by an eventual P–B4 with a gain of time.

8. . . .	PxN
9. 0–0	N–K1
10. B–K3	P–QR3

To keep my Knight out of Black's QN4, an unnecessary precaution. More precise is the immediate . . . P–KB4.

11. Q–N3	P–KB4
12. PxP	. . .

Better than 12. P–B3 P–B5 13. B–B2 P–KN4, when Black has fair chances of building up an attack.

12. . . .	PxP
13. P–B4	P–K5

To be considered is 13. . . . PxP 14. BxP P–K4 15. PxP e.p. BxP 16. QxP N–Q3 (16. . . . R–N1 17. QxRP R–N3 18. Q–R3 with no compensation for Black) 17. Q–B6, and Black would be insufficiently compensated for the pawn.

14. P–B5	N–B3
15. QR–Q1	K–R1
16. B–Q4	. . .

Unproductive is 16. P–Q6 BPxP 17. PxP PxP 18. B–B5 N–K1.

16. . . .	Q–K1
17. B–K5	N–Q2

Not 17. . . . P–B3? 18. P–Q6 PxP 19. RxP with great advantage because Black's QB becomes completely inactive.

18. BxBch	. . .

A lively position ensues after 18. BxP NxP 19. Q–R3 N–Q2 20. P–Q6 P–K4 (20. . . . PxP 21. BxQP R–B3 22. N–Q5 R–N3 23. N–B7, etc.) 21. N–Q5 PxP 22. RxP N–K4 with chances for both sides.

18. . . .	KxB
19. Q–N4	Q–N3
20. K–R1	Q–KB3

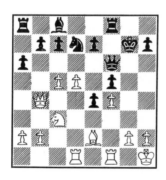

21. P–N4!   . . .

Up to now White has concentrated on the Queenside, but here he switches to the opposite wing. His principal intention is to anchor a pawn at KN5 in order to immobilize Black's forces.

21. . . .   P–QR4

21. . . . PxP 22. NxP Q–N3 23. BxNP costs a pawn. The next move is designed to deny White's Queen the important Q4 square after Black's Queen is chased away.

22. Q–R3   P–N3

The only way to try to develop Black's pieces and to avoid strangulation.

      23. P–N5   . . .

Unproductive is 23. BPxP QBPxP 24. PxP N–B4, and if 25. P–N4 PxP! 26. QxR PxN or . . . QxN with an unclear position.

      23. . . .   **Q–B2**

      24. P–B6   . . .

If 24. N–N5 NxP 25. NxP R–R2 26. N–N5 R–Q2, and Black's position has certainly not deteriorated.

      24. . . .   **N–B4**

      25. N–R4   . . .

Although I had the better game, I found it difficult to choose a promising continuation. I considered the obvious 25. P–N4 but discarded it; nevertheless, it is strong: 25. P–N4 PxP (if 25. . . . N–R3 26. PxP N–B4 27. Q–N2 RxP 28. N–Pch, etc.) 26. QxR B–R3 27. Q–R7 PxN 28. BxB P–B7 29. R–Q4. If in this line 26. . . . PxN 27. Q–R3 P–B7 28. Q–N2ch, etc. In either case, Black's compensation for the loss of material is insufficient.

      25. . . .   **NxN**

      26. QxN   **B–R3**

      27. BxB   **RxB**

      28. Q–Q4ch   **K–N1**

      29. Q–K5   **R–R2**

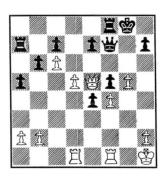

29. . . . R–B1 is inadvisable since this Rook is needed for defense on the Kingside. It is apparent that White has a substantial

edge at this point because Black's QR is out of play, but to find the means to break through is another story. The only feasible road to progress is to open the KN-file, and thus:

30. R–KN1	Q–N2
31. Q–K6ch	K–R1?

This gives me real winning chances. A better try is 31. . . . Q–B2. If 32. P–N6 (32. Q–Q7 Q–R4 with the annoying threat of . . . Q–B6ch) 32. . . . QxQ 33. PxQ (if 33. PxPch KxP 34. PxQ R–B3 35. R–N5 RxP, etc.) 33. . . . P–R3 34. R–Q7 R–K1 35. P–N7 R/2–R1, and if 36. RxBP QR–B1.

32. P–N6	R–B3

32. . . . P–R3 is necessary.

33. PxP!	QxRch

33. . . . QxP? 34. Q–B8ch. If 33. . . . RxQ 34. RxQ KxR 35. PxR KxP 36. R–Q7 brings about the same results as those in the game.

34. KxQ	RxQ
35. PxR	KxP
36. R–Q7	K–N2
37. RxPch	K–B3
38. R–K8	. . .

With a pawn to the good and Black's Rook apparently out of play, it should be easy for White to score the point, but . . .

38. . . .	P–R5!

Suddenly, Black's Rook comes alive, and White can do nothing about it. Very frustrating!

39. P–R4	R–R4
40. P–R5	R–Q4
41. P–R6	R–Q8ch
42. K–B2	R–Q7ch
43. K–K3	. . .

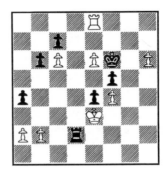

43. . . .   **R–Q8?**

In time trouble, my opponent makes the move which loses immediately. But if he had made the right move, could he have saved himself? The only move is 43. . . . R–Q6ch 44. K–K2 R–KR6, and now what? Can White win? Let's see.

The best for White is 45. R–KR8! KxP 46. P–R7 K–B3 (the only move, for if 46. . . . K–B2 47. R–QB8 RxP 48. RxPch) 47. R–B8ch K–N2 48. R–B8 KxP 49. RxPch K–N3 50. R–B8, and now Black has three possible continuations: (1) 50. . . . R–R2 51. P–B7 R–N2 52. P–R3 P–N4 53. K–K3 with Black in zugzwang; (2) 50. . . . R–R7ch 51. K–Q1 R–R8ch 52. K–B2 R–R7ch 53. K–B3 R–R6ch 54. K–N4 P–K6 55. P–B7 and wins; and (3) 50. . . . R–R2 51. P–B7 K–R4 (the best try) 52. K–K3 K–R5 53. K–Q4 K–R6 (if 53. . . . R–Q2ch 54. K–K5 R–R2 55. KxP P–K6 56. K–N6 P–K7 57. KxR P–K8=Q 58. R–KR8! and wins) 54. K–Q5 K–R5 (if 54. . . . R–Q2ch 55. K–K6, etc.) 55. K–Q6 RxP 56. RxR K–N6 57. K–K5, etc. To summarize: White can win even if Black puts up the best possible defense.

44. P–R7		**R–KR8**
45. P–R8=Qch		**RxQ**
46. RxR		**KxP**
47. R–Q8		**Forfeit**

Chapter 5

Open Lines

In the so-called romantic era of chess in the last century, White played the opening, and indeed the entire game, with but a single thought: checkmate! That such ambitions, which today many consider "primitive," were so often rewarded with success indicates that defensive technique in those days was not understood. White simply opened a few lines leading to the enemy King, often sacrificing a couple of pawns or a piece, and Black could only hope that White misplayed the attack. Black, of course, tried to do the same thing: he would, if given the chance, himself sacrifice material to get a mating attack.

With the development of defensive techniques, thanks in large part to Steinitz in the early days, it was discovered that mating attacks could be averted by the timely return of sacrificed material, simplification through exchanges, and the closing of critical lines.

In response, players had to be more subtle; they had to *prepare* their attacks by avoiding early simplification. Checkmate was still the idea, naturally, but the methods became more devious. Open lines still could not be dispensed with, but ideas about how, when, and where to open them and how to ensure control of them changed—progressed, if you like.

Take game 31, for example: in the middlegame White opens the QR-file—about as far as he could get from the enemy King—

and uses it to gain control of the seventh rank; only then is a mating attack possible. In game 32, White finally gains control of the QN-file, which enables him to win a pawn.

Games 33 and 34 show the use of open lines in focal-point strategy. In game 33 the combined pressure along the QB-file and the KB-diagonal against the specific square QB6 induces Black to give up a pawn voluntarily rather than have it taken from him, but White conquers the Queenside anyway. In game 34, the pressure by White's pieces against sensitive points in Black's position hinders Black's smooth development. Although White gains a sizable advantage, his impatience to win a pawn allows Black enough counterplay to draw the game.

In some situations open lines show to advantage in more general ways: game 35 demonstrates how Black's failure to take timely action against White's Bishops leads to ruin, whereas in game 36 we see a model of accurate defense against the opponent's two Bishops.

Finally, game 37 demonstrates the need to open lines when even solid advantages in space and material do not suffice for the win.

Game 31

File and Rank

There are all kinds of open lines—eight files, eight ranks, twenty-six diagonals, and trillions of permutations. This means that your ultimate objective, the checkmate of the enemy King, can be achieved in innumerable ways.

Since the safety of the King is—or should be—uppermost in the mind of every good player, your opponent should see to it that dangerous lines against his King are not opened, or at least that you do not control them exclusively if they are. It is profitable in such cases to open a line or two in a different area, where the opponent is often less vigilant or is himself trying to open lines. If you are able to control a file, use it to aim for the seventh rank because an attack along that rank, combined with pressure from a second direction, is one of the most difficult attacks to meet. For instance:

Maribor, 1967

KING'S INDIAN DEFENSE

S. Reshevsky	H. Westerinen
1. P–Q4	N–KB3
2. P–QB4	P–KN3
3. P–KN3	B–N2
4. B–N2	0–0
5. N–QB3	P–Q3
6. N–B3	N–B3
7. P–Q5	. . .

More usual is 7. 0–0 P–QR3 8. P–KR3 followed by 9. P–K4 or 9. B–K3.

7. . . .	N–QR4
8. N–Q2	P–B3!

A good move which refutes White's entire setup. The point is that White is unable to win a piece with 9. P–QN4 on account of 9. . . . NxQP! and Black's KB springs suddenly to life. Now White's KB becomes less effective and this casts suspicion on his entire system of development.

9. 0–0	PxP
10. PxP	B–B4

Having his Knight "trapped" after 11. P–QN4 doesn't bother Black at all because he has the adequate reply 11. . . . R–B1 12. B–N2 N–B5 with superior prospects.

11. N–N3	. . .

11. P–K4 B–N5 12. P–B3 B–Q2 13. Q–K2 R–B1 would inactivate White's KB without improving his chances.

11	NxN

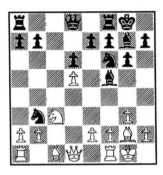

12. PxN   . . .

Playable and more natural looking is 12. QxN, but it seemed
to me that my play on the open Rook file would more than
compensate for the double pawn. This turns out to have been an
accurate assessment. Anyway, it was necessary to win this game;
I felt that, having obtained little if any advantage from the opening, I would have to seek winning chances by opening lines and
by trying to get the initiative.

     12. . . .   **Q–Q2**

With the intention of exchanging Bishops by continuing . . .
B–R6.

     13. P–K4   . . .

I could have prevented the exchange of Bishops but believed
that his was more useful than mine.

13. . . .	**B–R6**
14. Q–Q3	**BxB**
15. KxB	**P–QN4!?**

An interesting and enterprising move. My opponent tries to
seize the initiative on the Queenside, now that he no longer has
to worry about White's KB. His enterprise is commendable, but
he runs the risk of giving White strong pressure on the open
lines leading to his Queenside. His intention is to drive the Knight
from QB3 where it protects White's center.

     16. B–K3   . . .

I was tempted to play 16. QxP, but after 16. . . . QxQ 17. NxQ
NxKP 18. R–K1 (the only try, for if 18. RxP QR–N1 19. R–R5

N–B4 with the brighter prospects) 18. . . . N–B4 19. RxKP NxP
with advantage for Black.

16. . . .	P–N5
17. N–K2	. . .

Not 17. N–R4 since there the Knight would be out of play.

17. . . .	P–K3
18. R–R5!	. . .

This is the only means to keep up the pressure and prepares
to double Rooks on the QR-file. I had intended to continue with
18. PxP QxP 19. P–B3 P–Q4! 20. N–B4 Q–K4 21. B–Q4, but
Black unfortunately has the strong reply 21. . . . PxP.

18. . . .	PxP
19. PxP	. . .

White's pawn at Q5, though isolated, restricts the mobility of
Black's forces. I felt that the chances of my making progress were
good.

19. . . .	KR–K1

Black's immediate problem is his QRP which is exposed on an
open file and under pressure from two directions. His only course
is to apply counterpressure against White's QP. The purpose of
the text move is, therefore, to play . . . R–K4.

20. P–R3	. . .

Preventing . . . N–N5.

20. . . .	R–K4
21. KR–QR1	QR–K1

21. . . . R–R4 is bad on account of 22. N–B4, and 21. . . . Q–N2
is insufficient because of 22. RxP RxR 23. RxR QxPch 24. QxQ
RxQ 25. R–R8ch B–B1 26. B–R6 N–Q2 27. R–Q8 with a won
endgame.

22. RxP	. . .

White now has full control of the QR-file; in addition, he has
a Rook on the seventh rank, which makes it impossible for Black
to build up a counterattack and, at the same time, restricts
Black's mobility. White has the upper hand.

We see in this game the effect of control of an open file:
ultimate occupation of the seventh rank. It is not always possible
—or even necessary—to try to open files early in the game in

the vicinity of the enemy King, but control of a distant file serves the same purpose, especially when, as in this case, the opponent has insufficient compensation.

| 22. . . . | RxP |
| 23. N–Q4 | Q–B1 |

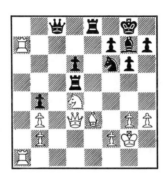

24. Q–B4 . . .

Forcing the exchange of Queens, thereby straightening out White's pawns.

24. . . . QxQ

If 24. . . . Q–Q1 or 24. . . . Q–N1, 25. N–B6 wins immediately, or if 24. . . . P–R4 25. R–B7 Q–N1 26. R/1–R7, with an overwhelming position.

25. PxQ	R–QB4
26. P–N3	P–R4
27. R/1–R6	. . .

Also sufficient is 27. N–N5 R–B3 28. R/1–R6 RxR 29. RxR, winning the QP, for if 29. . . . P–Q4, 30. P–B5 and the passed pawn cannot be stopped.

| 27. . . . | N–K5 |
| 28. N–N5 | R–B4 |

A desperate attempt to obtain some play on the Kingside. Futile also is 28. . . . R/4–B1 29. NxP NxN 30. RxN with little hope for Black.

| 29. NxP | NxN |
| 30. RxN | B–B1 |

31. R/6–R6	R–Q1
32. R–R8	R–Q6
33. P–B5	. . .

Simpler than 33. B–R6 K–R2 34. BxB R–Q7 35. B–B5 (not 35. P–N4 R/7xPch 36. K–N3 R/7–B6ch and draws by perpetual check, for if 37. K–N3? P–N4ch) 35. . . . RxB 36. R–KB6 K–N2 37. R–B3, with technical problems for White.

| 33. . . . | RxB |

Forced, for if 33. . . . RxNP 34. P–B6 R–B6 35. R–B8 followed by 36. R/6–R8, winning the Bishop (if 35. . . . K–N2 36. B–Q4ch). Now White's task is simpler.

34. PxR	RxP
35. R–Q8	K–N2
36. R–Q7	R–B7ch

Black's Rook is unable to protect his vital BP. If 36. . . . R–B4 37. P–K4 followed by 38. R/6–R7, winning the pawn.

37. K–B3	B–B4
38. R–QB6	R–B6
39. R/6–B7	RxPch
40. K–B4	P–N4ch
41. K–B5	. . .

The sealed move. When my opponent saw it, he resigned. The game might have continued: 41. . . . R–B6ch 42. K–K4 R–K6ch 43. K–Q5 B–N3 44. RxPch K–N3 45. R–N7ch K–R3 46. R–R7ch K–N3 47. R/B–N7ch K–B3 48. R–N7 and wins.

Game 32

Queenside Breakthrough

In most variations of the King's Indian Defense, White's chances lie in action on the Queenside, while Black's counterplay consists of aggressive action on the Kingside. White must, however, take care to secure his monarch's safety by keeping the critical lines near his King closed. Note in this game how Black is unable simultaneously to attack on the Kingside and to prevent White from taking control of the Queenside files.

Netanya, 1971

OLD INDIAN DEFENSE

S. Reshevsky	Y. Bleiman
1. P–Q4	N–KB3
2. P–QB4	P–Q3
3. N–QB3	QN–Q2
4. P–K4	P–K4
5. N–B3	B–K2
6. B–K2	0–0
7. 0–0	P–B3
8. R–K1	R–K1
9. B–B1	Q–B2

A good alternative is 9. . . . P–QR3, attempting to get counter-play with . . . P–QN4, and if 10. P–QR4 P–QR4.

10. P–KR3	. . .

A waiting move that also prevents . . . B–KN5.

10. . . .	N–B1

Black's plan becomes clear: he wants to bring his Knight to KN3 in an effort to initiate aggressive action on the Kingside.

11. B–K3	N–N3
12. P–Q5	. . .

Also possible is 12. P–QN4.

12. . . .	P–B4
13. P–R3	B–Q2
14. P–QN4	P–N3
15. R–N1	KR–N1
16. Q–B2	Q–B1
17. K–R2	N–R4
18. R–N3	. . .

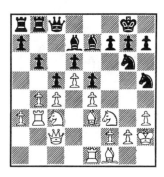

Feeling secure on the Kingside, White pursues his plan of preparing to open the QN-file by doubling Rooks on it. Note that Black's Rooks play only defensive roles.

18. . . .   **N–R5**

Exchanging pieces does not enhance Black's chances. He has to try opening a file of his own by 18. . . . P–B4, but after 19. PxP BxP 20. B–Q3 (also possible is 20. N–K4 N–B3 21. B–Q3) 20. . . . BxB 21. QxB N/3–B5 22. Q–B1 Q–B1 23. KR–N1, White has the advantage because he will soon open lines on the Queenside, whereas Black's KB-file is not really open and his pieces can easily be pushed back.

19. NxN   **BxN**
20. KR–N1   **Q–B1?**

An inexplicable move. Apparently Black has run out of ideas. Logical is 20. . . . P–N3 with the possibility of . . . P–B4. The suggested move also permits Black's Knight to move to N2 when attacked by White's KB.

21. PxP   **NPxP**
22. RxR   **RxR**
23. B–K2!   **N–B5**

24. B–N4! . . .

Does away with Black's stronger Bishop, which enables White's Queen to make inroads via his QR4 giving White access to important squares on the Queenside.

24. . . .	**BxB**
25. PxB	**B–K2**

Forced, since P–N3 was threatened.

26. P–N3	**N–N3**

Black's Bishop and Knight have clearly been inactivated. How, then, is he to meet White's invasion on the Queenside?

27. RxR	**QxR**
28. Q–R4	. . .

With the serious threat of winning the QRP with N–N5.

The White Queen can now make inroads into Black's position. The Queen is attacking the QRP and also threatening to reach the QB6 square where it will attack the QP and also cramp Black's position. Moreover, the Queen is in a position to reach the important K8 square if Black's Queen leaves the first rank. Black recognizes that the cost of protecting the QRP is too great, and so he gives control of the QN–file wholly to White.

28. . . .	**Q–QB1**

To be considered is 28. . . . Q–N7, but it would fail after 29. Q–K8ch [not 29. N–N5 because of 29. . . . B–N4! 30. NxQP P–KR3 31. N–B5 BxB 32. NxB N–B5 33. PxN (33. Q–B2 QxQ 34. NxQ N–Q6 35. K–N2 K–B1, with a very difficult endgame to win) 33. . . . PxP, and White would have no better than a draw

with 34. Q–K8ch K–R2 35. QxP followed by a perpetual check]
29. . . . N–B1 (if 29. . . . B–B1 30. N–N5 followed by NxQP and
wins) 30. QxB QxN 31. QxQP QxBP 32. BxP and wins. Neither
is 28. . . . Q–N3 sufficient (in order to meet 29. N–N5 with 29.
. . . P–QR3) because of 29. Q–B6 N–B1 (if 29. . . . QxQ 30.
PxQ B–Q1 31. N–Q5 and wins) 30. N–N5, and Black will be
slowly crushed.

29. QxP	QxP
30. Q–N8ch	B–B1
31. Q–N1	. . .

Not 31. P–R4 N–B5 32. PxN PxP, and White must guard
against the mate to follow after 33. B–Q2 P–B6. The only other
possibilities are 33. BxP and 33. Q–N1, either of which would
probably lead to a draw.

31. . . .   P–R4?

Played in time trouble and it loses quickly. The only try is 31.
. . . N–B5, after which White would have to play very accurately
in order to score the point. The correct continuation for White
is 32. Q–KB1 (if 32. PxN PxP 33. B–Q2 P–B6 34. Q–KB1 Q–R5ch,
and if 35. Q–R3 QxPch, etc.; if, in this same variation, 34. Q–KR1
B–K2 35. B–K3 B–B3 with the winning threat of . . . B–K4ch)
32. . . . Q–R4ch 33. K–N1 N–R6ch 34. K–N2 N–B5ch (if 34.
. . . Q–N5 35. P–B3) 35. PxN Q–N5ch 36. K–R2 PxP 37. Q–R3
QxQch 38. KxQ PxB 39. P–R4 (better than 39. PxP).

32. Q–Q1!   Q–B1

After the exchange of Queens, Black's position would be hopeless.

| 33. QxP | Q–R3 |

Black attempted to get play on the Kingside but without success. He now tries his luck on the other wing, but this, too, is doomed to failure.

34. N–N5	Q–R5
35. Q–K2	Q–N6
36. K–N2	B–K2
37. B–Q2	Q–B7
38. K–B1	. . .

White proceeds to untangle himself so that he will be in a position to advance his passed QRP.

| 38. . . . | P–B4 |

A last try for breath!

| 39. B–K1 | QxKP |

Neither is 39. . . . Q–N8 sufficient on account of 40. P–R4 PxP 41. P–R5 Q–R8 42. QxP N–B1 43. K–N2 B–Q1 44. B–B3 Q–R7 45. NxP, etc.

40. QxQ	PxQ
41. P–R4	N–B1
42. P–R5	N–Q2 and Resigns

Game 33

Duet for QB-file and KB

I usually have trouble scoring the full point against Grandmaster Arthur Bisguier; he is always alert tactically and wins many games thanks to his flair for counterplay. In the present game my pressure against QB6 and along the QB-file and my KB's diagonal, becomes unbearable for Black. He decides to sacrifice a pawn for counterplay, but this fails to materialize and White's conquest of the Black Queenside (and the pawns that go with it) ends the game.

U.S. Championship
New York, 1972

RETI OPENING

S. Reshevsky	A. Bisguier
1. N–KB3	P–Q4
2. P–KN3	N–QB3
3. P–B4	PxP
4. Q–R4	P–KN3
5. B–N2	. . .

If 5. N–K5? Q–Q4!

5. . . .	B–N2
6. N–B3	N–R3

Intending to post this Knight at Black's Q5.

7. QxBP	N–B4
8. 0–0	0–0
9. P–Q3	. . .

I considered 9. P–K3 (in order to prevent . . . N–Q5), but after 9. . . . P–K4 I would have trouble completing my development.

9. . . .	P–KR3

This is played to prevent N–KN5. Black intends to develop his Bishop to K3, not a safe square if White's Knight could jump to KN5. As we will see, this Bishop, which is so vital to the defense of the Queenside, is later exchanged for a White Knight, after which the Queenside collapses.

That's one of the reasons Black's QB is often called the "problem" Bishop.

10. B–Q2	P–K4
11. QR–B1	B–K3
12. Q–QR4	. . .

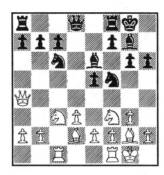

Black seems to have succeeded in developing, and the position may appear level to the superficial eye; but White enjoys an advantage because he controls the half-open QB-file while his KB is in a position to add to the annoying pressure against Black's Queenside.

| 12. . . . | N–Q3 |

A necessary retreat to prevent the maneuver N–K4–B5.

| 13. B–K3 | Q–Q2 |
| 14. KR–Q1 | . . . |

Intending to continue with P–Q4, which Black refuses to allow with his next move.

| 14. . . . | N–B4 |
| 15. B–Q2 | . . . |

15. N–K4 is worth considering.

15. . . .	N–Q3
16. B–K3	N–B4
17. B–B5	KR–Q1
18. N–Q2	. . .

The KB now comes into play. The combined pressure of White's Rook, Bishop, and Queen against QB6 and, indirectly, QN7 seriously cramps Black's activity. Compare the scope of the respective King Bishops.

In view of this, Bisguier decides to risk sacrificing a pawn in order to free his pieces. The risk is too high and the plan fails.

| 18. . . . | N/4–K2? |

The losing move: White simply accepts the pawn sacrifice, and Black receives insufficient compensation. I later asked Bisguier why he had chosen this move, and his answer was that he did not like his position anyway and decided to give up a pawn for possible counterplay. A better try is 18. . . . N/3–Q5 19. QxQ RxQ 20. BxNP R–N1 21. B–N2 RxP 22. P–K3 N–B7 (22. . . . N–N4 23. NxN RxN 24. B–B6, etc.) 23. N–B4 BxN 24. PxB RxRch 25. RxR, with advantage for White, but not necessarily a won game.

19. B/5xN		NxB
20. BxP		. . .

So that if 20. . . . QxQ 21. NxQ, protecting the QNP.

20. . . .		QR–N1
21. B–B3		. . .

Not 21. QxP? P–QB3, winning a piece.

21. . . .		RxP
22. QxP		. . .

True, Black has the advantage of the two Bishops, but that proves insufficient compensation for the extra passed pawn.

22. . . .		N–B4
23. P–K3		. . .

Preventing the incursion of the Knight to Q5. The White Queen pawn is immune to capture (23. . . . QxP? 24. N/2–K4).

23. . . .		B–B1
24. N–B4		. . .

Compelling Black to give up one of his Bishops and to open the Queen file.

24. . . .	BxN
25. PxB	Q–B1
26. P–B5	. . .

I considered 26. N–Q5 but rejected it because of 26. . . . P–QB3 27. N–B6ch (if 27. N–N6 RxRch 28. RxR Q–K3 with the possibility of . . . P–K5) 27. . . . K–N2 28. N–K4 (28. N–Q7? R–N2, and if 28. N–N4 RxRch 29. RxR Q–K3 with counterchances) 28. . . . Q–R1.

The purpose of the text move is to inactivate Black's Bishop.

| 26. . . . | P–R4 |

At the moment Black can undertake nothing; he has to await White's actions. White therefore has time to consolidate his position slowly and make his extra pawn count. Observe that the QB-file is no longer open: if White seems to have wrung all the advantage out of it that he can, look again eight moves from now.

| 27. Q–R3 | . . . |

Forcing the Rook from the seventh rank and thus spoiling any counterplay Bisguier may be hoping for.

27. . . .	R–N1
28. RxR	QxR
29. N–K4	N–N2

The Knight is accomplishing nothing where it is; so Bisguier tries to relocate it to a more favorable post.

| 30. Q–R6 | N–K3 |
| 31. R–Q1 | Q–B1 |

The only square. 31. . . . Q–K2? 32. R–Q7, winning the Queen.

| 32. Q–B6 | . . . |

The exchange of Queens would give Black counterplay. The text move gives me a lasting bind on the position.

| 32. . . . | B–N2 |
| 33. P–QR4 | . . . |

Now that Black's forces are immobilized, it is time to advance the passed pawn.

| 33. . . . | R–N7 |

Reaching the seventh rank—just a stab in the dark.

| 34. P–R5 | R–R7 |

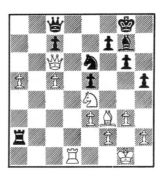

35. N–Q6! . . .

The crusher! Thanks to the nice vertical pin on the "closed" QB-file, Black's position falls apart.

     35. . . .   **Q–Q1**
     36. NxP   **Q–B3**

It appears that White is in trouble at this point: two pieces are attacked. But . . .

     37. N–N5!   . . .

Bisguier told me after the game that he had overlooked this move. 37. N–Q8 would have accomplished the same thing.

From the opening of this game the struggle has proceeded from the pressure exerted on the open QB-file or along the diagonal of White's KB. The QB-file has done its work; now the long white diagonals, marking a great "x" at White's Q5, do theirs.

     37. . . .   **NxN**
     38. B–Q5ch   . . .

The point!

     38. . . .   **K–R2**
     39. QxQ   **N–R6ch**
     40. K–N2   **Resigns**

Game 34

Restricting Opponent's Development

The Gruenfeld Defense is a pet opening of German Grandmaster Wolfgang Uhlmann. But Mark Taimanov of the USSR is certainly not unfamiliar with its nuances. He obtains a clear advantage in that his active pieces exert annoying pressure at various points. Becoming impatient, however (a characteristic of Taimanov), he goes for the win of a pawn and in so doing jeopardizes his advantage.

One of the values of controlling open lines is that eventually the opponent, unless he has full compensation, will be forced to make positional concessions or submit to an attack. "Cashing in" too soon, as Taimanov does for one measly pawn, is illogical because the type of advantage he holds at the time calls for increasing the pressure not releasing it.

USSR vs. the Rest of the World

Belgrade, 1970

GRUENFELD DEFENSE

M. Taimanov	W. Uhlmann
1. P–Q4	N–KB3
2. P–QB4	P–KN3
3. N–QB3	P–Q4
4. B–N5	N–K5
5. B–R4	P–QB4
6. BPxP	NxN
7. PxN	QxP
8. P–K3	B–N2
9. Q–B3	Q–Q1

Exchanging Queens advances White's development and emphasizes Black's problems with his KP.

10. B–N5ch	N–Q2
11. N–K2	0–0

Black has succeeded in castling but has had to lose a little time to protect his KP (9. . . . Q–Q1). His development is therefore somewhat retarded.

12. 0–0	P–QR3
13. B–Q3	R–N1

Black's KP remains a headache for him; otherwise, he could continue favorably with 13. . . . N–K4. With the text move Black seeks to free himself with . . . P–QN4, but White thwarts this easily. The cumbersome maneuvers by Black underscore the value of the aggressively posted White pieces.

14. P–R4   **P–N3**

14. . . . P–QN4 is now unavailing because of 15. PxP PxP 16. KR–N1, and the QNP falls.

15. KR–Q1   . . .

15. B–K4 would be met by 15. . . . N–B3 16. B–B6? B–N5 and wins.

15. . . .   **Q–K1?**

This causes Black serious difficulty. Mandatory is 15. . . . B–N2; then if 16. B–K4 BxB 17. QxB N–B3, or if 16. Q–R3 Q–K1, in both cases with a playable game.

16. B–K4!   . . .

White's Bishops enjoy open lines: the QB exerts pressure on the KP, and the KB halts the development of Black's pieces. White definitely stands better.

16. . . .   **P–K4**

If 16. . . . N–B3 17. BxN (not 17. B–N3 B–N5, and not 17. Q–B4 P–K4! 18. PxP NxB 19. QxN QxKP) 17. . . . PxB (if 17. . . . BxB 18. B–B6 B–Q2 19. BxB QxB 20. PxP) 18. B–B6 Q–K2 19. N–B4 with advantage.

17. B–QB6	Q–K3
18. B–N3	R–Q1
19. PxKP?	. . .

Taimanov is anxious to win a pawn, but as soon as he does he is confronted by serious problems. With 19. QR–N1, Black is placed in virtual zugzwang: for instance, if 19. . . . N–B1 20. PxKP RxRch 21. RxR BxP 22. N–B4 Q–B3 23. NxNP! and wins.

The text move leads to the exchange of several pieces and reduces White's advantage because it is precisely in the activity of those pieces that his advantage lies. And the extra pawn is not worth very much in an endgame with opposite-colored Bishops.

19. . . .	BxP
20. B–Q5	Q–K2
21. QxPch	QxQ
22. BxQch	KxB
23. BxB	R–N2

24. B–B4? . . .

As will be noted later, the text move is not the best since it gives Black an opportunity to gain a tempo with . . . P–KN4, attacking the Bishop. Consequently, correct is 24. B–N3. Although White is a pawn ahead, it is difficult to score the point because of the Bishops of opposite colors and the superior pawn structure Black enjoys on the Queenside.

24. . . .	R–K1
25. P–B3	P–B5
26. R–Q4	N–B4!

Sacrificing the pawn for counterplay. Unsatisfactory is 26. . . . P–QN4 27. PxP PxP 28. R–R6 N–B4 29. R–QB6 N–Q6 30. B–N5 or 30. B–R6 with good prospects.

27. RxP	B–K3
28. R–N4	P–QR4
29. R–N2	B–Q2
30. R/2–R2	N–N6
31. R–Q1	. . .

If 31. R–N1 N–B4.

31. . . .	N–B4
32. R–Q4	N–K3!
33. R–B4	. . .

Unavailing is 33. R–K4 on account of 33. . . . B–B3 34. R–K5 N–B4, winning the RP.

33. . . .	P–KN4!
34. B–Q6	N–B4

The point of Black's previous move. If 35. BxN B–K3, and White does not have the rejoinder 36. R–B4ch.

35. N–Q4	. . .

Preventing . . . B–K3.

35. . . .	NxP

Unsatisfactory for Black is 35. . . . RxP 36. BxN PxB 37. RxP R–R2 38. K–B2, winning the NP.

36. R/4xN	BxR
37. RxB	RxP

The pawns are equal, the opposite-colored Bishops are gone, and White retains a slight material advantage. In addition, Black's Rooks are not working together to make the most of their combined strength on open lines. White's next move solves this problem for Black.

38. N–N5?   . . .

White had a difficult choice here, and the text move relinquishes the advantage. Unsatisfactory also is 38. P–QB4 because of 38. . . . R–Q6 39. N–N5 (if 39. B–K5 R–K2 40. N–B6 R–K3, etc.; if 39. N–B5 K–K3; if 39. P–B5 PxP 40. BxP R–N7 with the double threat of . . . R–Q8 mate and . . . R/6–Q7, which White could not parry) 39. . . . R–Q2 40. B–B7 R–N6 (threatening . . . RxN) 41. BxP R–Q7, again with the double threat of mate and of doubling the Rooks on the seventh rank. But White could retain the advantage with 38. R–R3 R–K8ch (otherwise White could proceed with the consolidating 39. K–B2) 39. K–B2 R–QN8 40. P–QB4 with good prospects because Black has difficulty effecting concerted action by his Rooks.

38. . . .	R–K8ch
39. K–B2	R–QN8
40. P–QB4	R–Q2
41. B–K5	R–Q7ch
42. K–K3	RxP
43. K–K4	R–N5
44. RxR	PxR

45. N–Q4	K–K2
46. B–B7	. . .

Unsatisfactory is 46. K–Q5 K–Q2 47. P–B5 PxP 48. KxP P–N7
49. K–B4 P–R4 since White cannot make progress, for if 50.
N–N3, R–KB7. And if 46. K–B5 K–B2 47. P–R3 P–R3, and White
is stymied.

46. . . .	K–Q2
47. BxP	P–N6!

If 47. . . . RxP 48. P–B5 wins.

48. NxP	R–N7
49. B–K3	. . .

The piece cannot be saved, for if 49. N–B5ch K–B3 50. B–R7
R–R7.

49. . . .	RxN
50. BxP	R–QB6
51. B–B6	RxPch
52. K–B5	R–B7
53. P–R4	R–B7
54. P–B4	K–K1
55. K–N5	R–N7ch
56. K–R5	R–N3
57. B–N5	K–B2
58. P–B5	R–QB3
59. P–B6	K–K3
60. K–R6	R–B2
61. B–K3	

Draw

Game 35

Lines to the King

Levente Lengyel, conducting the Black pieces, chooses the
Nimzo-Indian Defense. In this opening White usually retains
the two Bishops against Black's Bishop and Knight. This is a
potentially dangerous situation for Black because in an open
position the Bishops attain their greatest power. So Black must

try to keep the position closed. But Black, failing to find the obvious solution, makes an inferior move on his 15th turn; he later told me that the move in fact had the approval of theoreticians. The practical value of the move is more accurately demonstrated by Black's resignation nine moves after making it.

Chess Olympics
Siegen, 1970

NIMZO-INDIAN DEFENSE

S. Reshevsky	L. Lengyel
1. P–Q4	N–KB3
2. P–QB4	P–K3
3. N–QB3	B–N5
4. P–K3	0–0
5. N–B3	P–QN3
6. B–Q3	B–N2
7. 0–0	P–Q4
8. B–Q2	. . .

An alternative is 8. PxP PxP 9. N–K5 B–Q3 10. P–B4 P–B4 11. B–Q2 N–B3.

8. . . .	PxP
9. BxP	P–B4
10. Q–K2	QN–Q2
11. KR–Q1	PxP
12. PxP	. . .

More promising than 12. NxP N–K4 13. B–N3 (13. B–R6 Q–B1) P–QR4 with the possibility of continuing . . . B–R3.

12. . . .	R–B1
13. B–Q3	BxN
14. BxB!	. . .

Superior to the usual 14. PxB Q–B2, and if 15. P–B4 BxN 16. QxB P–K4 with a good game for Black.

14. . . .	N–Q4
15. B–Q2	Q–B3?

A dubious move, to say the least. The simple 15. . . . Q–K2 is necessary, giving White only a slight positional advantage. Black is hoping for 16. B–KN5? N–B5! 17. Q–K3 N–R6ch! (not 17. . . . NxP 18. KxN BxNch 19. K–N1 and wins) with the better position.

       16. N–N5!   . . .

With open lines for the Bishops, White is able to undertake aggressive action against the King.

       16. . . .   **QxP?**

16. . . . P–N3 is mandatory, although after 17. N–K4 Q–K2 (not 17. . . . QxP 18. B–KR6 KR–Q1 19. N–Q6 and wins) 18. B–KN5 P–B3 19. B–KR6, White would have excellent prospects for an attack, since Black's King position would be considerably weakened.

       17. BxPch   **K–R1**
       18. B–K3!   . . .

The winning move, for this enables White's Rook to take part in the ensuing assault via Q4–KR4.

       18. . . .   **Q–K4**

There is no better. If 18. . . . Q–KR5 19. R–Q4 Q–R3 20. NxPch, etc. If 18. . . . Q–QB5 19. B–Q3 Q–KR5 20. P–KN3 and wins.

       19. Q–R5   . . .

Now that White has gained complete control of the KR-file, Black's monarch is at the mercy of White's forces.

       19. . . .   **N/4–B3**

with equal chances; and if 11. BxN QxB 12. PxP R–Q1, and Black would encounter no difficulty regaining the pawn.

11. . . .	PxP
12. BxP	N–K4
13. B–K2	N–N3

Finally disposing of the annoying pin.

14. B–N3	B–Q2
15. 0–0	B–B3

Now that Black has succeeded in developing the Bishop, I felt that White's two Bishops would confer only a minimal edge.

16. R–B1	Q–R4

I discarded 16. . . . QxQ 17. KRxQ KR–Q1 18. N–N5 BxN 19. BxB because of the substantial pressure exerted by the Bishops. Also unappetizing to me was 16. . . . QxQ 17. KRxQ P–R3 18. P–N4 (threatening P–QR4 and P–N5), and if 18. . . . N–Q4, then 19. NxN BxN 20. R–B7 QR–B1 21. R/1–QB1 with pressure.

17. Q–N3	P–R3

To prevent N–N5.

18. Q–N4	. . .

I expected 18. Q–R2 with the idea of continuing 19. P–N4. I intended to meet it with 18. . . . P–N4 19. P–N4 Q–N3.

Hort chooses to exchange Queens because Black's Queen and his other pieces are favorably posted, and he sees no chance of making progress in the middlegame. He therefore looks to the endgame, hoping that his two Bishops may be put to better use.

18. . . .	QxQ
19. PxQ	. . .

To appraise the ensuing endgame: White still has the two Bishops but is saddled with a doubled pawn. The Bishops can be a threat but the doubled pawn can be a liability. Black has no visible weaknesses, and at the moment White controls no open files and has no immediate prospects of making inroads. The position is approximately even.

This is not the same as saying that it is drawish, however. White's position does have possibilities, and it is up to Black to see that those possibilities do not become dangerous.

19. . . .	KR–Q1
20. KR–Q1	N–K2!

This Knight now begins to play an important role. It is headed for Q4 to attack the QNP and to keep the Queen file closed.

21. K–B1	N/2–Q4
22. R–Q4	. . .

So that if Black decides to exchange Knights, White's pawns will be undoubled. Black, of course, has no such intention.

22. . . .	QR–B1

Not bad, but more prudent is 22. . . . K–B1 to get the King to K2. Black should be ready to exchange Rooks on the Queen file if necessary.

23. QR–Q1	R–K1

24. P–K4 was the immediate threat.

24. NxN	. . .

Interesting but unproductive is 24. P–N5 NxN 25. PxB NxB (not 25. . . . NxR? 26. PxP NxNP 27. PxR=Q RxQ 28. BxP with good prospects) 26. PxP NxBch 27. RPxN R–N1 and wins.

24. . . .	NxN

24. . . . PxN gives Black an isolated pawn, and 24. . . . BxN permits White to get rid of his doubled pawn with 25. P–N5, for if 25. . . . P–QR4 then 26. P–N6 threatening to cut off Black's Rook by 27. B–B7.

25. P–K4	N–B2
26. P–B3	. . .

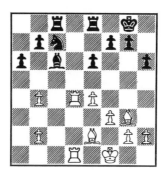

White plans to bring the Queen Bishop to KB2 after it is blocked by . . . P–K4. From KB2 the Bishop aims for QB5, where it can be useful in harassing the Black King. For instance, 26. . . . P–K4 27. R/4–Q2 P–B3 (in order to bring the Knight to K3) 28. B–B4ch K–B1 29. B–B2 (threatening 30. B–B5ch) N–K3 30. R–Q6, and Black is in an inextricable position. This is a serious problem for Black. One thing is certain: I have to bring my King to K2 and neutralize the White Rooks.

Hort and I each had about half an hour left for the remaining fifteen moves. A tense situation.

| 26. . . . | B–R5! |

To deprive White's Rooks of an important square on the Queen file.

| 27. R/1–Q2 | P–K4 |
| 28. R–B4 | . . . |

White has nothing better. If 28. R/4–Q3 P–B3 29. B–B2 N–K3 Black has nothing to worry about since White cannot get his KB to QB4. If 28. R–Q6 N–N4 29. R/6–Q5 (29. R–Q7 R–B8ch 30. K–B2 N–Q5 31. RxNP NxB 32. KxN B–N4ch 33. K–K3 P–B3 with equality because of the Bishops of opposite colors) 29. . . . R–B8ch 30. K–B2 P–B3 with no promising continuation for White. The effectiveness of Black's 26th and 27th moves now becomes apparent. The position does not promise much for the Bishops.

28. . . .	P–B3
29. B–B2	N–K3
30. P–KN3	K–B1

31. B–N6	K–K2
32. K–B2	B–N4
33. R/4–B2	. . .

Futile is 33. RxR RxR 34. BxB PxB 35. R–Q5 (35. K–K2 R–B3
36. B–K3 R–B5) 35. . . . R–B7ch 36. K–K3 RxNP 37. RxNP K–Q2
38. B–R5 K–B1 with the better prospects.

33. . . .	B–R5

Simpler is 33. . . . RxR 34. RxR BxB 35. KxB K–Q2 followed by
. . . R–QB1 with a draw.

34. R–B3	R–B3
35. RxR	. . .

White is unable to avoid the exchange of Rooks. If 35. B–K3
R/1–QB1 36. R/3–Q3 R–B7.

35. . . .	BxR
36. K–K3	P–N4

Imperative in order to prevent P–B4 followed by P–B5, which
enables White's QB to reach the important square QB5 and
thereby harass Black's King.

37. B–B1	R–QB1
38. R–QB2	R–QR1

Any other Rook move costs a pawn by BxP.

39. R–Q2	R–QB1
40. B–R3	R–QR1
41. B–B5	R–KN1

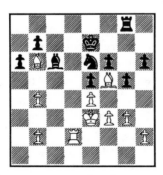

The adjourned position. With the tension removed and
thorough analysis by both sides to follow, I felt that I would be
able to hold the position; my feeling proved justified.

42. K–B2 . . .

I expected the sealed move to be 42. R–Q1; actually, it didn't make any difference what Hort sealed. The only way White can make progress is to effect P–R4 in an attempt to seize control of the KR-file. If 42. R–Q1 B–N4 43. R–KR1 (43. P–R4 is meaningless because of 43. . . . PxP 44. PxP R–KN1 with Black in control of the file) 43. . . . R–QB1! (threatening . . . R–B7 with the idea of . . . R–K7 mate) 44. B–B5ch K–B2 45. P–R4 P–N3 (or even 45. . . . R–Q1 threatening . . . R–Q6ch) 46. BxP R–B7, etc.

42. . . .	**B–N4**
43. R–Q1	**R–KR1**
44. K–K3	**P–KR4**
45. P–R4	. . .

Otherwise 45. . . . P–R5.

45. . . .	**PxP**
46. PxP	**R–KN1**

Draw

Black threatens . . . R–N7, and if 47. K–B2 N–B5 again threatening . . . R–N7(ch). Best for White is 47. BxN, which leads to a simple draw because of the Bishops of opposite colors.

Game 37

The "Impregnable" Defense

Sometimes, despite gaining a substantial advantage, you find that your opponent can "stonewall it"; that is, he can set up a position in which the lines are closed and which has the appearance of impregnability. Such positions can be frustrating to the player who must win, and they tax his ingenuity to the utmost degree.

In this game, Black attempts to set up such a position, even giving up material for that purpose, when he recognizes that he is on the verge of losing. White, despite his material superiority, knows he must have new open lines in order to make his superiority count. Patient maneuvering is out of place in this kind of situation.

Maribor, 1967

BENONI DEFENSE

S. Reshevsky	L. Crepinsek
1. P–Q4	N–KB3
2. P–QB4	P–B4
3. P–Q5	P–K4
4. N–QB3	P–Q3
5. P–K4	B–K2
6. B–Q3	O–O
7. P–KR3	N–R3
8. P–R3	. . .

The purpose of this move is not to prevent . . . N–QN5 but to be in a position to play P–QN4 after Black plays . . . N–QB2, and thereby to initiate action on the Queenside before Black does the same with . . . P–QR3 and . . . P–QN4. While this is a reasonable plan, it precludes castling long with the idea of Kingside attack because of the insecurity of the White King on the Queenside after the pawn moves. To be seriously considered, therefore, is 8. N–B3 followed by Q–K2 in preparation for Queenside castling.

8. . . .	N–K1
9. KN–K2	P–KN3
10. O–O	N–N2
11. P–B4	P–B3?

I was very happy to see this reply since I thought that I would encounter little difficulty in scoring the point. The text obviously reduces Black to passivity. Imperative is 11. . . . P–B4; I intended to continue 12. KPxP NPxP (12. . . . BxP 13. P–KN4 BxB 14. QxB with advantage) 13. B–K3 with good positional prospects.

12. P–B5	P–KN4

With the false hope of being able to block action on that wing.

13. P–KR4	Q–K1
14. P–KN4	P–R3

Unavailing is 14. . . . P–R4. There would follow 15. K–N2 NPxP (15. . . . RPxP 16. PxP PxP 17. N–N3 N–R4 18. NxN QxN 19.

R–R1 followed by QxP) 16. R–R1 PxP 17. RxP with an over-whelming position.

15.	K–B2	K–B2
16.	R–R1	R–R1
17.	B–K3	B–Q2
18.	Q–Q2	N–B2
19.	P–N4	. . .

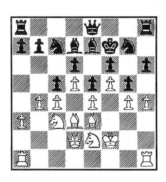

To deprive my opponent of obtaining counterplay with . . . P–N4, for then 20. NPxP QPxP (if 20. . . . QNPxP 21. BxBP QPxP 22. P–Q6ch) 21. BPxP NxNP 22. BxN BxB 23. P–Q6 followed by 24. Q–Q5ch and wins. After the text move, White's position is powerful, Black's counterchances nil.

19.	. . .	P–N3
20.	R–KR2	N–R3
21.	Q–N2?	. . .

I made this move in an effort to retain the possibility of action on the Queenside, but it gives Black an opportunity to react on the Kingside because White's pressure on the KNP is relieved. Correct is 21. P–N5 N–B2 22. QR–R1 R–KB1 23. PxP RPxP 24. R–R7 with an irresistible attack since White would be in a position to mass all of his forces on the KR-file and to penetrate unhindered.

21.	. . .	P–R4!
22.	RPxP	KBPxP

23. PxRP	**RxP**
24. QR–R1	**R–R5**

The only defense. After 24. . . . RxR 25. RxR followed by an eventual Q–Q2, the KNP would be lost.

The next phase of the game revolves around the struggle for control of the KR-file. If White wins this struggle the game will be his; if Black gets the file, he could draw.

25. P–N5	**N–B2**
26. Q–B1	**Q–R1**
27. Q–KN1	. . .

Threatening 28. RxR PxR 29. Q–N6ch followed by P–B6.

27. . . .	**Q–R4**
28. N–N3	**Q–R2**
29. N–B1	**N–R4**

If 29. . . . R–KN1 30. N–Q2 (not 30. BxNP because of 30. . . . NxBP) 30. . . . P–N5 (if 30. . . . N–R4 31. N–B3 RxR 32. QxR) 31. RxR BxRch 32. K–K2 N–K1 33. Q–R2 R–KR1 34. B–B2 and wins, for if 34. . . . Q–R4 35. QxB.

30. BxNP	**RxRch**

31. NxR!	. . .

After 31. QxR BxB 32. QxNch QxQ 33. RxQ R–KN1, White's task would be difficult, even though he would be a pawn ahead. Black's two Bishops and his control of the KN-file would afford him drawing chances. The text move appears to be bad but has a subtle point.

Game 38
A Calculation Error

Almost every decisive game depends on errors. In fact, when someone tells you that he outplayed his opponent to win, what he means is that he forced his opponent to make errors. None of the breathtaking sacrificial combinations we all admire would have been possible without at least one error by the victim. So-called positional masterpieces themselves depend on certain lapses of judgment by the loser, even if this is no more than a poor choice of opening. Tartakower was correct to say that a game of chess is won by the player who makes the next-to-last mistake.

An instructive error is made by Mednis in this game. His position at the time of his mistake is no worse than White's, but in calculating a short tactical sequence he fails to notice a good move at my disposal, or at least he fails to recognize its consequences. His 32nd move is based on the sound principle of double attack: he gives check and at the same time attacks an unprotected Rook. But, because of time pressure, he doesn't see that the Rook cannot be taken because his Queen is in danger. A simple oversight, yes. But it should serve as a warning. Emanuel Lasker admonished students not to be satisfied with a good move but to look for a better one.

U.S. Championship
New York, 1972

GRUENFELD DEFENSE

S. Reshevsky	E. Mednis
1. P–QB4	N–KB3
2. P–KN3	P–B3
3. B–N2	P–Q4
4. N–KB3	P–KN3
5. 0–0	B–N2

6. PxP	**PxP**
7. P–Q3	. . .

A different system. The usual continuation is 7. P–Q4, leading
to a symmetrical type of position, which, contrary to general
belief, offers White chances for a minimal positional advantage.

7. . . .	**0–0**
8. N–B3	**N–B3**
9. B–B4	. . .

The Bishop here prevents Black's . . . P–K4, which would
enable him to control the central squares.

9. . . .	**P–KR3**
10. R–B1	**P–K3**

Blocking his QB. Black is afraid to continue 10. . . . B–B4
because of 11. N–K5. To be considered is 10. . . . N–KR4 11.
B–Q2 P–K4 with lively play.

11. N–QR4	. . .

Intending to post this Knight favorably on QB5.

11. . . .	**R–K1**
12. N–K5	. . .

Preventing the freeing . . . P–K4.

12. . . .	**NxN**
13. BxN	**B–Q2**

Better is 13. . . . P–N3 (to keep White's Knight out of QB4)
followed by . . . B–N2.

14. N–B5	**B–B3**
15. Q–N3	**R–K2**

Insufficient is 15. . . . P–N3. White would then make inroads
into Black's position with 16. N–R6 R–QB1 17. R–B2 (intending
to double Rooks on the QB-file) with considerable pressure.

16. R–B2	**N–K1**

Black has to get rid of White's strongly posted QB.

17. BxB	**NxB**
18. P–K4	. . .

White's superior control of space is beginning to tell.

18. . . .	**N–K1**

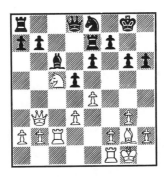

19. KR–B1? . . .

Much stronger is 19. P–K5, creating a powerful bind in the center which leaves Black's position completely lifeless and almost impossible to defend. After 19. P–K5, White can proceed with 20. P–Q4 and afterward choose between positional play on the Queenside or aggressive action on the opposite wing.

19. . . .	N–B3
20. Q–B3	. . .

Again 20. P–K5 is more potent.

20. . . .	P–K4!

Finally, an aggressive move, which affords Black counterplay.

21. Q–K1	PxP
22. PxP	Q–N3
23. Q–K3	K–N2
24. Q–R3	Q–Q1

If 24. . . . R–Q1 25. N–R4 (the enticing 25. NxP RxN 26. RxB QxP does not offer White too much) 25. . . . Q–B2 26. N–B3 with the annoying double threat QxP and N–Q5.

25. Q–K3	Q–N3
26. Q–R3	Q–Q1

I marked time while my opponent hinted at a draw. But I was determined to try for a win even at the risk of losing.

27. Q–N4	. . .

This move does not really change the complexion of the game, but it does entice Mednis to become more confident and more aggressive.

27. . . .	Q–N3
28. Q–B3	R–Q1
29. Q–R3	R/2–K1
30. R–B3	R–Q7

| 31. R–N3 | Q–Q1 |
| 32. NxP | R–Q8ch? |

The losing move. Mednis, in serious time trouble, makes the normal-looking and tempting move, a check which also attacks White's unprotected Rook. He expects 33. RxR; he would then have a promising game after 33. . . . QxRch 34. B–B1 NxP with the threat of 35. . . . N–Q7. But Mednis overlooks White's intended reply. Also unplayable is 32. . . . BxN 33. RxB Q–Q5 34. QxP with no counterplay for Black. 32 . . . Q–Q5 is correct. If then 33. R–B1 BxP 34. R–N4 Q–Q4 35. BxB NxB 36. QxP? N–N4 with the menacing threats of . . . N–R6 and . . . N–B6ch. The only plausible continuation for White (after 32. . . . Q–Q5!) is 33. Q–B5 BxP 34. QxQ RxQ (if 34. . . . PxQ 35. N–Q6!) with approximate equality.

33. B–B1!   . . .

The move Mednis did not take into account.

33. . . .   **BxN**

Interesting but unavailing is 33. . . . Q–Q7. There would follow 34. RxR (not 34. RxB? Q–K7 and wins) QxR 35. N–Q6 R–K3 (if 35. . . . R–Q1 36. R–Q3 Q–K8 37. P–B3, which stops Black's threats and leaves White a pawn to the good. Note that

in this line 37. N–B5ch PxN 38. RxR B–N4! 39. Q–B8ch K–N3
40. PxPch KxP wins for Black.) 36. R–Q3 Q–K8 37. P–B3 with
advantage.

34. RxR	QxR
35. RxB	NxP
36. QxP	. . .

Now that Black's imaginary threats have been exhausted, White
emerges with a pawn plus and two passed pawns.

36. . . .	Q–B6
37. B–K2	Q–B3

Not 37. . . . QxB? 38. RxPch with mate to follow.

38. Q–K3	N–Q3
39. R–N6	Q–K2
40. Q–B5	R–Q1
41. P–QR4	. . .

Since Black's pieces are immobilized, the advance of this
pawn, even without the aid of the QNP, suffices to win.

41. . . .	N–B4
42. QxQ	NxQ
43. P–R5	N–Q4
44. R–N7	R–QB1
45. P–R6	R–B8ch
46. K–N2	R–B7
47. P–R7	Resigns

Game 39

Poetic Justice

As I point out in another chapter, the quality of a piece is measured by its mobility. Look at the position after White's 28th move: his Bishop on QN7 has no way out and has lost all of its power. White, who until this move had been enjoying a considerable advantage, gave it all away for the sake of winning one pawn. His error, of course, was his failure to see Black's reply, which won not only the unfortunate Bishop but the Exchange as well. His lapse in judgment was to consider his advantage to be worth only a pawn.

The reader would be deprived of an enjoyable game if that were all. Only a few moves later Black returns the compliment as well as most of his advantage—and for the same reason: overconfidence resulting in careless calculation.

And still more: insisting on a loss, White makes yet another tactical mistake in the endgame and tosses away a draw. The endgame, by the way, is instructive; note especially the paradoxical maneuver on Black's 52nd and 54th moves to win an important tempo.

Interzonal Tournament

Petropolis, 1973

SICILIAN DEFENSE

S. Kagan	S. Reshevsky
1. P–K4	P–QB4
2. N–KB3	P–Q3
3. P–Q4	PxP
4. NxP	N–KB3
5. N–QB3	P–QR3
6. P–KN3	. . .

Kagan always plays this against the Najdorf variation. The move has merit, and Black must play precisely in order to obtain equality. In another game, Geller, as Black, drifted into a losing position in this variation, but Kagan blundered and lost.

6. . . .	P–K4

Also playable is 6. . . . P–K3 7. B–N2 B–Q2 followed by . . . N–B3.

7. KN–K2	B–K2
8. B–N2	B–K3
9. P–QR4!	. . .

To prevent . . . P–QN4 and also to be in a position to put a bind on the Queenside by continuing P–R5.

9. . . .	QN–Q2
10. 0–0	R–QB1

Better is 10. . . . P–QN3, preventing P–R5.

11. P–R3	0–0
12. K–R2	Q–B2
13. P–R5!	. . .

Preventing Black's Knight from reaching his QN3 square.

13. . . .	KR–Q1
14. B–K3	P–R3

After White's P–R5, Black cannot free himself with . . . P–Q4 (since his Knight cannot occupy QN3). The text is a waiting move.

15. Q–Q2	B–B1
16. KR–B1	. . .

16. . . .	P–QN4
17. P–KN4	. . .

17. PxP e.p. NxNP 18. RxP B–B5 gives Black good play.

17. . . .	**N–B4**

Intending . . . Q–N2, exerting pressure on the KP and preparing for the freeing . . . P–Q4, but White refuses to allow that.

18. N–Q5	**BxN?!**

Wiser is 18. . . . NxN 19. PxN B–Q2, and if 20. P–N4 (threatening 21. B–N6 after the Knight is displaced) 20. . . . N–R5 with better prospects than those offered by the actual move.

19. PxB	**R–K1**
20. N–N3	**P–K5?**

Permitting White to post his QB on a very favorable square. Correct is 20. . . . Q–N2, attacking the QP immediately and threatening 21. . . . P–K5. This would reduce White's immediate chances for attack. After 20. . . . Q–N2 21. P–N5 PxP 22. BxP N–R2, Black's position would be tenable, although White would enjoy a slight edge.

21. B–Q4!	. . .

Prevents . . . R–K4 and places the Bishop where it will be most useful in an onslaught against Black's King.

21. . . .	**N/4–Q2**

The retreat of this Knight is imperative now for defensive purposes.

22. P–N5	**PxP**
23. QxP	**Q–N2**

Black is confronted with two problems: meeting the impending attack and protecting his KP. The text move seeks to remove the possibility of an imminent assault and to exchange his weak KP for White's QP; however, as a consequence White's Bishops become strong. There is no better choice.

24. P–QB3	**QxP**
25. QxQ	**NxQ**
26. BxKP	. . .

White's roaming Bishops obviously give him a considerable advantage.

26. . . .	**N–B5**
27. B–N7	**R–N1**

28. BxRP?? . . .

A losing move. Correct is 28. B–QB6 KR–Q1 (if 28. . . . . QR–Q1 29. B–N6) 29. R–Q1, retaining the advantage.

      28. . . . **N–Q6**

      29. P–N4 . . .

White does not see what is coming; otherwise he would try 29. B–R7, although after 29. . . . R–R1 30. BxP NxR 31. BxN R–K2, Black has a winning position. To no avail is 29. R–Q1 (or KR–QN1 or R–B2, etc.) on account of 29. . . . N/6–B4, winning the wandering KB. White's loss of the Exchange, however, is only part of his problem.

      29. . . . **NxR**

      30. RxN **P–Q4!**

And now the threat of 31. . . . R–K3, winning the Bishop, cannot be met.

      31. N–B5 **R–K3**

      32. BxQNP **RxB**

Black is now a Rook ahead, for which White has two pawns. Kagan might have resigned here, but his stubbornness proves justified!

      33. R–KN1 **P–N3**

      34. N–K3 . . .

34. . . .   B–N2??

Black now begins to make a few bad moves, which throws away his advantage. Almost any other move is sufficient for victory. For example, 34. . . . N–K4 threatens to dispose of the well-posted Bishop with 35. . . . N–B6ch or 35. . . . N–B3.

35. BxB	KxB
36. N–B5ch	K–B3
37. N–Q4	R–N1

Better is 37. . . . R–N2 38. NxR KxN (or even 38. . . . PxN) 39. P–R6 R–R2 40. P–N5 K–Q3, winning easily.

| 38. NxR | PxN |

Better is 38. . . . KxN to get the King to the Queenside faster.

| 39. R–QR1 | K–K4? |

Another inaccuracy. Usually it is preferable to bring the King toward the center but not in this case. Correct is 39. . . . K–K2 to hasten to the Queenside. Play might have continued 40. P–R6 N–N3 41. P–R7 R–QR1 42. R–R6 N–B1 43. R–B6 K–Q2 and wins.

40. P–R6	R–QR1
41. P–R7	N–N3
42. R–R6	. . .

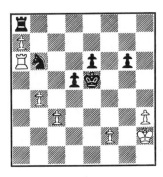

The adjourned position. Strangely enough, this endgame is not a win for Black even though he is a piece ahead.

| **42. . . .** | **N–B1** |

Unappetizing is 42. . . . N–B5 43. P–N5 P–N4 44. K–N3, and with his Rook activated, Black cannot hope to make progress.

| **43. R–B6** | **NxP** |

There is nothing else. Not 43. . . . K–B4, trying to advance the KP, because of 44. RxN RxR 45. P–N5–6–7 and wins.

| **44. R–R6** | **R–QB1** |

Otherwise, White will advance his QNP.

| **45. RxN** | **RxP** |

And now an interesting Rook-and-pawn ending has been reached. With correct play it should be drawn.

46. K–N2	**P–Q5**
47. R–KN7	**K–B4**
48. R–B7ch?	**. . .**

Wasting valuable time and allowing Black's King to help his QP advance more easily. Correct is 48. P–B3 R–N6 49. R–N7 K–B5 (49. . . . P–Q6 50. K–B2) 50. R–B7ch K–K6 51. R–K7 P–Q6 52. RxPch K–Q7 53. K–B2 K–B7 54. R–Q6 R–B6 55. K–K3 R–B1 56. P–N5 and draws.

| **48. . . .** | **K–K5** |

The King, with the aid of the Rook, will promote the advance of the passed QP. White fails to recognize this possibility and neglects to take countermeasures by advancing his QNP.

| **49. R–B6** | **K–Q6** |

50. RxKP	K–B7
51. R–Q6	. . .

51. RxP loses immediately: 51. . . . P–Q6 52. R–Q6 P–Q7 53. RxPch (otherwise 53. . . . R–Q6 and queens) KxR and wins because the White King is not able to advance rapidly enough.

51. . . .	P–Q6
52. K–B3	. . .

So that if 52. . . . P–Q7ch, then 53. K–K2.

52. . . .	K–B8!

With the threat of 53. . . . P–Q7ch 54. K–K2 R–B7 and wins.

53. K–N4	P–Q7
54. P–R4	K–B7!

Threatening 55. . . . R–Q6. The text move gains a tempo on 54. . . . P–Q8=Qch.

55. RxPch	KxR
56. K–N5	R–B3
57. P–B4	K–K6
58. P–B5	PxP
59. KxP	K–Q5
60. P–R5	K–Q4
61. P–N5	R–Q3
62. K–N5	K–K3
63. K–N6	R–Q8
64. P–R6	R–N8ch
65. K–R7	K–B2
	Resigns

Game 40

Underestimated Opponent

Most young players of talent have a very sharp tactical sense; they try everything, analyze long, forced variations, and enjoy complicated positions where anything can happen. Such players are very dangerous opponents for older masters who prefer to rely on general positional considerations and their feeling for position, saving the effort of long calculations for when it is really needed. This game is an example: Ivkov, probably in time pressure, "feels" that his mating net will bring him victory, but what is needed more than feeling is calculation.

The game also illustrates the advantage of opposite-colored Bishops to the player with the initiative. Black's Bishop travels on black squares and attacks White's KB2, also black. White's white-squared Bishop can't defend the attacked point, and this factor weighs heavily against him when he avoids a drawish continuation in pursuit of a nonexistent win.

Interzonal Tournament

Sousse, 1967

RUY LOPEZ

B. Ivkov	H. Mecking
1. P–K4	P–K4
2. N–KB3	N–QB3
3. B–N5	P–QR3
4. B–R4	N–B3
5. 0–0	B–K2
6. R–K1	P–QN4
7. B–N3	P–Q3
8. P–B3	0–0
9. P–KR3	N–QR4
10. B–B2	P–B4
11. P–Q4	Q–B2
12. QN–Q2	N–B3
13. PxBP	PxP
14. N–B1	. . .

Considered best is 14. N–R2 so that later, after White's N–B1, when Black attacks White's Queen with . . . R–Q1, White can play it to KB3 instead of to K2 as in this game.

14. . . .	B–K3
15. N–K3	QR–Q1
16. Q–K2	P–B5
17. N–B5	BxN

| 18. PxB | KR–K1 |
| 19. N–N5 | . . . |

The text achieves nothing. More promising is 19. B–N5, as I played against Eliskases in Argentina in 1966.

19. . . .	N–N1
20. B–K3	QN–Q2
21. P–QR4	N–B4
22. PxP	PxP
23. BxN	. . .

Forced because of the threat of 24. . . . P–K5 followed by . . . N–Q6. But in giving up the Bishop, White has to be reconciled to no more than equality.

23. . . .	BxB
24. P–QN4	B–N3
25. N–K4	. . .

Forced, for if 25. QR–Q1 RxR 26. P–K5 27. NxKP NxN 28. BxN Q–K4 29. R–K1 QxQBP with a won position. But now Black is able to secure control of the important Q–file.

25. . . .	NxN
26. BxN	R–Q3
27. KR–Q1	KR–Q1
28. RxR	QxR
29. R–R8	. . .

To be considered is 29. P–N4 K–B1 30. K–N2, and if 30. . . . Q–Q7 31. Q–B3, with an equal position.

29. . . .	RxR
30. BxR	P–N3
31. B–K4	K–N2
32. P–N3	Q–Q2
33. Q–B3	Q–Q7
34. P–B6ch?	K–R3
35. K–N2	Q–K8

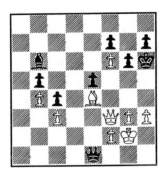

36. P–R4??   . . .

The losing move. Ivkov attempts to set up a mating net with
P–N4–N5, but he underestimates his opponent. He could draw
easily with 36. B–Q5. There would follow 36. . . . P–K5 (other-
wise BxKBP) 37. BxKP BxP 38. Q–B4ch (if 38. QxB QxBch 39.
K–R2 P–N4 followed by . . . K–N3, and the KBP would be lost,
giving Black excellent winning chances) 38. . . . P–N4 39.
Q–B5 Q–N8ch 40. K–B3 QxPch 41. K–K2 Q–K6ch 42. K–B1 (42.
K–Q1 Q–K8ch 43. K–B2 Q–K7ch 44. K–N1 Q–Q8ch 45. K–R2
Q–N6ch, etc.) 42. . . . Q–K8ch, etc.

Probably time pressure played a part here. The amount of
calculation Ivkov needed—and no doubt didn't have time for—
should have warned him against entering such an intricate continuation, especially against a tactically alert player like Mecking.
It is true, however, that at the time of this game Mecking was
only a talented fifteen-year-old; perhaps this can be offered as
testimony in Ivkov's defense.

36. . . .		**BxP**
37. Q–N4		**B–K6**
38. Q–B8		. . .

Unsatisfactory is 38. Q–Q7 B–B5 39. PxB QxBch 40. K–N1
Q–K6ch 41. K–N2 PxP 42. QxBP Q–K7ch 43. K–N1 (43. K–R3
Q–B6ch 44. K–R2 Q–N6ch 45. K–R1 QxPch 46. K–N2 P–B6
and wins) 43. . . . P–B6 44. Q–N7ch K–R4 45. QxRPch K–N5
46. QxPch KxP 47. Q–R6ch K–N5 48. Q–N6ch K–B5 49. Q–R6ch
K–B4 and wins.

I suspect that Ivkov missed some subtlety here when he made his 36th move.

38. . . .	Q–B7ch
39. K–R3	QxP
40. P–N4	K–N2
41. P–N5	Q–B8ch
42. B–N2	Q–Q6
43. K–N4	B–B7
Resigns	

Game 41

Mate First

Would you rather have three pawns or a piece? If you have any experience, you will answer, "It depends on the position." Pawns are great in the endgame, when they can be advanced and promoted without being bothered by too many tactical threats. (See Reshevsky–Seidman, game 10, and Larsen–Bobotsov, game 57.) When you're being mated, however, your passed pawns can't help much.

That's the story of this game. To avoid a difficult defense, Najdorf exchanges a piece for three pawns. Najdorf is a great competitor who hates defense and loves tactical play; given that, his decision is the best practical solution and cannot be considered unsound.

Such material imbalances create certain special problems. Correct play for the side with the piece, especially when Queens and other pieces are present, is to use his extra piece energetically to keep his middlegame initiative. Each breathing space given the opponent is a chance for him to advance his pawns or try to simplify the position. The side with the pawns, generally, should head for the endgame. In other words, the above question is best answered: "In the middlegame take the extra piece; in the endgame take the pawns."

Mar del Plata, 1968

SICILIAN DEFENSE

Palermo	M. Najdorf
1. P–KB4	N–KB3
2. N–KB3	P–KN3
3. P–KN3	B–N2
4. B–N2	0–0
5. P–Q3	P–B4
6. 0–0	N–B3
7. P–K4	P–Q3

A variation of the Closed Sicilian has been reached. White will attempt to attack on the Kingside by pushing pawns, while Black will seek counterplay on the opposite wing. This usually affords the opportunity for tactical play all over the board and an exciting game.

| 8. P–QR4 | . . . |

More usual, and better, is 8. N–B3.

8. . . .	R–N1
9. N–B3	P–QR3
10. N–R4	N–Q5

Preferable is 10. . . . N–K1 11. P–B5 P–K3, preventing the advance P–KN4.

| 11. P–B5 | P–K3 |
| 12. P–KN4 | . . . |

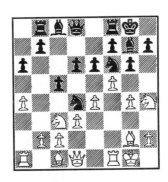

| 12. . . . | N–Q2 |

Unplayable is 12. . . . NxKP 13. NxN KPxP (13. . . . QxN? 14. B–N5, trapping the Queen) 14. PxP (14. N–N5, attempting to retain the piece, fails on account of 14. . . . PxP followed by . . . P–R3) 14. . . . QxN 15. B–N5 Q–R4 16. QxQ PxQ 17. P–B6 B–R1 18. P–B3 with great advantage. 12. . . . N–Q4 is met by 13. P–N5 NxN 14. PxN N–B3 15. P–B6 with a stranglehold.

13. P–N5	**B–K4**

Black must avoid allowing his Bishop to be locked in after P–B6.

14. P–B6	**P–N4**

Unavailing is 14. . . . P–R3 15. N–B3 NxNch (if 15. . . . PxP 16. NxB followed by 16. BxP) 16. QxN PxP 17. BxP, and Black is in a hopeless position. Black therefore starts his Queenside counterplay.

15. PxP	**PxP**
16. N–B3	**P–N5**
17. N–K2	**. . .**

To be considered is 17. NxB NxN (17. . . . NPxN 18. NxN PxP 19. BxP BxN 20. BxN PxB 21. Q–N4–R4) 18. N–K2.

17. . . .	**NxN/6ch**
18. BxN	**. . .**

White should continue with the attack immediately by playing 18. RxN, and if 18. . . . P–R3 19. Q–K1 PxP 20. BxP (threatening Q–R4 followed by R–R3) BxBP 21. RxB NxR 22. Q–R4 with a won position. If 18. . . . P–R4 (trying to blockade the position) 19. R–R3 followed by B–B3 and an eventual BxRP. The text slows the attack somewhat.

18. . . .	**P–R3**
19. P–R4	**. . .**

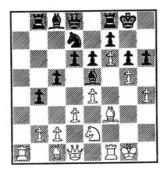

19. . . .	NxP

Otherwise White can line up his pieces on the Kingside at will and crash through to victory. 19. . . . P–R4 would lose sooner or later to BxRP with a mating attack. Najdorf decides to trade the Knight for three pawns, which is normally sufficient compensation. His sacrifice, if it can be called that, is not surprising since his dislike of defense is well known. His choice does offer long-range chances, but the endgame is still far off.

20. PxN	QxP
21. K–N2	. . .

Of course not 21. BxP QxP, winning.

21. . . .	BxP

Better than 21. . . . QxP 22. R–R1 Q–B3 23. BxP BxP 24. BxR BxR 25. BxP, etc.

22. BxP!	BxR

Inadvisable is 22. . . . R–K1 because of 23. R–R7 with serious pressure on the KBP. If 23. . . . QxP 24. Q–Q2 B–B3 (to prevent B–N5) 25. R–KR1.

23. BxR	B–K4

23. . . . KxB 24. QxB QxP (if 24. . . . QxQ 25. RxQ with the better chances for White in the ensuing endgame) 25. R–R1 Q–N4ch 26. K–B2 with the dangerous threat of R–R8ch followed by Q–N7 or Q–R7.

24. B–R6	QxP
25. R–R1	Q–K2
26. Q–Q2	B–Q2

Inadvisable is 26. . . . P–N6 27. R–QN1 P–N7 28. P–B3 Q–N2 29. P–Q4 B–R1 30. P–K5 P–Q4 31. B–N5 followed by B–B6 with mating threats. Black's counterplay is slow to materialize, and his potential passed pawns are still potential. White has the initiative.

27. B–B4	**B–N2**

Better is 27. . . . B–KB3, preventing White's next move.

28. B–N5	**B–KB3**

Forced, for if 28. . . . P–B3 Black's KB remains out of play, and if 28. . . . Q–K1 29. Q–B4 followed by Q–R4 is more than unpleasant for Black. The following exchange eliminates Black's best piece; 27. . . . B–KB3 would have avoided this.

29. BxB	**QxB**
30. Q–R6	**Q–N2**

Black's task is difficult. White was threatening to win material with 31. Q–R7ch and Q–R8. 30. . . . B–K1 is a better try.

31. Q–R2!	. . .

White's Queen is better than Black's, so why exchange?

31. . . .	**P–K4**

Of no help is 31. . . . R–N3 32. Q–R4 (threatening to penetrate Black's position with the Queen via K7 or Q8) 32. . . . P–N4 33. Q–N4 followed by N–N3–R5.

32. R–R1	**Q–B3**
33. Q–N3	**K–N2**
34. B–N4	**B–K1**

Preferable is 34. . . . B–N4 with the intention of continuing with . . . P–B5 and obtaining a passed pawn. If 35. R–R1 R–KR1 with good drawing chances.

35. Q–K3	. . .

35. . . .   **K–N1?**

Permits White's pieces to make inroads into Black's defenses via the dark squares, which were weakened by the exchange of Bishops on the 29th move. With 35. . . . Q–R5, Black can stop White's progress by keeping control of the dark squares. If 36. B–B3 Q–R3 37. QxQch (37. Q–B2 Q–N4ch 38. N–N3 B–N4, etc.) 37. . . . KxQ 38. R–R6 P–N6 39. PxP RxP 40. RxP B–N4 winning the QP (41. N–B1 R–B6), after which White has no winning chances.

        36. Q–R6   **B–N4**

        37. R–KB1   **Q–N2**

37. . . . Q–K2 38. R–KR1 and wins.

        38. Q–N5   **P–B5**

        39. Q–K7   **Q–B1**

Unsatisfactory is 39. . . . PxP on account of 40. RxP QxR 41. B–K6 and wins.

        40. Q–B7   **. . .**

Threatening 41. B–K6.

        40. . . .   **R–K1**

        41. PxP   **B–R5**

        42. N–N3   **. . .**

Unproductive is 42. R–B1 Q–R3 (threatening . . . Q–Q7) 43. QxP Q–N4 44. K–B3 (44. K–R3 K–N2, and if 45. QxNP? R–R1ch 46. K–N3 B–Q2) 44. . . . R–Q1 45. QxNP BxP 46. RxB R–Q6ch 47. K–B2 Q–R5ch 48. K–B1 QxB with at least a draw, for if 49. Q–N8ch K–R2 50. QxP Q–B6ch 51. K–K1 Q–R8ch 52. K–B2 R–B6 mate.

42. . . .	BxP
43. Q–R5	. . .

Not 43. B–Q7 R–K2 44. QxP? Q–Q1.

43. . . .	P–N6
44. Q–Q2	Q–K2
45. R–KR1?	. . .

The correct try for a win is 45. B–Q1 BxB 46. RxB, and Black's QNP could be attacked by White's forces without visible counterplay for Black. White is still looking for a mate, but he underestimates Black's chances. Typical of tactical struggles, the game could go either way suddenly.

45. . . .	Q–B3
46. B–Q7	Q–B5!
47. Q–K2	. . .

If 47. QxQ PxQ 48. BxR PxN 49. B–B6 P–N7 with winning chances.

47. . . .	R–R1
48. R–KB1	. . .

48. . . .	Q–N4?

This move can be explained only by time trouble. Correct is 48. . . . R–R7!, which wins. After 49. RxQ PxR 50. K–B3 PxN 51. KxP (51. P–K5 P–KN7 and wins) 51. . . . R–R8, White is unable to stop Black's QNP except by heavy material sacrifice. If 49. RxQ PxR 50. K–B3 PxN 51. P–K5 P–KN7 and wins.

Another try for White, after 48. . . . R–R7!, is 49. K–R3, but

Black can counter with 49. . . . Q–R3ch 50. K–N4 P–B4ch 51.
BxP (51. PxP BxPch 52. NxB PxNch followed by . . . RxQ; if
51. NxP Q–R4ch) 51. . . . PxBch 52. NxP (52. RxP R–R8 53.
Q–KB2 B–Q8ch; if, in this line, 53. R–N5ch K–R1 54. R–R5
QxRch followed by . . . B–Q8) 52. . . . Q–N3ch 53. K–R3 (53.
K–R4 BxP) Q–R2ch 54. K–N4 (54. K–N3 B–Q8 55. QxB Q–R7ch
56. K–N4 R–N7ch 57. K–B3 Q–R6ch; if instead 56. K–B3 Q–B5
mate) 54. . . . B–Q8 55. QxB R–N7ch 56. N–N3 (56. K–B3
Q–R6ch) Q–N3ch with mate to follow.

| 49. Q–B3 | Q–K2 |

Better is 49. . . . R–KB1, and if 50. B–K6 P–N7 51. BxPch
K–N2, and Black wins. White's best after 49. . . . R–KB1 is 50.
B–R4, but after 50. . . . P–B4 51. PxP PxP, the chances would
be even.

| 50. Q–N4 | R–R2 |

White's threat of 51. N–B5 is too strong, and Black's position
becomes untenable. If for instance 50. . . . P–N7 51. N–B5 Q–B1
52. B–K6 P–N8=Q 53. RxQ BxR 54. QxPch K–R1 55. Q–R5ch
K–N1 56. BxPch QxB 57. N–R6ch and wins.

51. N–R5	RxB
52. N–B6ch	K–N2
53. Q–R4	BxPch
54. K–N3	. . .

Not 54. QxB QxN 55. RxQ KxR with a probable draw.

54. . . .	Q–Q1
55. Q–R7ch	K–B1
56. NxB	. . .

Also good is 56. NxRch QxN 57. Q–R8ch K–K2 58. Q–R4ch
winning the Bishop.

Black now has four pawns for a piece, but his King is in a
mating net.

56. . . .	P–N7
57. Q–R8ch	K–K2
58. Q–R4ch	K–B1
59. N–B6	R–N2
60. Q–R8ch	K–K2
61. N–Q5ch	Resigns

Game 42

Draw Sacrifice

A tactical opportunity is often the only hope when all seems lost. I could cite many last-minute "miracles"—enough to fill a book —but the same message is spoken by all of them: "miracles" happen only when they are permitted to happen. The only truly won game is the one that is posted on the scoreboard as such. If your opponent makes a desperate try and it works, no excuse in the world is going to change that ½ to a 1.

Moral: Every plan should include a consideration of the opponent's plan. See also Szabo–Tukmakov, elsewhere in this volume.

Soviet Interclub Team Tournament
1969

KING'S INDIAN DEFENSE

R. Kholmov	M. Tal
1. P–Q4	N–KB3
2. P–QB4	P–KN3
3. N–QB3	B–N2
4. P–K4	P–Q3
5. N–B3	0–0
6. B–K2	QN–Q2
7. B–K3	P–K4
8. 0–0	R–K1
9. P–Q5	N–N5
10. B–N5	P–KB3
11. B–R4	N–R3
12. N–Q2	. . .

Inadvisable is 12. P–QN4 P–R4 13. P–QR3 P–KN4 14. B–N3 P–KB4 15. KPxP PxP 16. PxP RxR 17. QxR P–K5 18. N–Q2 NxP with advantage for Black. To be considered, however, is 12. N–K1–B2–K3.

12. . . .	N–B2
13. R–K1	. . .

More aggressive is 13. P–QN4 to promote an eventual P–QB5.

13. . . .	P–KR4
14. P–KR3	. . .

14. P–B3 coupled with bringing the Bishop to KB2 is a good alternative.

14. . . .	B–R3
15. N–B1	B–N4
16. B–N3	. . .

Since the mobility of this Bishop will now be limited, it is wiser to exchange: 16. BxB NxB 17. P–QN4 with pressure on the Queenside.

16. . . .	P–R5
17. B–R2	P–KB4
18. B–Q3?	. . .

Good is 18. PxP PxP 19. P–B4 BxP (19. . . . PxP 20. Q–Q4 Q–B3 21. Q–B2 Q–R3 22. N–N5 with advantage) 20. BxB PxB 21. Q–Q2, recovering the pawn with advantage, for if 21. . . . Q–N4 22. N–N5.

18. . . .	N–B3
19. Q–B2	N–R3?

Permitting White to open up the position; or, knowing Tal, *wanting* White to open it up. 19. . . . P–B5 locks in White's KB and gives prospects for an attack.

20. PxP	PxP
21. P–B4	PxP
22. RxRch	QxR
23. Q–B2	N–R4
24. R–K1	Q–Q1

Wiser is 24. . . . Q–B2 25. N–K2 B–Q2 26. NxP N–B3.

25. N–K2	Q–B3
26. NxP	N–N2

Preventing R–K8ch and, by avoiding NxN, keeping White's QB inactive.

27. P–B5	N–B2

28. PxP? . . .

Up to now Kholmov has played well, but with the text move he gives up most of his advantage. With 28. R–B1 (threatening to penetrate to the seventh rank), he could increase the pressure. The idea behind his next few moves is to create tactical threats against Black's weak pawns. But tactical play is Tal's daily bread.

28. . . .	**PxP**
29. N–K3	**B–Q2**
30. N–K6	**NxN**
31. PxN	**BxP**
32. NxP	**BxP?**

A dangerous decision. Safer is 32. . . . N–K4.

The reduced number of pawns in this position means that the pieces of both players are very active and there are many tactical chances.

33. Q–B3	**B–K3**

It is unwise for Black to attempt to protect the QNP: 33. . . . R–N1 34. N–K7ch K–B1 35. Q–K4 with the serious threat of 36. Q–R7, among other things.

34. QxP	**R–KB1**
35. R–KB1	**N–K4**
36. BxN	. . .

The mate threat 36. NxQP doesn't work because of 36. . . . B–K6ch.

36. . . .	**PxB**

Not 36. . . . QxB? 37. N–R6ch followed by mate.

37. QxP	**R–B2**
38. Q–N8ch	. . .

White should try 38. Q–B5 B–KB5 (if 38. . . . Q–K2 39. P–QN4 followed by 40. B–B4) 39. N–Q6 R–B1 40. B–B4 BxB 41. QxBch K–R1 42. R–Q1 with difficulty for Black. White is trying to get too much out of the little advantage he has left.

38. . . .	**R–B1**
39. Q–N4	**B–KB5**
40. N–K7ch	**K–N2**
41. N–N6	**. . .**

Unproductive is 41. Q–K4 because of 41. . . . Q–R3 (not 41. . . . QxN? 42. Q–R7ch K–B3 43. Q–N6 mate). 41. K–R1, however, still gives White some play. Now Tal seizes the opportunity to force a draw.

41. . . .	**B–K6ch**
42. K–R2	**QxR!**
43. BxQ	**RxB**
44. Q–K7ch	**. . .**

Better than 44. NxP which permits 44. . . . B–N8ch and draws.

44. . . .	**KxN**
45. QxBch	**K–R2**
46. P–KN4	**. . .**

Unavailing is 46. Q–Q7ch K–R1 47. Q–K8ch K–R2 48. Q–R5ch K–N1 49. Q–N4ch (49. QxRP B–N8ch *wins*) K–B1.

46. . . .	**R–B7ch**
47. K–R1	**R–B8ch**

Draw

Chapter 7

Pieces, Good and Bad

The only good piece is a working piece. A piece that is undeveloped, out of play, passive, or hampered by pawns is not a good piece.

Obviously, if you entertain hopes of defeating a majority of your opponents, you must play with full force; that is, with all your pieces working. This means that in your planning at every stage of the game you must pay careful attention to the effectiveness of your pieces compared with those of your opponent.

One of the errors inexperienced players are often guilty of—even grandmasters do it once in a while—is to attack prematurely by thrusting a few pieces and pawns in the general direction of the enemy King without regard for the situation of the other pieces. The punishment for this unwarranted aggression is backward development, resulting from exchange or elimination of the small attacking force, leaving the other pieces uncoordinated or undeveloped. Game 43 is like that, but here Black gets ideas about the Queenside before completing his development. It takes two bad errors by White to let Black off the hook. Game 44 is another example of the evils of incomplete development.

Pieces are tools with which each player tries to effectuate his own plans while hindering those of his opponent. It often happens during the course of the struggle that a piece may find itself far from its most effective post because the scene of battle has shifted. Plans do change. You must be alert to the opportunities such situations offer, and you must never fail to consider your opponent's opportunities in this respect. Sometimes a sharp move in an unexpected corner can prove embarrassing for the opponent whose forces are massed for some purpose elsewhere. Those pieces will then be unable to adapt readily to the requirements of the new situation. See game 45.

The trouble with weak pawns and weak squares is that they have to be watched over by pieces, which are then not free to participate in more fruitful endeavors. Such passive pieces usually cannot meet two distinct simultaneous threats. That's what happens in game 46.

In a game of attack and defense, like chess, when neither side is able to gain an advantage a balanced state of inactivity is reached. But usually an enterprising player will find an unexpected move, even a sacrifice, to upset the balance and create winning chances. In game 47, a sudden pawn move opens new vistas for White's pieces and at the same time throws Black's into confusion.

Every amateur is familiar with the power of the two Bishops working together. Their strength lies in their mobility; as a team they rake the board in four directions and at great distances. The terror such Bishops can inspire in even the staunchest foe is illustrated in game 48, where the redoubtable Spassky prefers to give up a pawn rather than let his opponent keep the Bishops.

But Bishops are not always good. The rule that applies to all other pieces applies as well to them: a good Bishop is a working Bishop. Game 49 aptly demonstrates the differences between White's good Bishop and Black's bad one.

Pawn structure has a lot to do with whether a piece is to be considered good or bad. If your only Bishop and your opponent's pawns are on squares of the same color, your Bishop is probably very good—unless your own pawns are on the same color, too, which can be bad. The point is that a Bishop, otherwise very effective, cannot attack anything which is not on the same color square. When your pawns and your Bishop are on the same color, the Bishop's mobility, and hence its strength, is seriously reduced. Game 50 illustrates.

Bishops are most often favored over Knights because of the great difference in mobility. There are times, however, when the pawns and other pieces limit the activity of the Bishop; in such cases the short-stepping Knight can be superior. See game 51 to see how the Bishop dominates the Knight in an open position, and game 52 to see how effective the Knight can be in a congested position. In the endgame, too, the Bishop is usually better. In game 53 the Knight is clearly outclassed because its mobility is limited, but when the Knight is active, as in game 54, the Bishop suffers.

Knights function best in the center, as do most pieces, because that is where they achieve maximum range. This is particularly important for the Knight because of its natural limitations: it is the only piece (besides the King) that cannot travel more than two squares on a single move. A Knight at or near the edge of the board is obviously restricted. Game 55 illustrates the difference between a central Knight and one on the flank. In game 56 we see a rather common positional theme in the King's Indian Defense (and in other openings): the use of K4 as a Knight outpost, a particularly effective post in the King's Indian because of the pawn structure.

Knights in the endgame, again because of their limited range, are not very effective when the opponent has separated passed pawns. This is why White can sacrifice a piece in game 57. In game 58, on the other hand, White has only one passed pawn, which, until he errs, Black blockades effectively with his Knight.

Rooks need open files. They usually come into active play only after the opening, when some pawns and pieces have been exchanged and the position indicates which files are likely to be opened. Game 59 shows the differences between working and idle Rooks, and why the latter should always be avoided.

Queens, too, need open lines, but because of their great power in all directions they can often function well even in closed positions, especially when tactical opportunities are present. As is the case with all pieces, control of crucial squares or groups of squares has a profound bearing on potential activity. Game 60 is an example.

Finally, game 61 exemplifies a fairly common situation: Queen against Rook and minor piece in the endgame. Such situations present certain special problems, and the student should take the time to familiarize himself with the characteristic strategies for both sides.

Game 43

Premature Action

Since activity and mobility are desirable in pieces generally, the side that can complete its development and at the same time prevent the opponent from completing his will have the advantage, other things being equal. In this game, Black attempts a Queenside action before he is fully developed. As a result, he gets a nearly lost position. At the critical moment, however, White errs and allows Black to get his pieces into play, leading to equality and a draw. Compare the position before White's 22nd move with that after Black's 26th for a graphic illustration of the value of development.

Interzonal Playoff Match
Los Angeles, 1967

KING'S INDIAN DEFENSE

S. Reshevsky	L. Stein
1. P–Q4	N–KB3
2. P–QB4	P–KN3
3. N–QB3	B–N2
4. P–K4	P–Q3
5. P–B3	P–B3
6. B–K3	P–QR3

Intending 7. . . . P–QN4, making it inadvisable for White to castle on the Queenside. This explains White's next move.

7.	P–QR4	P–QR4

Preventing P–R5 and enabling Black to anchor his QN at QN5, if this should become desirable.

8.	B–Q3	N–R3
9.	KN–K2	0–0
10.	0–0	P–K4
11.	Q–Q2	N–Q2

Stein embarks now on a faulty plan to obtain play on the Queenside with the Queen and two Knights. The plan is faulty because he lags in development, whereas White is fully developed and ready to begin Kingside operations. Indicated is 11. . . . N–QN5 to force White's Bishop to QN1 before his QR is developed.

12.	QR–Q1	PxP
13.	NxP	N/2–B4
14.	B–N1	Q–N3

Black is now ready to harass the Queenside pawns with . . . Q–N5.

15. P–B4!   . . .

White disregards the threat to his pawns and proceeds with an attacking plan. The immediate threat of P–B5 is very serious for Black since it would entomb his KB. If 15. . . . Q–N5 16. P–B5 B–K4 (if 16. . . . QxBP 17. B–R6!) 17. N–B3 QxBP 18. NxB PxN 19. B–R6 R–K1 20. PxP RPxP 21. B–R2 N–N6 22. Q–KB2, etc.

| 15. . . . | **P–B4** |
| **16. PxP** | **PxP** |

Not 16. . . . BxP 17. BxB PxB 18. N–K6 with great advantage.

| **17. P–KN4!** | . . . |

So that if 17. . . . PxP 18. Q–QB2.

| **17. . . .** | **N–N6** |

The only try. If 17. . . . BxN 18. BxB PxP 19. P–B5 with a winning attack.

18. NxN	**QxN**
19. B–Q4	**BxBch**
20. QxB	**Q–N5**

Again forced, for if 20. . . . QxNP 21. R–B2 Q–N5 22. PxP Q–B4 23. R–N2ch K–B2 24. R–N7ch K–K1 25. N–K4 and wins.

| **21. KR–K1** | **Q–B4** |

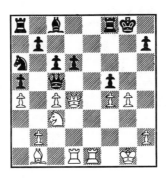

21. . . . PxP is met by 22. BxPch followed by R–K7ch, leading to mate. The activity of White's pieces in this phase of the game, compared to Black's inactive forces on the Queenside, obviously refutes Black's idea of move 11.

| **22. QxQ?** | . . . |

An illogical move, bringing Black's Knight into play and losing an important tempo. After 22. P–N5, Black's plight would be unbearable. His QP would be lost eventually, and Black's Bishop and QR would remain undeveloped. With my Rooks well located and my opponent saddled with an isolated KBP, I would win easily. Now Black's Knight is able to take part in the defense and his Bishop joins the party.

22. . . .	NxQ
23. RxP	. . .

Better is 23. P–N5 B–K3 (if 23. . . . R–Q1 24. R–K5!) 24. RxP BxP 25. R–K5.

23. . . .	PxP
24. R–K5	. . .

This looked so good to me that I didn't search for a better continuation on my 22nd turn. Black comes up with a surprising reply.

24. . . .	N–K3!

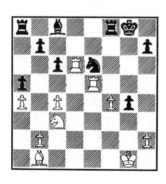

25. R–R5?   . . .

The final mistake, tossing away the win for good. If 25 R/6xN BxR 26. RxB RxP Black has good drawing chances: for example, 27. R–K7 R–B2 28. RxR KxR 29. BxP R–Q1 followed by . . . R–Q7; or 27. N–K4 R–Q1 28. B–B2 R–Q5 29. P–N3 P–R4 or K–B2 with no chance for White to make progress.

However, White can maintain his advantage with 25. N–K2. If 25. . . . NxP 26. NxN RxN 27. R–R5 R–B2 28. R–Q8ch K–N2 (if 28. . . . R–B1 29. RxRch KxR 30. RxP B–K3 31. R–R8ch B–N1 32. B–R7 and wins) 29. RxPch K–B3 30. RxRch KxR 31. B–B5 and wins. If 25. . . . N–N2 26. N–N3 (preventing the development of the Bishop at B4), and if 26. . . . RxP 27. N–R5 NxN (if

27. . . . R–B1 28. R–KN5, or 27. . . . R–B2 28. R–Q8ch R–B1 29.
N–B6ch) 28. RxN as above.

25. . . .	**NxP**
26. RxRP	**. . .**

I had intended 26. R–N5ch K–R1 27. R–R6 but overlooked 27.
. . . N–R6ch, winning the Rook and defending the RP.

26. . . .	**B–K3**

With the development of the Bishop, Black's worst problems
are over. His KR, Bishop and Knight pose some threats to the
White King.

27. RxNP	**QR–N1**

Better is 27. . . . N–R6ch 28. K–N2 (28. K–R1 R–B8ch 29.
K–N2 R–N8 mate) 28. . . . R–B6 (threatening perpetual check
with . . . N–B5ch) 29. B–Q3 (if 29. N–K2 R–B7ch 30. K–N3
RxN) 29. . . . RxB 30. RxR N–B5ch. The only way to avoid
the perpetual check is 29. R–Q1, but after 29. . . . QR–KB1 30.
B–K4 R–K6, Black would have excellent counterplay.

28. RxR	**RxR**
29. K–B2	**. . .**

More promising is 29. R–Q2 BxP 30. K–B2 R–KB1 31. K–K3
with good prospects since Black's scattered pawns would be
vulnerable.

29. . . .	**RxPch**
30. K–K3	**. . .**

Unproductive is 30. K–N3 N–R4ch 31. K–R4 RxPch 32. K–N5
N–N2 33. RxP P–N6 with equality.

30. . . .	**N–N7ch**
31. K–Q4	**R–Q7ch**
32. K–B5	**. . .**

After 32. B–Q3, Black can draw either by 32. . . . N–B5 33.
K–K3 RxBch 34. RxR NxR 35. KxN K–B2 36. K–Q4 K–B3 37.
K–B5 K–K4 or by 32. . . . B–B4 33. N–K4 BxN 34. KxB N–K8.

32. . . .	**RxR**
33. KxR	**BxP**
34. KxP	**. . .**

If 34. K–B5 B–N6 35. K–N6 N–R5 36. KxP BxP 37. KxB
N–B6 and draws. If 34. B–K4 N–K6 to be followed by . . . N–B8.

34. . . .	N–K6
35. N–K4	K–N2
36. N–B2	. . .

Insufficient is 36. N–N3 K–B3 37. K–N6 K–N4 38. KxP B–N6 39. K–N4 BxP 40. KxB K–R5 with an easy draw.

36. . . .	B–K7
37. B–Q3	BxB
38. NxB	N–B8
39. K–N5	NxP
40. KxP	N–B6
41. K–N6	N–Q7

Draw

Game 44

Sleeping on the Job

Another case of backward development. White seems to have no particular reason for delaying the development of his Queenside pieces. He soon allows Black to open the game advantageously, and, in the end, White's Knights appear ludicrous, like the night watchman who wakes up after the burglars have escaped with the loot.

Netanya, 1971

SICILIAN DEFENSE

H. Westerinen	S. Reshevsky
1. P–K4	P–QB4
2. N–KB3	P–K3
3. P–Q4	PxP
4. NxP	N–QB3
5. N–N5	. . .

Fischer's favorite; it requires accurate play by Black.

5. . . .	P–Q3
6. B–KB4	P–K4
7. B–K3	P–QR3

In my opinion, the only move. 7. . . . N–B3, as played by Taimanov against Fischer in their 1971 match, gives White a strong position after 8. B–N5.

8.	N/5–B3	N–B3
9.	B–K2	B–K2
10.	0–0	0–0
11.	P–B3	P–QN4
12.	Q–Q2?	. . .

The only attempt for White to get an advantage is 12. P–QR4 P–N5 13. N–Q5 or immediately 12. N–Q5.

12.	. . .	R–N1
13.	R–Q1	. . .

White's plan is too slow and unproductive. Again the correct continuation is 13. P–QR4 followed by N–Q5 after 13. . . . P–N5.

13.	. . .	R–K1
14.	B–B1	P–R3

Preventing an eventual B–KN5.

15.	K–R1	Q–B2
16.	Q–B2	N–QR4

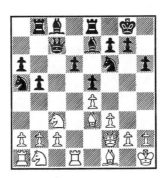

17. P–QN3? . . .

Creating a lasting weakness on the Queenside. Necessary is 17. B–Q3 N–B5 18. B–QB1, and although Black would have the superior position, White could put up strong resistance, which he is not able to do after the text move.

17. . . .	**B–K3**
18. **B–Q3**	**KR–Q1**

In preparation for . . . P–Q4, opening up the game. White can do nothing to stop it.

19. **B–Q2**	**N–B3**
20. **N–K2**	**P–Q4**
21. **PxP**	**NxP**
22. **Q–N3**	. . .

This accomplishes nothing. Wiser is 22. QN–B3 N/4–N5 23. B–K4 P–B4 24. BxN QxB, and although Black still would have the better game, White would have better chances for survival than after the text move.

22. . . .	**N–B3**
23. **P–QR3?**	. . .

A better try is 23. QN–B3 (this piece has to be developed at all cost), and if 23. . . . N–QN5 24. P–B4. Obviously 23. BxRP is impossible on account of 23. . . . N–KR4, winning a piece.

23. . . .	**N–KR4**
24. **Q–B2**	**BxNP**
25. **BxRP**	. . .

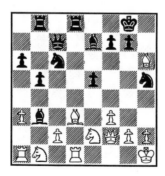

25. . . .	**P–K5!**

The pawn sacrifice shatters White's defenses.

26. **PxP**	**N–K4!**

With the double threat of . . . PxB and . . . N–N5. Black's superior forces on the Q- and QB-files added to his threats against the King make White's position untenable. This situation resulted from White's neglecting to develop his Queenside pieces.

        27. B–KB4   . . .

There is nothing more promising. If 27. B–Q2 or 27. B–B1, then 27. . . . N–N5 28. Q–N1 B–B4 and wins. If 27. B–K3 B–B3 28. N–Q4 N–N5 29. Q–N1 NxB, etc. If in this line 28. B–Q4 N–N5 29. Q–N1 RxB 30. NxR (if 30. PxB RxB 31. RxR BxR) 30. . . . BxN and wins.

27. . . .	**NxB/6**
28. RxN	**NxB**
29. NxN	. . .

Against 29. QxN, Black has the choice of 29. . . . QxP or 29. . . . QxQ 30. NxQ B–B3 31. P–B3 B–B5 32. RxRch RxR and wins because White is not able to parry the annoying threat of . . . R–Q8ch.

29. . . .	**RxR**
30. NxR	**QxP**
31. QxQ	. . .

If 31. Q–B1 R–Q1 32. N–B2 B–B3.

31. . . .	**BxQ**
32. N–N4	**B–B3!**
33. NxB	**BxR**
34. NxB	**R–Q1**
35. N–B3	**R–Q6**
Resigns	

Game 45

Surprised Pieces

Heart and mind, body and soul, pieces and pawns: each an indivisible pair. In chess, the logical progression of the game—the plans, the tactics, the attacks and defenses—must involve pieces and pawns working together. Not only must they support one another concretely and tactically, they must also depend on one another strategically; that is, a certain type of pawn structure calls for a certain type of piece deployment. A breakthrough prepared and executed by pawns loses its force when the pieces are not poised to exploit the new situation.

So it is in this game. Kim Commons, a promising young American master, first fails to play P–K5 at a propitious moment, when the complications are favorable to him; and on his very next move he radically changes the course of the game, but unfavorably, for his pieces are not ready to exploit the changed situation. Perhaps he was seized by a sudden inspiration. More likely, he was a little overambitious, a frequent characteristic of young players. Whatever the cause, his 24th move comes as a great surprise—to his own pieces.

72nd U.S. Open

Ventura, 1971

KING'S INDIAN DEFENSE

K. Commons	S. Reshevsky
1. P–Q4	N–KB3
2. N–KB3	P–KN3
3. P–B4	B–N2
4. P–KN3	P–B4

4. . . . P–B3 followed by . . . P–Q4 leads to a symmetrical position with few prospects for either side.

5. P–Q5	P–Q3
6. B–N2	0–0
7. 0–0	N–R3
8. N–B3	N–B2
9. B–B4	P–QR3
10. P–QR4	R–N1
11. P–R5	P–QN4
12. PxP e.p.	RxP
13. R–R2	. . .

So far, all well known. In order to break White's control of the center, Black must attempt to get in . . . P–K3. There is some difficulty involved in achieving this.

13. . . .	R–K1

The immediate 13. . . . . P–K3 costs a pawn: 14. N–QR4 R–N1 15. PxP, etc.

14. N–QR4   **R–N1**

To be considered is 14. . . . . R–N2, and if White proceeds, as he does in the game, with 15. P–N3, then Black can continue with 15. . . . . P–K3 16. PxP NxP 17. BxP? (17. QxP RxP) R–Q2.

     15. P–N3   **B–B4**
     16. N–K1   **Q–B1**
     17. P–B3   **B–R6**

     18. P–K4   . . .

If 18. BxB QxB 19. NxP? (19. P–KN4 P–KR4!) P–N4, winning a piece.

     18. . . .   **BxB**
     19. KxB   **Q–N2**
     20. R–R3   **N–R4**
     21. B–K3   **P–K3**

My objective is finally achieved but not without possible danger.

     22. P–KN4   **N–B3**

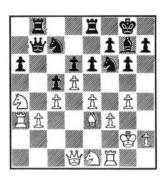

23. B–B4!?   . . .

To be seriously considered is 23. P–K5. For if 23. . . . QPxP 24. NxP Q–B1 25. P–Q6 R–Q1 26. PxN5 N–Q2 (26. . . . N–R4 27. P–Q7) 27. PxN and wins. In response Black's best course is 23. . . . N/3xQP 24. PxN NxP 25. B–Q2 BxP; Black would have three pawns for the piece, with about even chances.

| 23. . . . | PxP |
| 24. BxP? | . . . |

My young opponent is looking for complications. Correct is simply 24. KPxP, maintaining the pressure on the QP and keeping Black's position cramped and defensive. His pieces, particularly his Knights, are not well situated for the type of position that now arises. The QN will be out of play on the Queenside, the other one passive.

24. . . .	PxKP!
25. NxP	Q–B3
26. BxN	QxB

26. . . . QxN 27. B–Q6!.

| 27. NxRP | Q–K2 |

Both of White's Knights are clumsily placed, especially the one at QR6, and his King is precariously posted; Black's pieces, on the other hand, are actively situated, and he also has a potential passed pawn.

| 28. NxR | . . . |

28. R–R2 is a better try. Black can then continue 28. . . . R–R1 (threatening . . . Q–N2) 29. P–N4 Q–K3! 30. P–QN5 QxP with advantage.

28. . . .	QxR
29. PxP?	. . .

Giving up a piece is tantamount to resignation. He should try 29. N–Q7 so that if 29. . . . PxPch 30. QxP (not 30. NxP because of 30. . . . NxP). I would have played 29. . . . P–K6 30. NxNch BxN 31. Q–K2 QxP with advantage.

29. . . .	RxN
30. P–K5	Q–N7ch
31. R–B2	QxKP
32. N–B3	Q–B5
Resigns	

Game 46

Passive Pieces

This interesting game illustrates a strategic idea that is very popular today: Black's sacrifice of the QNP in order to gain a powerful initiative on the open lines on the Queenside. Geller finally wins the pawn back and retains a clear positional profit: far more active pieces and safer pawns. In fact, White's QBP is a major factor in the immobilization of White's Rook and Knight, and it is this forced inactivity that allows Black's King to walk in with decisive threats. The final maneuver, when Black tucks his Rook into a corner where it apparently has the least possible activity, is amusing.

Interzonal Tournament

Palma de Majorca, 1970

KING'S INDIAN DEFENSE

W. Uhlmann	Y. Geller
1. P–Q4	N–KB3
2. P–QB4	P–KN3
3. N–QB3	B–N2
4. P–K4	P–Q3

5. B–K2	0–0
6. B–N5	P–B4
7. P–Q5	P–KR3
8. B–B4	. . .

8. B–Q2 or 8. B–K3 seems preferable.

8. . . .	P–R3
9. Q–Q2	K–R2
10. N–B3	. . .

In view of Black's next move, White should continue 10. P–QR4, and if 10. . . . Q–R4 11. R–R3, preventing . . . R–QN4.

10. . . .	P–QN4!
11. PxP	PxP
12. BxNP	Q–N3
13. B–K2	. . .

Better is 13. B–Q3, adding protection to the KP.

13. . . .	Q–N5

14. P–K5?	. . .

Necessary is 14. 0–0, and if 14. . . . NxKP 15. NxN QxN 16. B–Q3 Q–QN5 17. Q–K3, with a chance for counterplay by continuing with P–KR4–5.

14. . . .	N–R4
15. B–N3	B–R3
16. BxB	. . .

Relatively better chances are offered by 16. 0–0 NxB 17. RPxN PxP 18. BxB RxB 19. Q–K2. The text move expedites Black's development.

16. . . .	RxB
17. PxP	PxP
18. 0–0	N–Q2

Black's activity on the QR- and QN-files sufficiently compensates for the pawn.

19. QR–K1	NxB
20. RPxN	N–N3
21. R–K2	. . .

21. R–K4 can be satisfactorily met by 21. . . . BxN 22. Q–K2 Q–R4 23. PxB QxRP.

21. . . .	N–B5
22. Q–Q3	KR–QR1
23. P–N3	. . .

23. P–R3 is refuted by 23. . . . NxRP. White's problem is the pressure against his Queenside pawns.

23. . . .	QxN
24. QxQ	BxQ
25. PxN	RxP

| 26. RxR | . . . |

Nothing is achieved by 26. R–K7 K–N2 27. R–N1 (threatening R/1–N7) 27. . . . B–N5 (threatening . . . R–B7 followed by . . . R/1–R7), and if 28. N–K1 R–R8 29. RxR RxR 30. K–B1 R–B8 and wins.

| 26. . . . | RxR |

The endgame is strategically difficult for White: his Rook and Knight are inactive and the QBP is in danger. Moreover, Black's

Rook and Bishop occupy favorable posts. White's Knight has no safe square except KB3, where it does nothing to defend the QBP, and the danger to that QBP forces the Rook to remain behind in a passive position.

27. R–B1	B–B3?

Stronger is 27. . . . B–N5; see the next note.

28. K–B1?	. . .

Necessary is 28. R–N1 threatening to attack Black's QP with R–N6, and if 28. . . . R–R3 29. P–N4 (preventing . . . P–R4), and Black's chances of progress would be substantially reduced.

28. . . .	P–R4!
29. N–K1	. . .

Even now, 29. R–N1 is worth a try.

29. . . .	P–N4
30. R–B2	R–R8
31. K–K2	K–N3
32. N–B3	. . .

The Bishop is obviously much stronger than the Knight, which has no useful targets here and will soon be compelled to mark time, hopping around sadly in a small space. White has no choice but to wait for Black to proceed with his plan.

32. . . .	K–B4

The Black King now walks in unmolested and becomes the major factor in Black's victory.

33. N–Q2	P–N5
34. N–B1	B–Q5
35. N–Q2	. . .

White is virtually in zugzwang. If 35. N–K3ch BxN 36. KxB (36. PxB K–K5 is no improvement) R–R6ch 37. K–K2 K–K5 followed by . . . K–Q5 and wins easily.

35. . . .	R–KN8
36. N–N3	B–K4
37. N–Q2	RxP

Can he get away with this? What is he doing to his Rook?

38. K–B1	R–R7
39. K–N1	R–R6
40. N–B1	P–R5

The point.

41.	K–N2	PxP
42.	PxP	. . .

42. NxPch BxN 43. PxB K–K5 44. R–B2 K–Q6 45. R–B4 P–B4
is no better for White.

42.	. . .	K–K5
43.	R–B2	P–B3
44.	R–R2	R–R1
	Resigns	

Game 47

A Thorn in the Center

In the middlegame a White passed pawn suddenly darts ahead
and throws the Black forces into turmoil. The Pawn itself does
not survive the battle, but its effect on the enemy camp is like
that of a lion's leaping into a pack of gazelles. Snapping in both
directions and also threatening to advance farther in search of
bigger game, the pawn brings chaos to the enemy forces which
must try to capture it and at the same time stay out of its way.

The pawn, though finally lost, has a salutary effect on White's
pieces; with brighter prospects, they encounter little difficulty in
creating enough new threats to force Black to sacrifice material.

72nd U.S. Open
Ventura, 1971

NIMZO-INDIAN DEFENSE

S. Reshevsky		A. Spiller
1.	P–Q4	N–KB3
2.	P–QB4	P–K3
3.	N–QB3	B–N5
4.	P–K3	P–QN3
5.	N–K2	. . .

More usual is 5. B–Q3 B–N2 6. N–B3, etc., but the text move is
a good alternative, getting away from the trodden path.

5. . . .	**P–B4**
6. P–QR3	**B–R4**

Better than 6. . . . BxNch 7. NxB 0–0 8. P–Q5 with a strong bind for White.

7. R–QN1	**N–R3**

7. . . . N–B3 is more frequently seen, but the text move is not bad because it offers Black's QB greater freedom once it is posted at QN2.

8. N–N3	**. . .**

Preferable is 8. B–Q2 B–N2 9. N–N3 or 9. N–B4.

8	**0–0**

Why not 8. . . . B–N2, slowing down the development of White's KB?

9. B–Q3	**BxNch**
10. PxB	**P–Q3**
11. 0–0	**B–N2**
12. Q–K2	**N–N1**
13. P–K4?	**. . .**

A mechanical move. Stronger is 13. P–B4 which hinders . . . P–K4.

13. . . .	**P–K4**

14. P–Q5	**. . .**

Here I missed the very promising continuation 14. P–B4! BPxP (if 14. . . . PxBP 15. BxP White gets a strong position without having to give up a pawn for it) 15. PxQP PxQP 16. P–K5 PxP (a

better defense is 16. . . . R–K1, but after 17. N–B5 PxP 18. PxP
QN–Q2 19. B–B4 with good prospects) 17. PxP R–K1 18. RxN!
PxR 19. Q–N4ch with a winning attack, for if 19. . . . K–B1 20.
B–R6ch K–K2 21. N–B5ch, etc., and if 19. . . . K–R1 20. Q–B5
K–N1 21. QxPch K–B1 22. N–B5 followed by mate. Note how in
these variations the White pieces are very well focused on the
Kingside, able to generate a mating attack with hardly any
further preparation. Black's pieces, on the other hand, are inactive.

The text move permits a blockade by Black which limits the
activity of White's pieces.

14. . . .	B–B1
15. P–B4	PxP
16. BxP	N–N5

A good move which attempts to prevent White from breaking
through with P–K5.

17. P–R3	. . .

To be considered nevertheless is 17. P–K5, and if 17. . . . PxP
(17. . . . R–K1? 18. P–K6) 18. BxP R–K1 19. B–B7!.

17. . . .	N–K4
18. BxN	. . .

The Knight is too well placed and must be eliminated.

18. . . .	PxB
19. Q–R5	. . .

I now faced the problem of where to concentrate my forces.
Neither wing appeared to offer great prospects. I finally decided
to try the Kingside, and, if that proved unfruitful, my next
strategy would probably be to attempt action on the Queenside
by advancing by QRP to R5. The text move is a feeble attempt
to weaken the Black King's defenses.

19. . . .	P–B3
20. R–B2	. . .

In order to be in a position to double the Rooks on the KB-,
QR-, or Q-file. I left myself the option because I didn't know yet
where the Rooks belonged. This will depend on the setup of
Black's forces.

20. . . .	N–B3
21. N–B1	. . .

Not 21. PxN QxB, attacking the Rook and the Knight.

| 21. . . . | N–K2 |
| 22. N–K3 | N–N3 |

Intending of course an eventual . . . N–B5.

| 23. P–N3 | Q–K1? |

My opponent is apparently satisfied with his position and becomes complacent, ignoring the possible advance of White's
passed QP; otherwise he would blockade with . . . Q–Q3.

| 24. P–KR4 | . . . |

Meeting Black's immediate threat of 24. . . . . N–B5, which
would net him a pawn.

| 24. . . . | B–Q2 |
| 25. Q–Q1 | . . . |

In order to answer . . . B–R5 with B–B2. I am not averse to
exchanging Bishops when mine is less active than my opponent's.
The exchange would also increase my chances of anchoring my
Knight at KB5.

| 25. . . . | N–K2 |

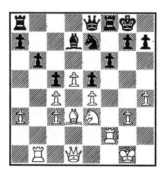

His Knight having become useless at N3, Black decides to relocate it, but wiser is 25. . . . N–N1 and N–B2, where it could be
better utilized to control the vital Q3 square.

| 26. P–Q6! | . . . |

An ambitious advance since it appears that the pawn may
eventually be surrounded and captured. I had to assess the

possibilities very carefully. I decided that I could defend the pawn sufficiently and long enough to enable me to launch some kind of attack since Black's pieces would be tied up trying to win this pawn. I considered the alternative 26. R–QR2 to be followed by P–R4–5, but I decided to break through on the Q-file because it was closer to the Black King and therefore offered a quicker decision.

As so often happens, a pawn move like this opens up broad new vistas for the pieces which could not be otherwise obtained so economically.

26. . . .	N–B3

If 26. . . . N–B1 27. B–K2, and if 27. . . . Q–K3? 28. B–N4 costs Black a piece (28. . . . K–B2 29. BxB and 30. Q–Q5ch). After 26. . . . N–B1, the Knight and the QR remain out of play.

27. P–R5	. . .

The main purpose of this move is to prevent . . . Q–N3; I also wanted to locate my Knight at KB5 without allowing its dislodgment by . . . P–N3, which, after the text move, would weaken Black's King position irreparably.

27. . . .	R–Q1
28. R–Q2	B–K3
29. B–K2	Q–B2
30. B–N4!	. . .

The purpose of this strong move is to dispose of Black's Bishop so that I can anchor my Knight at KB5. Once having reached this square, the Knight gives me a stranglehold on the position, which enables me to develop numerous effective threats.

30. . . .	BxB

Black's best try is 30. . . . BxP, but after 31. P–Q7 N–R4 32. R–Q6 (threatening NxB followed by B–K6) K–R1 33. N–Q5 BxN 34. RxB, Black's chances of defense are very poor. The reasons are the strength of the QP and the inactivity of the Black pieces, the latter a direct result of the former.

31. QxB	R–Q2

This loses, but there is no satisfactory reply. Best under the circumstances is 31. . . . N–N1 (to prevent P–Q7) 32. N–B5 K–R1

33. N–K7 KR–K1, followed by . . . N–Q2 or . . . R–Q2, but Black's position would be cramped and untenable in any case.

    32. N–B5   . . .

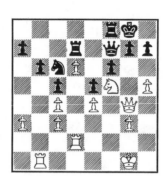

And now the double threat of N–R6ch and N–K7ch cannot be parried. Note the great strength of a Knight on a central square, which I will discuss later in this chapter.

    32. . . .   **K–R1**

    33. N–K7!   . . .

The winning move. Black must lose the Exchange.

    33. . . .   **RxN**

If 33. . . . N–N1 34. N–N6ch PxN (otherwise White wins the Exchange and the game) 35. PxP followed by Q–R5ch, etc.

    34. PxR   **NxP**

    35. R–Q7   **P–B4**

    36. PxP   **QxKBP**

    37. QxQ   **NxQ**

    38. R–KB1   **K–N1**

    39. RxP   . . .

The rest is not difficult. Black could resign at this point.

    39. . . .   **NxP**

    40. RxRch   **KxR**

    41. R–N7   **N–K7ch**

    42. K–B2   **NxP**

    43. RxQNP   **K–B2**

    44. R–QR6   . . .

44. K–K3 also does the trick, but the fastest way is to promote the advance of the QRP.

44. . . .	**P–N4**
45. PxP e.p.ch	**. . .**

Slows down the NP.

45. . . .	**PxP**
46. P–R4	**N–QBch**
47. K–K2	**N–N7**
48. P–R5	**NxP**
49. R–R8	**Resigns**

Game 48

Two Bishops

It often happens that a player is so fond of his advantageous position that he is reluctant to transpose to a winning endgame. Yet, that is how chess games are won: more space in the opening is translated into the initiative, which leads to better piece placement, which leads to enemy weaknesses, which results in attack or material gain, etc.

This game is a good example. White's opening initiative consists of his slightly more active pieces which exert pressure on Black's isolated QP. To get rid of the pressure, Black gives his opponent the advantage of the two Bishops. The Bishops soon become so threatening that Black is willing to give up a pawn to deprive White of one of them.

Sochi, 1966

NIMZO-INDIAN DEFENSE

V. Korchnoi	B. Spassky
1. P–Q4	N–KB3
2. P–QB4	P–K3
3. N–QB3	B–N5
4. N–B3	P–B4

| 5. P–K3 | 0–0 |
| 6. B–Q3 | P–QN3 |

This is Spassky's favorite variation of the Nimzo-Indian Defense. He resorted to it several times in the 1966 Piatigorsky tournament with relative success. It has also been a favorite of Bobby Fischer's.

| 7. 0–0 | B–N2 |
| 8. N–QR4 | . . . |

Accepted as the best attempt to obtain an opening advantage in this variation. The threat is 9. P–QR3 followed by 10. PxP.

| 8. . . . | PxP |
| 9. PxP | B–K2 |

Otherwise 10. P–B5 would be embarrassing for Black.

| 10. B–B4 | . . . |

More popular today is 10. R–K1 P–Q3 11. P–QN4, followed by fianchettoing the Bishop.

10. . . .	P–Q3
11. R–K1	QN–Q2
12. N–B3	P–Q4

Moving this pawn a second time is illogical. More prudent is 12. . . . R–K1 followed by N–B1–N3 while waiting for White to undertake something.

| 13. Q–K2 | N–R4 |
| 14. B–Q2 | N/4–B3 |

Indicating a willingness to split the point; however, Korchnoi is not content with a "grandmaster draw."

| 15. N–KN5! | . . . |

So that if 15. . . . P–KR3, White could win with 16. NxKP PxN 17. QxPch R–B2 18. B–N6 Q–KB1 19. BxRch QxB 20. QxB.

15. . . .	**R–K1**
16. PxP	. . .

Unsound is 16. NxBP KxN 17. QxPch K–B1 18. PxP B–N5 19. Q–R3 BxN 20. PxB BxP 21. BxP NxB 22. QxN N–B3, and in this case three pawns do not compensate for the piece.

16. . . .	**PxP**
17. Q–B3	**P–KR3**
18. N–R3	**B–N5**

Spassky tries to relieve the pressure on his QP, but in doing so he gives his opponent the advantage of the two Bishops. To be considered is 18. . . . P–R3 19. P–R4 (otherwise Black would continue with . . . P–QN4 and . . . N–N3–B5 with good prospects) 19. N–N1, to be followed by . . . N–B3–QN5.

Black's maneuver leads rather suddenly to a clear White advantage. The White Bishops enjoy clean open lines, whereas Black's pieces are passive and he sorely misses the KB.

19. Q–N3	**BxN**
20. PxB	**K–R1**
21. P–B3!	. . .

White's Bishops are free to roam the various sectors of the board and thus offer him the enviable choice of either aggressive or positional action. Black's Bishop, on the other hand, is out of play.

In depriving Black's Knight access to his K5, Korchnoi limits the mobility of Spassky's pieces considerably and thus keeps his KB's diagonal open.

21. . . .	**RxRch**
22. RxR	**Q–KB1**
23. B–B5	. . .

Ineffective is 23. Q–B7 on account of 23. . . . Q–QN1 24. QxQch RxQ 25. R–K7 K–N1 followed by . . . R–K1.

23. . . .	**R–K1**
24. N–B4	**RxRch**
25. QxR	**Q–Q1**

25. . . . Q–R6 loses to 26. BxN NxB 27. Q–K8ch N–B1 28. QxP, etc.

26. P–KR4 . . .

With Black completely on the defensive, Korchnoi proceeds to initiate action on the Kingside, intending to create weakness in Black's camp.

26. . . . **K–N1**

27. B–B1 . . .

To deny Black the simplification he could get with . . . K–B1 followed by . . . Q–K2.

27. . . . **N–N1**

Relocating this Knight to a more favorable post.

28. B–QR3 . . .

The Bishops now occupy important lines, restricting Spassky's activity and compelling him to defend rather than actively seek counterplay.

28. . . . **N–B3**

29. P–N4 **Q–N1**

30. B–B1 . . .

30. N–Q3 is out of the question because of 30. . . . P–N3, and 30. Q–K3 is unappetizing because of 30. . . . N–QR4.

30. . . . **Q–K1**

31. Q–B2 . . .

Unproductive is 31. QxQch NxQ 32. NxP NxP 33. N–K7ch K–B1, etc.

31. . . . **N–Q1**

The Knight is needed on the Kingside for defensive purposes. Spassky's task is difficult indeed.

32. P–N5		PxP
33. PxP		N–R2
34. P–N6		N–B1
35. PxPch		QxP
36. Q–B2		B–B3
37. N–N2		B–Q2
38. N–K3		. . .

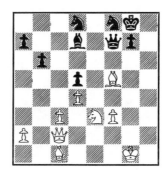

	38. . . .	**BxB?**

Understandably anxious to simplify, considering that he has been defending patiently for several hours. Correct, however, is 38. . . . P–N3 39. BxB NxB, and White would have difficulty making substantial progress; the continuation 40. NxP QxN 41. QxPch K–R1 is unproductive.

39. QxB	**QxQ**
40. NxQ	**K–B2**

Spassky decides to give up his RP. He discarded 40. . . . N–B3 because of 41. N–K3 N–K2 42. B–R3 N/B–N3 43. K–B2 K–B2 44. K–N3 K–K3 45. K–N4 P–R3 46. K–N5 K–B2 47. N–N2, which, when followed by N–B4 or N–R4, renders Black's position indefensible.

41. N–Q6ch	**K–K3**
42. N–N5	**. . .**

One of the pawns has to go, for if 42. . . . N–B3 43. N–B7ch K–Q3 44. B–B4ch followed by NxP.

42. . . .	**K–Q2**
43. NxP	**N/B–K3**
44. N–N5	**N–N2**
45. K–B2	**N–Q3**
46. N–R3	**. . .**

After an exchange of Knights, White could make no progress despite the pawn plus.

46. . . .	**N–QB2**
47. B–B4	**N/B–N4**

| 48. BxN | NxB |
| 49. K–K3 | K–K3 |

After 49. . . . K–B3 50. K–B4, Black could resign. Although a pawn ahead, Korchnoi still has his work cut out for him. Knight endings can be extremely difficult and the win elusive.

| 50. N–B2 | P–KN4 |
| 51. K–Q3 | P–N4 |

It is wiser not to advance this pawn, since now it becomes more susceptible to attack.

52. N–K3	N–B2
53. K–B2	N–Q1
54. K–N2!	. . .

Leaving in reserve an extra tempo which could prove necessary. After 54. K–N3 N–B3 White could not maneuver his Knight because of . . . K–B4, but now after 54. . . . N–B3 55. K–N3, Black's only reasonable move is 55. . . . K–Q3, leaving the Knight free to maneuver. White could, of course, play P–R3, but why exhaust the only reserve tempo move when it is not necessary?

54. . . .	N–B3
55. K–N3	K–Q3
56. N–Q1	K–K3
57. N–B2	K–B3

Unavailing now is 57. . . . K–B4 58. N–Q3 P–N5 59. PxPch KxP 60. N–K5ch NxN 61. PxN K–B4 62. K–N4 and wins.

58. N–Q3	K–K3
59. K–N2	K–Q3
60. N–B5	N–R4
61. K–B2	N–B5

If 61. . . . N–B3 62. N–R6 N–R4 63. K–Q3 N–B3 64. K–K2 and K–B2–N3.

62. N–Q3	K–K3

If 62. . . . N–R4 63. N–K5 K–K3 64. K–N2 K–B3 65. K–R3 and K–N4.

63. K–N3	N–Q7ch
64. K–N4	N–N8

Hopeless is 64. . . . NxP 65. KxP P–N5 66. K–B6, and if 66. . . . P–N6 67. N–B4ch K–B4 68. NxP. White's Knight would be able to get back in time to stop Black's pawn.

65. N–B2	K–B4
66. N–R3	P–N5

Spassky is lost and makes a last stab. Inadequate is 66. . . . K–B3 on account of 67. N–N1 K–B4 68. N–K2 N–Q7 69. KxP NxP 70. P–R4, etc.

67. PxPch	KxP
68. N–B2ch	K–B6
69. N–Q1	K–K7
70. KxP	KxN
71. K–N4	K–B7
72. P–R4	Resigns

The pawns cannot be stopped, for if 72. . . . NxP 73. P–R5 N–K7 74. K–B5, etc. A fine performance by Korchnoi.

Game 49

Good Bishop, Bad Bishop

In this instructive endgame watch how Black's dark-squared Bishop is able to accomplish so much unlike White's which is reduced to preventing the advance of a pawn—and that only temporarily. An important factor is that the pawns of both players are on squares the same color as their Bishops. But whereas Black's Bishop is free to travel outside the confines of his pawn cage, White's is not. Of course, Black's material advantage and his passed pawns rather limit White's opportunities, but still the difference in Bishops is striking.

The endgame is in several stages: first, Black forces White to advance a pawn, releasing a square Black needs to penetrate; second, another White pawn, on the opposite wing, is forced to advance, becomes weaker and gets captured; third, the Black King moves to penetrate as originally planned, tying up the White King; fourth, Black advances his passed pawn unmolested by White's King, which, as we have just noted, is busy preventing Black's King from penetrating; finally, Black's King returns to the other side and forces White into zugzwang to effect penetration.

Chess Olympics
Lugano, 1968

Black to play

B. Jansson	O. Panno
50. . . .	B–B3
51. B–Q1	. . .

White should not play NxB because his King could not then prevent Black's King from entering KN4 and his remaining Bishop would be inferior to Black's.

| 51. . . . | B–N2 |

52. K–B3	**B–R3**
53. B–B2	**B–B8**

The end of stage one: Black has forced the advance of the QRP so that when Black's King reaches QR4 it will be able to penetrate via QN5.

54. P–QR4	**B–B5**

Now Black begins to concentrate on the KRP, which in advancing becomes more vulnerable.

55. P–R4	**B–Q7**
56. K–K2	**B–R4**
57. K–B2	**B–Q1**
58. B–Q3	**K–Q2**
59. P–KR5	. . .

Forced, for if 59. K–N3 K–B2 followed by . . . K–N3–R4, etc.

59. . . .	**BxN**

If 59. . . . PxP 60. NxPch PxN 61. BxBch K–B2 62. P–R5 K–Q3 63. B–B8 and draws. Black's Bishop has done its work: the King is ready to penetrate the Queenside, and Black is two pawns up.

60. BxB	**PxP**

End of stage two. Now white has to hurry over to the Queenside.

61. K–K2	. . .

The only defense against Black's threat of making inroads with the King via QR4.

61. . . .	**K–B2**
62. K–Q3	**K–N3**
63. K–B2	**K–R4**
64. K–N3	. . .

End of stage three. White's King arrives on the Queenside just in time; but Black now makes preparations for his King to reach the opposite side. White's problems are just beginning.

64. . . .	**P–R5**
65. B–N2	**B–N4**
66. B–B3	. . .

There is no way to stop the advance of the RP, for if 66. K–R3 B–Q7 67. K–N3 (67. B–R3 P–K5) B–N5, forcing White's Bishop to move which allows one of the passed pawns to advance.

| 66. . . . | P–R6 |
| 67. B–R1 | P–R7 |

End of stage four. There follows a brief period of inactivity while Black decides on his best approach.

68. B–N2	B–R5
69. B–R1	B–K8
70. B–N2	B–N6
71. B–R1	B–B5
72. B–N2	B–R3
73. B–R1	K–N3

After some Bishop probes, the King is ready to return to the other side, where its penetration into the enemy's camp will be effected.

74. K–B2	K–B2
75. K–Q3	K–Q2
76. K–K4	K–K2
77. K–B5	K–B2
78. B–K4	P–R4

To prevent any action by White on that wing by P–R5 and B–B8. An unnecessary precaution.

79. B–R1	B–B1
80. B–N2	K–N2
81. K–N5	B–K2ch
82. K–B5	. . .

White's position is indefensible. If 82. K–R5 K–B3 83. B–K4 P–R8=Q 84. BxQ K–B4 and wins. If 82. K–N4 K–B3 83. K–N3 (83. B–K4 B–B1 84. B–R1 B–N2 85. B–K4 B–R1 86. B–R1 P–K5 87. BxP K–K4 88. B–R1 K–Q5 and wins) 83. . . . K–B4 84. KxP K–B5 and wins.

| 82. . . . | K–R3 |
| 83. B–B3 | B–B1 |

A waiting move. If 84. K–N4 K–N3, followed by . . . K–B3 and . . . P–K5, etc. If 84. B–R1, the Black monarch advances via KR4.

| 84. K–B6 | B–N2ch |
| 85. K–B5 | . . . |

Insufficient is 85. K–K7 K–N4 86. KxP K–B5 followed by . . . P–K5.

| 85. . . . | B–R1! |

Now White is in zugzwang!

86. B–N2	K–R4
87. B–R1	K–R5
88. K–K6	K–N5
89. KxP	K–B5
90. K–K6	P–K5
	Resigns

If 91. P–Q6 B–K4 92. P–Q7 B–B2. An instructive endgame.

Game 50

A More Equal Bishop

Some Bishops are more equal than others (to paraphrase George Orwell). The theme of the ending of this game is the relative effectiveness of two Bishops, the White one able to attack the opponent's pawns which are all on white squares, the Black one able to do nothing useful because White's pawns are all on black squares. The qualities of good and bad, when speaking of Bishops, always depend on the pawns. The lesson here is easy to teach but not so easy to put into practice: place your pawns on squares the opposite color of your Bishop. Or: when going into an endgame with a more-or-less fixed pawn structure, get rid of the Bishop that is the same color as the squares your pawns are on.

7th Match Game

Porec, 1968

NIMZO-INDIAN DEFENSE

L. Portisch	B. Larsen
1. P–Q4	N–KB3
2. P–QB4	P–K3
3. N–QB3	B–N5
4. P–K3	0–0
5. B–Q3	P–Q4

6.	N–B3	PxP
7.	BxP	P–B4
8.	0–0	N–B3
9.	P–QR3	B–R4
10.	Q–Q3	P–QR3
11.	R–Q1	P–QN4
12.	B–R2	B–N2?!

In the first game of this match and in the eighth game of the Gligoric–Tal match in the same year, Black played 12. . . . P–B5. There followed in both games 13. Q–K2 Q–K1 in order to effect . . . P–K4 immediately. Apparently Larsen is not satisfied with this continuation, but the text, though not necessarily worse, does not seem to be an improvement either.

13.	PxP	BxN
14.	Q–B2	. . .

Not 14. PxB QxQ 15. RxQ N–K5 regaining the pawn with a good position.

14.	. . .	Q–K2
15.	QxB	KR–Q1

Winning an important tempo. White is in no position to retain the pawn since he must prevent Black from obtaining control of the Q-file. This is the idea behind Black's 12th move.

16.	B–Q2	N–K5
17.	Q–B2	NxQBP
18.	B–K1	. . .

18. B–B3 is meaningless because of 18. . . . N–R5, and 18. P–QN4 N–R5 19. B–N3 QR–B1 20. BxN N–K4 favors Black.

18.	. . .	N–R5
19.	QR–B1	RxR
20.	RxR	R–QB1

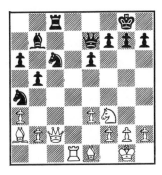

White seems to stand better here because of the two Bishops, although at the moment they are not too well placed. Black's Knight on R5 is well posted. White's QNP is under pressure, and he is compelled to pay attention to its protection.

21. B–N1		P–N3
22. Q–K2		Q–B3

22. . . . P–K4 is unattractive on account of 23. P–K4 followed by B–R2, where the Bishop would exert pressure.

23. R–Q7		B–R1
24. P–QN4		N–K4

24. . . . Q–R8 is satisfactorily met by 25. Q–R2, and if 25. . . . QxQ 26. BxQ with the superior endgame. If 24. . . . N–B6 25. Q–N2 N–Q4 26. QxQ NxQ 27. R–Q1 with the better position. The exchange of Queens would give White a distinct advantage in both cases because of the two Bishops.

25. NxN		QxN
26. R–Q4		. . .

To prevent the Queen's penetration at QR8.

| | 26. . . . | N–B6 |

A misjudgment. With his usual optimism, Larsen overrates his position and decides to play for a win. Wiser is 26. . . . R–B8 27. R–Q1 (not 27. R–Q8ch K–N2 28. RxB RxB 29. RxP N–B6 30. Q–Q2 N–K5 31. Q–K2 Q–B6 32. K–B1 N–Q7ch 33. K–N1 RxBch 34. QxR N–B6ch) 27. . . . RxR 28. QxR Q–R8 29. Q–Q8ch K–N2 30. Q–Q4ch QxQ 31. PxQ with no advantage for White because of the isolated QP.

27. BxN	RxB
28. Q–N2	Q–N4
29. P–N3	R–B1
30. Q–Q2	B–B6
31. B–Q3	. . .

The Bishop must get to B1 to defend the light squares. At the moment, Black's Bishop seems to be the better of the two because it is "doing" something. But look at the pawns! Black's are all on the same color squares as his Bishop, and all of White's are on the opposite color of his Bishop. Later on this will be the decisive factor; now, however, White must take care to protect his King and avoid exchanging Bishops, for therein lies his end-game win.

31. . . .	P–K4
32. R–Q7	Q–N5

Interesting but unsound is 32. . . . R–Q1 33. BxQNP RxR 34. BxR Q–Q1 35. Q–Q3 B–B3 (if 35. . . . B–N5 36. B–N5, and if 35. . . . P–K5 36. Q–Q5 Q–B3 37. Q–Q4) 36. B–B5, and Black has insufficient compensation for the pawn.

33. B–B1	K–N2
34. Q–Q6	Q–B4

Black has no time for 34. . . . R–R8 on account of 35. QxKPch K–R3 36. RxP with mating threats.

| | 35. R–B7 | . . . |

Understandable since he wants to reach a favorable Bishop ending.

35. . . .	RxR
36. QxR	B–Q4?

Giving White a chance to breathe. Correct is 36. . . . P–KR4, and White would have great difficulty in making any progress. If 37. Q–Q6 Q–B3, and if 37. P–KR4 P–N4.

37. P–B4	PxP
38. QxP	QxQ?

In time trouble, Larsen goes astray. The text permits White to rid himself of the isolated KP; moreover, it helps White's King to reach the center. The correct course is 38. . . . Q–B3 followed by . . . P–N4, forcing White to exchange Queens and leaving him with the isolated KP.

39. KPxQ	K–B3

Just the ending White wants. Now *his* Bishop is the powerhouse and Black's is passive.

40. K–B2	. . .

40. . . .	K–B4?

This loses, but the position cannot be held in any case. The best try is 40. . . . K–K3. There could follow 41. K–K3 K–Q3 42. K–Q4 P–B4 43. B–Q3 B–B3 44. B–B2 B–Q4 45. B–Q1 with Black in zugzwang; for if 45. . . . B–K3 46. B–B3 (threatening B–N7) B–B1 47. B–Q5 threatening to attack the Kingside pawns, and if 45. . . . B–B3 46. B–N3.

Black's troubles stem from having all his pawns on white squares against which White's Bishop applies great pressure. White's pawns, on the other hand, are invulnerable to attack by Black's Bishop. The position clearly illustrates the disadvantage

of having your pawns on the same color squares as your only
Bishop.

| 41. K–K3 | K–N5 |
| 42. K–Q4 | . . . |

Now White's King is in a position to attack the pawns on
either side. The Black King's action is confined to one side only.

| 42. . . . | B–N2 |
| 43. K–K5! | . . . |

The winning move. Incorrect is 43. K–B5 on account of 43. . . .
K–B6 44. K–N6 B–B1 45. K–B7 B–K3 46. K–N7 B–B5 47. B–R3
P–B4 48. KxP P–R4 49. K–R5 K–B7 50. P–R4 PxP 51. KxP K–N8
52. P–N5 BxPch 53. KxB KxP and wins.

| 43. . . . | P–KR4 |

There is nothing better. If 43. . . . P–B4 44. K–B6 K–B6 45.
K–N7 K–B7 46. KxP KxB 47. KxP K–N7 48. P–KR4 B–B6 49.
P–R5 BxPch 50. KxB KxP 51. K–N5, etc. Or 43. . . . K–B6 44.
K–B6 B–Q4 45. B–R3 P–KR4 46. P–B5 PxP 47. K–N5 K–B7 48.
BxP K–N7 49. KxP KxP 50. P–N4 K–N6 51. K–N5. And if 43. . . .
K–B6 44. K–B6 K–B7 45. B–Q3 K–N7 46. KxP KxP 47. P–N4
K–N6 48. P–B5 KxP 49. P–B6, etc.

44. K–B6	B–Q4
45. B–Q3	K–R6
46. P–B5	KxP

If 46. . . . PxP, White has 47. KxP KxP 48. K–B4 K–R6 49.
B–K2 P–R5 50. B–N4ch, etc.

| 47. K–K5 | P–N4 |

Desperation. If 47. . . . B–B6 48. PxP PxP 49. K–B4 B–N5 50.
BxKNP followed by B–K4–N7. If 47. . . . B–B3 48. PxP PxP 49.
BxKNP KxP 50. BxP, and Black's Queenside pawns fall prey to
White's King.

| 48. KxB | KxP |
| 49. P–B6 | . . . |

The rest is simple.

49. . . .	P–R5
50. K–K5	P–R6
51. K–B5	K–R5
52. B–K4	P–R7

If 52. . . . P–N5 53. K–B4 P–N6 54. K–B3 P–N7 55. K–B2, and the Bishop would be free to devour the Queenside pawns.

53. B–Q5		**P–N5**
54. K–B4		**K–R6**
55. B–R1		**P–N6**

55. . . . K–R5 56. B–N2 P–N6 57. K–B3, etc.

56. K–B3		**K–R5**
57. B–N2		**Resigns**

Game 51

Good Bishop, Bad Knight

The advantage of Bishop over Knight is mainly one of mobility. In an uncluttered position the Bishop can accomplish several things at once while the Knight, more limited in scope, has to be content with modest goals. In crowded positions, however, the situation is reversed: the Bishop cannot flex its muscles and is often uselessly passive, whereas the Knight can take its sweet time creating threats or snapping up loose pawns.

The endgame below is an example of the Bishop's obvious superiority in open positions. The ability of White's Bishop to simultaneously create long-range threats and keep the enemy Knight trapped in a corner is decisive in this game.

Netanya, 1969

NIMZO-INDIAN DEFENSE

S. Reshevsky	M. Damjanovic
1. P–Q4	N–KB3
2. P–QB4	P–K3
3. N–QB3	B–N5
4. P–K3	P–B4
5. B–Q3	P–Q4
6. N–B3	0–0
7. 0–0	N–B3
8. P–QR3	QPxP

9. BxP	B–R4
10. Q–Q3	P–QR3
11. R–Q1	P–QN4
12. B–R2	B–N2
13. PxP	BxN
14. Q–B2	Q–K2
15. QxB	N–K5

In Portisch–Larsen (game 50) Black played 15. . . . KR–Q1, winning a tempo but still not achieving full equality.

16. Q–B2	NxQBP
17. P–K4!	. . .

Gligoric, in a 1967 game, tried developing his QB at Q2 which proved insufficient. The text move allows the Bishop more scope.

17. . . .	KR–B1

My opponent consumed a lot of time for this move, and it is his best. White was threatening to weaken Black's KP by 18. B–N5 P–B3 19. B–K3, etc.

18. B–KB4	. . .

If 18. B–KN5 Q–B1!. The text move threatens B–Q6 immediately.

18. . . .	N–R5
19. Q–Q2	R–Q1
20. Q–K2	. . .

I was tempted to seize the stronghold Q6 by playing 20. B–Q6, but after 20. . . . Q–B3 21. P–K5 Q–N3 22. B–N1 P–B4 23. PxP e.p. QxP, Black's pieces become active.

20. . . .	RxRch
21. RxR	R–Q1
22. R–QB1	P–R3
23. B–KN3	. . .

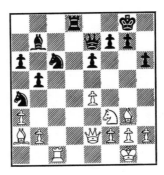

Threatening to weaken Black's position with 24. B–R4. Although White enjoys the advantage of the two Bishops, at the moment he is not in a position to capitalize on this minute theoretical superiority because there is no discernible weakness in Black's camp. In addition, Black's Knight is well posted at R5, bearing down on the NP.

23. . . .	N–Q5
24. NxN	RxN
25. P–B3	. . .

Protecting the pawn and enabling the QB to get to KB2 where it will be more effective.

| 25. . . . | Q–N4 |
| 26. R–B2 | . . . |

26. R–B7 is inadvisable on account of 26. . . . R–Q7 27. Q–K1 Q–Q1 with serious threats.

26. . . .	R–Q2
27. B–B2	Q–Q1
28. P–KN3	. . .

Better than 28. P–R3 because the King on an open diagonal at R2 would not be so safe as at N2.

| 28. . . . | N–N3 |

Since the Knight can be driven away at will, Black decides to retreat voluntarily and regroup his forces. Black's problem is his inactive Bishop. Futile is 28. . . . R–Q8ch 29. K–N2 R–QR8 30. P–N3 N–N3 31. Q–Q2 QxQ (31. . . . N–Q2 32. B–Q4) 32. RxQ N–B1 33. B–B5 with an easily won position.

29. K–N2	N–B1
30. B–K3	. . .

In order to be able to play R–Q2 and exchange Rooks. Each exchange further underlines the ineffectiveness of Black's Bishop.

30. . . .	N–K2
31. R–Q2	N–B3
32. RxR	QxR
33. Q–Q2	. . .

My chances will be better with the Queens off the board.

33. . . .	QxQch

Damjanovic must have felt that he could hold the endgame because he didn't hesitate to make this move. Preferable is 33. . . . Q–K2, in which case I might have tried to weaken his Queenside pawns by playing 34. B–N3 followed by 35. P–QR4. Now Black's only good piece is his Knight. But not for long!

34. BxQ	. . .

34. . . .	K–B1?

A costly strategical error. Black should try to post his Knight at QB5 by continuing 34. . . . N–K4. This failure condemns his Knight to passivity.

35. B–B3!	. . .

Immobilizing the Knight and exerting pressure against the KNP.

35. . . .	P–K4
36. B–Q5	. . .

This long-dormant Bishop finally comes into play dramatically. Black cannot dislodge it without paying a price.

36. . . .	P–B3
37. P–B4	PxP
38. PxP	K–K1
39. K–B3	N–Q1

Black has to exchange Bishops even though it means giving White a passed pawn. Now watch how useless Black's Knight is when there are threats both in the center and on the Kingside.

40. K–N4	BxB
41. PxB	N–N2
42. B–N4	. . .

The sealed move. This is necessary in order to keep the Knight out of play.

42. . . .	P–N3

The best try. If 42. . . . K–B2 43. P–B5 P–N3 44. PxPch KxP 45. P–KR4 P–R4ch 46. K–B4 K–B2 47. P–N3 K–N3 48. P–R4 K–B2 49. PxP PxP 50. K–K4 K–N3 51. P–Q6, etc. If in this line 48. . . . P–R4 49. B–B3 PxP 50. PxP N–B4 51. B–Q4 NxP 52. P–Q6 K–B2 53. K–B5 and wins.

43. P–B5	P–N4

44. P–QR4!	. . .

The winning move. It had to be made at this moment while the Black King was not protecting the KBP. Dubious is 44. K–R5 K–B2 45. KxP P–R4 46. B–B3 N–Q3 47. BxRP NxPch 48. K–R5

N–K6 49. P–Q6 K–K3 50. B–N4 N–B8 51. P–R3 N–N6ch 52. K–N6 N–K7 with drawing chances.

| 44. . . . | K–B2 |

If 44. . . . PxP 45. K–R5 P–R4 46. B–R3 keeping the Knight imprisoned.

| 45. PxP | PxP |
| 46. K–R5 | Resigns |

Black's position is hopeless. For if 46. . . . K–N2 47. P–R3 K–R2 48. B–K7 K–N2 49. P–N4 K–B2 50. P–Q6, etc.

Game 52

A Delicate Balance

Another demonstration of the advantages of Bishop over Knight. In this case White wins the endgame by "stalemating" the Knight at the edge of the board. Of considerable help is the fact that Black's King is behind White's passed pawn, always an inferior position.

Interzonal Tournament

Palma de Majorca, 1970

TARRASCH DEFENSE

S. Reshevsky	B. Ivkov
1. P–Q4	N–KB3
2. P–QB4	P–B4
3. N–KB3	. . .

3. P–Q5, leading to the Benoni, is more usual.

3. . . .	P–K3
4. N–B3	P–Q4
5. BPxP	KPxP
6. P–KN3	N–B3
7. B–N2	B–K2
8. 0–0	0–0
9. PxP	BxP

10. N–QR4	B–K2
11. B–K3	R–K1
12. R–B1	B–KN5

The purpose of this move is to exert indirect pressure on White's KP and to provoke P–KR3, thereby slightly weakening White's KNP.

| 13. B–B5 | . . . |

A good alternative is 13. N–B5 BxN 14. BxB N–K5 15. B–K3 Q–Q2 16. Q–R4, as in the Hort–Ivkov game from the same event.

13. . . .	N–K5
14. BxB	QxB
15. P–KR3	. . .

If 15. QxP QR–Q1 16. Q–QN5 BxN followed by . . . N–Q5 with promising play.

| 15. . . . | BxN |

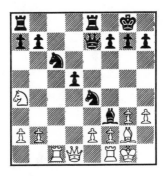

| 16. PxB! | . . . |

It is usually inadvisable to double one's pawns, but in this case it is important to drive away Black's Knight after which I will be able to exert substantial pressure against the isolated pawn with my Bishop.

16. . . .	N–B3
17. P–B4	QR–B1
18. R–K1	QxRch

Ivkov is too eager to reach the endgame. Preferable is 18. . . . Q–Q3, preventing the immediate advance of the KNP.

19. QxQ	RxQch
20. RxR	K–B1
21. R–Q1	N–K2
22. N–B3	R–B4

Better than 22. . . . R–Q1. The text move offers Black the possibility of . . . P–QN4–5 followed by the Rook's penetration to the seventh rank.

23. P–KN4	P–KR3
24. P–N5	N–R4
25. BxP	NxP
26. PxP	PxP

Not 26. . . . NxPch on account of 27. K–R2 NxP 28. P–R7 N–N3 29. R–Q4 P–B4 30. BxP K–K2 31. B–B3 with the threat of K–N2.

27. BxNP	NxPch
28. K–B1	N–B5
29. B–K4	P–QR4
30. R–Q7	P–R4
31. R–N7	P–B4
32. B–B3	P–KR5
33. P–R4	N/2–N3
34. R–N5	R–K4
35. N–K2	N–Q6

36. B–R5   . . .

Virtually forcing Black's next move, which gives White a passed pawn.

36. . . .	RxR

If 36. . . . K–N2, White can continue with 37. P–B4 to force the exchange of Rooks while the King is farther away from White's passed pawn.

37. PxR	N/3–K4
38. P–N3	P–R6
39. P–B4	N–KN5

Not 39. . . . N–Q2 because of 40. B–N6, winning the BP and KRP without any compensation for Black.

40. P–N6	N–K6ch
41. K–N1	N–B4
42. B–B3?	. . .

Stronger is 42. N–Q4! K–K2 (42. . . . N–Q4? 43. N–K6ch NxN 44. P–N7 queening) 43. B–B3 K–Q3 44. K–R2 with good winning chances.

42. . . .	N–B7!

Preventing N–Q4.

43. P–N7	N–Q2
44. B–B6	N–N1
45. B–N5	K–K2
46. K–R2	K–Q3
47. KxP	K–B2
48. B–Q3	N–K6
49. K–N3	KxP
50. K–B3	N–Q4
51. BxP	. . .

White is finally a pawn ahead, but a forced win is still not evident due to the scarcity of material. If Black succeeds in exchanging pawns, he can sacrifice a Knight for the remaining pawn and, since Bishop and Knight cannot win against a Knight, Black would draw.

| 51. . . . | K–N3 |
| 52. K–K4 | NxP?! |

An impatient decision which gives White some chances. Safer is 52. . . . N–B2, and if 53. K–K5 N–B3ch 54. K–Q6 N–N4ch 55. K–Q7 N/4–Q5 56. NxN NxN 57. B–K6 K–B4 58. P–B5 NxBP 59. BxN K–N5 60. B–K6 P–R5 and draws. If 53. B–N4 K–B4 54. P–B5 N–Q2 and Black should draw; and lastly, if 53. K–Q4 K–N4 54. K–B3 N–Q4ch, etc.

53. KxN	K–B4
54. B–B2	K–N5
55. K–K3	N–Q2
56. K–Q4?	. . .

Imperative is 56. K–Q2, where the King would avoid Black's tempo-winning checks.

56. . . .	N–B4
57. N–B1	P–R5
58. N–R2ch	K–R6
59. P–N4	. . .

| 59. . . . | N–N6ch? |

The losing move. Correct is 59. . . . N–K3ch. If 60. K–K5 KxN 61. KxN (if 61. BxP K–R6) P–R6 62. B–K4 K–N6 63. P–N5

P–R7 64. B–Q5ch K–N5 and draws. And if 60. K–B4 KxN 61.
BxP K–R6 62. B–Q7 N–B2 63. B–B8 K–R5 64. K–B5 K–R6, and
White is unable to advance his pawn without having it taken.
Note however that if White had made the correct move on his
56th turn, Black would not have this possibility.

60.	K–B3	KxN
61.	B–B5	K–R6

Against 61. . . . N–B8, White has 62. B–K6ch K–N8 63. B–B4
P–R6 64. P–N5 N–K7ch 65. K–Q3 N–B5ch 66. K–K4, etc.

62.	P–N5	N–B4
63.	P–N6	K–R7
64.	K–N4	N–N2
65.	KxP	N–Q1
66.	B–K4	K–N7
67.	K–N4	K–R7
68.	B–Q5ch	K–N7
69.	K–B5	K–R6
70.	K–N5	. . .

Before reaching this position, I thought that I would encounter
no difficulty in scoring the point, but I suddenly saw that 70.
K–Q6 would not suffice because of 70. . . . K–N5 71. K–B7 K–N4!
72. B–R2 K–R3 73. B–B4ch K–R4, and if now 74. B–K2 N–K3ch
draws. If I had the position of move 74 but with Black to move,
I would win, but I could not bring about such a position by force.
I therefore repeated moves in order to reach the time control.

I found out later that my predicament caught the fancy of
many experts during the game, and analysis of the position was
going on outside the playing hall. There was a wide divergence
of opinion as to the outcome of the game. Can White stalemate
the Black Knight and simultaneously keep the Black King away
from the pawn?

70.	. . .	K–N7
71.	K–N4	K–B7
72.	K–B4	K–N7
73.	K–N4	K–B7
74.	K–B5	K–B6

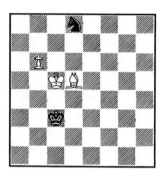

| | 75. B–K4 | K–N6 |
| | 76. B–B5 | N–N2ch |

If 76. . . . K–R5 77. B–Q7ch K–R4 78. B–B8 K–R5 79. K–Q6 is the same as in the actual game.

	77. K–B6	N–R4ch
	78. K–N5	N–N2
	79. B–B8	N–Q1
	80. K–B5	K–R5
	81. K–Q6	K–R4
	82. K–B7	K–N4
	83. B–R3	Resigns

For if 83. . . . K–R3 84. B–B1ch K–R4 85. B–B4 and wins. If 83. . . . K–R4 84. B–N4 K–N4 85. B–K2ch K–B4 86. B–B4 and wins. Exponents of the Bishop must certainly be pleased with the Bishop's performance in this endgame.

Game 53

Another Good Bishop

If the previous game warmed the hearts of Bishop-lovers, this one should do even more; for whereas last time the Knight was severely restricted and White had a passed pawn, this time the Knight is free to roam and White doesn't get a passed pawn until the game is just about over. And still the Bishop triumphs.

Interzonal Tournament
Sousse, 1967

SICILIAN DEFENSE

S. Reshevsky	M. Matulovic
1. N–KB3	P–QB4
2. P–K4	. . .

This must have come as a surprise to Matulovic, for this was the first and only time I played a King's pawn opening in this event. I had experimented with this opening in the Maribor tournament just prior to the Interzonal so as to be ready to use it here if I felt it expedient.

I wanted to get the same variation with White that Geller had against Matulovic earlier in the tournament, but I didn't want to tip my hand by playing 1. P–K4, a rare opening in my practice. I had noted earlier that Matulovic invariably answer 1. N–KB3 with 1. . . . P–QB4, so I decided to "trick" him into playing the Sicilian.

2. . . .	N–QB3
3. P–Q4	PxP
4. NxP	P–K3
5. N–N5	P–Q3
6. P–QB4	. . .

In order to obtain a bind in the center and restrict Black's development.

6. . . .	N–B3
7. QN–B3	P–QR3
8. N–R3	B–K2
9. B–K2	0–0
10. 0–0	P–QN3
11. B–K3	B–N2
12. R–B1	. . .

A good alternative is 12. P–B4 (keeping the Knight out of K4) followed by B–B3.

12. . . .	N–K4
13. Q–Q4	N/4–Q2
14. P–B3	. . .

Not the best move since it allows Black counterplay by enabling him to effect the freeing . . . P–Q4. Correct is 14. KR–Q1.
I was worried about 14. . . . P–K4 15. Q–Q3 N–B4, attacking the
Queen and the KP, but I didn't realize that after 16. BxN QPxB
17. Q–B3 Q–B2 18. N–B2, followed by N–K3–Q5, I would have
had the advantage.

| 14. . . . | R–K1 |

The threat is now 15. . . . P–Q4 16. BPxP PxP 17. PxP B–B4.

| 15. B–B2 | . . . |

Although the text move gives Matulovic the opportunity to
equalize, I see no promising alternative. If 15. Q–Q2 P–Q4 16.
BPxP PxP 17. PxP NxP 18. NxN BxN/4 19. QxB BxN, and if 20.
B–QB4 Q–K2 with equality. If 15. N–B2 P–Q4 16. BPxP PxP 17.
PxP B–B4 18. Q–Q3 RxB 19. NxR Q–K2 with a speculative attack.
If 15. N–R4 P–Q4, and the NP is immune to capture because of
. . . B–B4. Also 15. KR–Q1 P–Q4 16. P–K5 fails on account of 16.
. . . B–B4 17. Q–B4 N–R4, etc.

15. . . .	P–Q4
16. BPxP	PxP
17. PxP	B–B4
18. Q–KR4	. . .

Slightly better is 18. Q–Q2 BxBch 19. RxB P–QN4 20. N–B2
N–N3 21. P–Q6.

18. . . .	NxP
19. QxQ	QRxQ
20. N/R–N1	. . .

I discarded 20. N–K4 on account of 20. . . . N–B5, attacking the
KB and the Knight.

| 20. . . . | N–B5 |
| 21. KR–K1 | . . . |

21. B–B4 is bad because of 21. . . . N–K4, and 21. B–Q1 is out of the question because of 21. . . . N–Q6.

| 21. . . . | **K–B1?** |

Not the best move. With 21. . . . NxBch 22. RxN RxR 23. NxR BxBch 24. KxB N–B4 25. K–B1 P–QR4 followed by . . . B–R3, Black can pose serious problems for White. After this move, I became optimistic that Matulovic would continue his weak end-game play.

22. QR–Q1	P–QN4
23. P–QR3	BxBch
24. KxB	N–B4
25. RxR	RxR
26. R–Q1	RxR
27. NxR	N–N6
28. B–B1	. . .

I elected to retain the Bishop. White has a slight edge at this point but certainly not enough to win. His mild pressure against the Queenside pawns requires only that Black be alert.

28. . . .	K–K2
29. N/N–B3	K–Q3
30. K–K3	K–K4
31. P–N3	N–Q4ch
32. NxN	BxN
33. N–B3	B–B3
34. N–R2	K–Q3
35. N–N4	B–N2

36. P–B4	P–R3
37. B–Q3	N–B4
38. B–B2	B–B1
39. N–R2	B–K3
40. N–B3	. . .

| 40. . . . | B–N6? |

At last, the mistake I was hoping for. With 40. . . . P–B4, Black would have a tenable position despite a slight disadvantage. I have come to the conclusion lately that it often pays to continue in equal positions, especially in the endgame where many players are more likely to go astray.

41. N–K4ch!   . . .

Black has to lose a pawn. If 41. . . . K–Q4 42. NxN BxB 43. NxP K–B5 44. N–B7 B–R5 45. K–Q2 followed by N–K8 and wins without great difficulty.

| 41. . . . | NxN |
| 42. BxB | P–B4 |

To no avail is 42. . . . N–B3 43. K–Q4! N–N5 (43. . . . K–K2 44. K–B5 N–Q2ch 45. K–B6 with an eventual K–N7, etc.) 44. P–R3 N–B7 45. BxP NxP 46. K–K3 P–N4 47. B–R5 with the Knight trapped.

| 43. B–B2 | N–B4 |

White wins the endgame easily after 43. . . . K–Q4 44. BxNch PxB 45. P–KN4 K–B5 46. P–KR4 K–N6 47. P–B5 KxP 48. P–N5 KxP 49. P–B6, etc.

44. BxP	K–Q4
45. P–QN4	N–R5
46. B–B8	. . .

Forcing matters. I didn't like 46. B–B2 because of 46. . . . K–B5.

46. . . .	N–B6
47. K–Q3	. . .

Better than 47. BxP K–B5 followed by . . . K–N6. Black also has at his disposal 47. . . . K–B3 followed by . . . N–N8.

47. . . .	N–N8
48. BxP	NxP
49. B–N7ch	K–Q3
50. B–K4	N–B5
51. K–Q4	. . .

With his King on this square where the Black Knight is unable to bother it with checks, White can operate on both wings at will.

51. . . .	N–N3

If 51. . . . N–Q7 52. B–N2 N–N6ch (if 52. . . . N–B5 53. B–B1 N–R6 54. K–B3 K–Q4 55. K–N3 and wins) 53. K–B3 N–B8 54. B–B1 N–R7ch 55. K–N3 N–B8ch 56. K–N2 with the Knight trapped.

52. P–R4	N–B1

The poor Knight is no match for the Bishop.

53. P–N4	N–K2
54. P–R5	N–B1

Forced, for if 54. . . . N–N1 55. B–Q3 (if after the text move 55. B–Q3, then 55. . . . N–R2 threatening to drive the King back

with . . . N–B3ch) 55. . . . K–B3 56. K–K5 N–B3 57. B–K2
followed by K–K6–B7.

55. P–N5	N–K2
56. P–B5!	. . .

Unproductive is 56. PxP PxP 57. P–B5 N–N1 58. B–Q3 N–B3,
and if 59. B–K2 N–Q4. White would still have chances to win
with 59. BxP, but victory is not assured.

56. . . .	PxP
57. P–B6	PxP
58. P–R6	P–B4
59. P–R7	N–N3
60. BxP	N–R1
61. B–Q3	K–K2 and Resigns

Matulovic sealed his last move and resigned later. White can
win as follows: 62. K–B5 K–B2 63. KxP K–N2 64. K–B6 N–B2
65. K–B7 N–K4 66. B–B1 P–N5 67. P–N5 N–N3 68. P–N6 N–K2
69. B–N2 and the pawn queens.

Game 54

Active Knight

Bishops are not *always* superior to Knights. In positions where
a Knight has good posts from which to influence the play it can
be better than a Bishop, even when the Bishop is unrestrained
by pawns. The centralized Knight in this endgame embodies
many threats because of its freedom to jump from one good
square to another. Black's Bishop must try to stop at least some
of these threats, so it becomes defensive and passive, not a
Bishop's ambition.

Playoff Match
Chicago, 1973

ENGLISH OPENING

S. Reshevsky	L. Kavalek
1. N–KB3	P–KN3

2. P–B4	B–N2
3. N–B3	P–QB4
4. P–Q4	PxP
5. NxP	N–QB3
6. N–B2	. . .

An alternative is 6. P–K3, which leads to a positional type of game. I was looking for one which offers complications.

6. . . .	P–Q3
7. P–K4	N–R3?

The merit of this move is questionable. Black is trying to prepare for . . . P–B4 and intends to recapture on B4 with his Knight, but the Knight move offers White attacking possibilities. The main drawback of the text move is that the Knight is awkwardly posted. Preferable is either 7. . . . P–B4 or 7. . . . N–B3.

8. B–K2	P–B4
9. P–KR4!	. . .

A surprising move for me. Positional play is my forte, but when the situation demands it, I veer away from conservative continuations. The idea behind the text move is to discourage my opponent from castling on the Kingside because of the impending threat of opening the KR-file with P–R5.

9. . . .	PxP
10. P–R5	. . .

Better than 10. NxP N–B4 11. P–R5 Q–R4ch 12. B–Q2 Q–K4 compelling White to retreat his Knight (13. N–B3).

10. . . .	B–B4
11. PxP	PxP
12. N–K3	N–B2
13. RxRch	BxR

14. P–KN4   . . .

The pawn has to be regained. I considered 14. NxB PxN 15.
Q–Q5 or 15. B–R5 and finally 15. P–KN4, but Black has adequate
replies.

14. . . .   **B–K3**

Unappetizing for Black is 14. . . . BxNch 15. PxB B–K3 16.
R–N1 with strong action on the Queenside.

15. Q–B2   **N–N4**

To be considered is 15. . . . Q–R4 16. B–Q2 Q–K4, but after
17. NxP QxP 18. QxQ BxQ 19. R–N1 B–N2 20. RxP, White's
chances would be very good.

16. NxP   **N–Q5**

It appears that Black's forces are making an incursion into
White's position, but this soon proves illusory.

17. Q–Q3   **N/4–B6ch**
18. K–B1   **Q–R4**

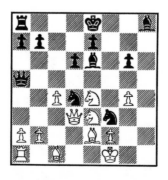

19. BxN	NxB
20. B–Q2	. . .

The threat of . . . Q–K8ch has to be parried. Both 20. Q–Q1 N–K4 and 20. Q–K2 N–Q5 waste time for White.

20. . . .	NxBch

Possible is 20. . . . Q–R3 21. B–B3 N–K4 22. Q–K2 0–0–0 23. P–N3 with a complicated position.

21. NxN	BxQNP?

A mistake which causes Black many problems, not the least of which, paradoxically, is the reduction of the scope of this Bishop. Necessary is 21. . . . K–B2 or 21. . . . B–B2. In either case, White's two Knights would be superior to the two Bishops.

22. R–N1	. . .

Of course not 22. QxPch B–B2, winning material.

22. . . .	B–K4

Another misjudgment. Correct is 22. . . . B–B3 to prevent White's strong 25th move.

23. RxP	. . .

With White's Rook on the seventh rank, White's Knights and the Queen are able to begin a concerted action against Black's exposed King. The initiative White has gained as a result of Black's ill-advised 21st move gives him attacking chances against Black's King, which in turn force the Bishops into defensive roles not at all suited to their nature.

23. . . .	K–B2
24. N–B3	R–R1

A desperate attempt by Kavalek to obtain immediate counteraction against White's King, but Black's position is already untenable, for if 24. . . . B–B3 White could make substantial progress with 25. P–N5 B–N2 (25. . . . BxP 26. R–N5) 26. QxP, etc.

25. N–N5ch	K–B3

The King can be easily menaced by White's forces here, but Black has no good alternative.

26. NxB	R–R8ch

Trying for a perpetual check, but there is to be none.

27. K–N2	R–R7ch
28. K–B3	. . .

The King is headed for K4 where it will be safe from attack and will also serve well to restrict the mobility of the opponent's King.

28. . . .   **R–R6ch**

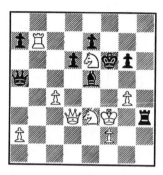

If 29. K–K2 QxPch 30. Q–B2? RxNch and wins.

    29. K–K4!   . . .

This is the reply I planned when I made my 25th move, N–N5ch. The King is safe in the middle of the board!

    29. . . .   **KxN**

    30. Q–Q5ch   . . .

Forcing an ending in which Black's pieces become completely immobilized.

    30. . . .   **QxQch**

    31. NxQ   **K–B2**

There is no good alternative. If 31. . . . R–R2 (31. . . . B–B3 32. N–B4ch) 32. P–B4 B–B3 33. P–N5 B–R1 34. RxRP, and Black would have no constructive moves.

Note the difference between this position and Uhlmann–Geller, game 46, in which the Knight was inferior mainly because it had no permanent points of support in the center. Here the Knight's many available squares make it superior to the Bishop, which has relatively little influence.

    32. RxPch   **K–B1**

    33. P–B5   . . .

33. RxP also wins, but the text move expedites matters.

    33. . . .   **R–R6**

    34. P–B6   **R–R5ch**

35. K–B3	R–QB5
36. P–B7	B–B3
37. R–Q7	Resigns

38. NxB and 38. R–Q8ch cannot both be prevented. The Knight even stops desperation checks.

Game 55

Good Knight, Bad Knight

Tartakower once wrote that after planting a Knight in the center you can go to sleep. This is not to be taken literally, of course, but it contains more than a germ of truth. From the center a Knight commands maximum terrain; for example, on Q5 it controls QN4 and QN6, QB3 and QB7, KB4 and KB6, K3 and K7. No other piece can make that claim.

Tartakower might also have said (though he didn't) that "a Knight on the rim looks dim," a commonly heard cliché which, again, is fundamentally true. A Knight on Q5 controls eight squares, on QR4 only four—half as many. That's what makes the difference in this game.

Netanya, 1971

IRREGULAR OPENING

| S. Reshevsky | S. Kagan |
| 1. P–QN3 | . . . |

I believe this was the first time I ever used this opening. It is one of Larsen's favorites, and certainly no worse than other first moves.

1. . . .	N–KB3
2. B–N2	P–KN3
3. P–N3	B–N2
4. B–N2	0–0
5. N–KB3	P–Q3
6. P–Q4	B–Q2?!

For the purpose of playing 7. ... Q–B1 followed by ... B–KR6 and exchanging Bishops, but this idea uses several tempos, slowing Black's development. Wiser is 6. ... P–K4 7. PxP KN–Q2, recovering the pawn with a playable position.

7. 0–0	**Q–B1**
8. R–K1	**B–R6**
9. P–K4	**. . .**

An alternative is 9. B–R1 to retain the Bishop.

9. . . .	**BxB**
10. KxB	**P–K4**

Insufficient for equality. A better try is 10. ... R–Q1 11. Q–B1 P–B4 12. P–Q5 P–K4.

11. PxP	**KN–Q2**
12. N–B3	**NxP**

Wiser is 12. ... PxP, and if 13. N–Q5 Q–Q1 followed by ... P–QB3.

13. N–Q5	**. . .**

From this dominating square in the center, the Knight threatens the QBP and the squares K7 and KB6. All of these threats play their parts, some of them made clear only in the notes.

13. . . .	**N–B3**
14. NxN	**BxN?**

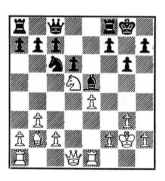

Imperative is 14. ... PxN. I then intended 15. Q–Q2 followed by QR–Q1, when White would have a distinct positional plus.

15. Q–B1!	**. . .**

White now seriously threatens to gain control of Black's KB3 square, thereby menacing the safety of the King.

15. . . .	**Q–Q1**
16. **P–KB4**	**BxB**
17. **QxB**	. . .

The dark squares in Black's camp, pressured by White's Queen and Knight, compel Black to engage in cumbersome maneuvers in an attempt to avoid an immediate catastrophe.

17. . . .	**P–B3**
18. **QR–Q1**	**R–B2**

Black has difficulty developing his QR. This is the only try. Obviously, Black's pieces lack coordination.

19. **P–QN4!**	. . .

Opening a drive to promote a breakthrough in the center with P–K5, beginning with the dislocation of Black's Knight, after which Black's stubborn defense collapses.

19. . . .	**P–QR3**
20. **P–QR4**	**Q–KB1**
21. **P–N5**	**PxP**
22. **PxP**	**N–R4**

22. . . . N–K2 loses the QBP, and 22. . . . N–Q1 keeps the QR imprisoned (it has no prospects on the QR-file). But the Knight is certainly no threat on QR4, and it never moves from here, playing no further part in the game.

23. **Q–B3**	. . .

White has a clear advantage because of his superior development. His Rooks are posted on the Q- and K-files; the Knight is anchored at Q5. Black's pieces, on the other hand, are only defensively placed. White is poised for a breakthrough at K5.

23. . . .	**P–N3**

Insufficient is 23. ... P–B3 24. N–N6 R–R2 25. R–QR1 Q–Q1
26. N–B4 P–N3 27. NxN RxN 28. RxR PxR 29. QxQBP R–B2 30.
Q–Q5ch K–N2 31. P–B4. Also, 23. ... P–B3 24. N–N6 R–R2 25.
P–K5 BPxP 26. PxP PxP 27. RxP favors White.

24. P–K5   . . .

The long-planned advance, which opens the position and exposes the Black monarch to various threats. It is instructive to
note how rapidly Black's position crumbles after this breakthrough, but it is not surprising: compare the Knights and the
Queens.

24. . . .   **BPxP**

Black is compelled to dispose of this pawn; otherwise P–K6
would be crushing.

25. PxP   **PxP**

An attempt to simplify would fail: 25. ... R–B7ch 26. K–N1
Q–B6 (26. ... R–B6 27. QxP, and Black cannot continue 27. ...
R–B1 because of 28. N–K7ch) 27. QxQ RxQ 28. NxBP followed
by PxP.

26. QxKP   **Q–N2**

If 26. ... R–B7ch 27. K–N1 Q–B6 28. N–B4 (not 28. N–K7ch
K–B2! 29. Q–K6ch K–N2) 28. ... RxBP 29. R–KB1 Q–B6 30.
Q–K6ch K–R1 31. R–Q7 and wins.

27. N–K7ch   **K–B1?**

Loses quickly. Necessary is 27. ... K–R1; but after 28. QxP,
White's victory cannot be denied.

28. Q–Q5!   . . .

Winning the Exchange by force, for if 28. . . . R–N1 29. Q–Q8ch.

28. . . .	**R–K1**
29. NxPch	**QxN**
30. RxRch	**K–N2**

30. . . . KxR 31. Q–Q8 mate.

31. R–Q4	**QxBPch**
32. K–R3	**Resigns**

For if 32. . . . Q–B4ch (the only attempt to ward off mate) 33. R–N4ch K–R3 34. R–K6ch K–R4 35. R–K5.

Game 56

Knight on K4

In many "Indian" defenses White's K4 square is strategically vital. If Black allows a White pawn to remain there, he will find it more difficult, if not impossible, to undermine the White pawn on Q5. If he removes it by playing . . . P–KB4 and then . . . BPxKP, White's K4 becomes available for White's pieces; in addition, White's diagonal QN1–KR7 remains open, along which his KB and Queen can create serious threats to the Black King.

In this game, Black chooses to exchange pawns on White's K4 and somewhat simplifies the position. But White's Knight occupies the K4 stronghold and dominates the board. Although the second half of the game (from move 42) is a Rook-and-pawn endgame, the middlegame theme is White's good Knight against Black's bad Bishop. As in many similar situations arising from this type of opening, White's Knight on K4 threatens Black's weak QP and also keeps an eye on the dark squares on Black's Kingside —all of which Black's only minor piece, his King Bishop, is committed to defending passively. Black's resulting lack of counterplay allows White to effect a decisive penetration with his King and Rook.

Chess Olympics

Lugano, 1968

KING'S INDIAN DEFENSE

S. Reshevsky	M. Najdorf
1. P–QB4	N–KB3
2. N–QB3	P–KN3
3. P–K4	P–Q3
4. P–Q4	B–N2
5. P–B3	0–0
6. B–K3	P–K4
7. P–Q5	. . .

An alternative is 7. KN–K2 N–B3 8. Q–Q2 or 7. . . . P–B3 8. Q–Q2, but the text move is simpler and makes it harder for Black to achieve equality.

7. . . .	N–R4
8. Q–Q2	P–KB4
9. 0–0–0	N–Q2
10. B–Q3	N/2–B3
11. KN–K2	PxP

11. . . . P–B5 12. B–KB2 followed by P–KN4, forcing an opening of lines, obviously favors White. The text move begins a plan to destroy White's center pawns. This succeeds to some degree, but it also eventually weakens Black's QP thus giving White's Knight a beautiful post on K4.

12. NxP	. . .

12. PxP N–N5 13. B–N5 B–B3 accomplishes nothing for White.

12. . . .	NxN
13. BxN	. . .

13. PxN blocks White's KB and occupies K4 with a pawn, and after 13. . . . B–N5 followed by . . . BxN and . . . N–B5, White would have to fight for equality.

13. . . .	N–B3
14. B–QB2	B–B4
15. N–N3	. . .

Better than 15. P–KN4 BxB 16. QxB P–K5 or 16. . . . N–Q2.

15. . . .	**BxB**
16. QxB	**. . .**

16. . . .	**Q–K1**

With the idea of continuing . . . P–B3 or . . . P–B4 so that if PxP then . . . QxP. In the Gheorghiu–Gligoric game, which was being played at the same time (in fact on the very next board), Black played 16. . . . P–B4, and after 17. PxP e.p. PxP 18. P–KR4 Q–R4 19. K–N1 P–K5 20. P–R5 Q–K4 21. NxP NxN 22. B–Q4 Q–K2 23. BxB KxB 24. P–R6ch K–B2 25. KR–K1, Black's position became hopeless. Black's opening setup, sponsored by Russian analysts, must therefore be reassessed.

17. B–N5	**P–B4**
18. PxP e.p.	**QxP**
19. BxN	**BxB**
20. N–K4	**B–K2**
21. R–Q5	**. . .**

White's strategy becomes clear. He obtains a well-posted Knight against his opponent's inactive Bishop. The text move is designed to prevent the freeing . . . P–QN4 and, at the same time, to increase the pressure against the QP.

21. . . .	**QR–B1**
22. P–QN3	**QxR**
23. PxQ	**RxQch**
24. KxR	**K–B2**

A deceptive-looking position. Although it appears that Black has achieved complete equality and has no further worries, in fact White has at his disposal the possibility of a breakthrough on either wing. His Knight, in addition to pressuring Black's QP and being posted to get quickly to any new battlefield, keeps Black's Bishop in a passive position, favoring White's chances for a breakthrough.

| 25. R–QB1 | K–K1 |

If Black succeeds in exchanging Rooks, which he may try by . . . R–B1, White would retain equally good prospects, whereas Black's chances for counterplay would be even further reduced.

26. K–Q3	K–Q2
27. P–QN4	P–QR3
28. P–QR4	R–QR1

To activate the Rook after 29. P–N5 PxP.

| 29. R–QN1 | . . . |

Intending an eventual P–QR5 and P–QN5.

| 29. . . . | B–Q1 |
| 30. P–R3 | . . . |

A waiting move.

30. . . .	R–B1
31. P–R5	R–R1
32. N–Q2	P–N3?

Najdorf feared 33. N–B4 followed by 34. P–N5, but the position resulting from those moves offers better defensive prospects than the one that follows the text move.

33. PxP	BxP
34. R–QR1	B–Q1
35. N–B4	R–R2

Black's position is untenable. Najdorf is completely on the defensive; his Rook is inactive, his Bishop without prospects. White, on the other hand, has all the winning chances; his Rook exerts pressure on the QRP, and his Knight (which cannot be dislodged) is in a position to help promote the QNP while at the same time it attacks the QP.

| 36. R–R4? | . . . |

Short of time, I missed the following simple win: 36. P–N5 P–QR4 37. P–N6 R–N2 (37. . . . R–R3 38. R–QN1; if 37. . . . R–R1 38. P–N7 R–N1 39. R–QN1 P–R5 40. K–B3 K–B2 41. N–R5 P–R6 42. R–N5 B–R5 43. K–N3 B–B7 44. KxP B–N3 45. K–R4 BxN 46. KxB RxP 47. RxRch KxR 48. K–N5 P–N4 49. P–N3 P–R4 50. P–R4 and White has the opposition; if, in this line, 43. . . . B–K8 44. N–B4, etc.) 38. R–QN1 and wins.

The text move frees Black's Bishop and considerably reduces White's winning chances.

36. . . .	R–R1
37. P–R4	P–KR4
38. P–N5	P–R4
39. P–N6	R–N1
40. RxP	BxP
41. NxBch	. . .

After 41. R–N5 B–B2 42. RxR BxR, there would be little reason for either side to play on. Now that Black's Bishop has become active, it is at least equal to White's Knight and must be eliminated if White cherishes any hopes of winning.

41. . . .	RxN
42. R–R7ch	K–K1
43. R–KN7	R–N5
44. RxP	RxP

Completely unsatisfactory for Black is 44. . . . R–Q5ch 45. K–K3 RxP 46. R–R6, since White's three pawns would advance faster than Black's two.

45. RxQP	K–B2
46. K–K3	R–Q5
47. P–N3	. . .

47. R–KR6 RxP 48. RxP K–B3 49. P–N4 R–KB5 leads to a draw.

47. . . .	R–Q8
48. K–K4	R–K8ch
49. K–B5	R–K6

50. R–B6ch?   . . .

Again missing a win: 50. R–Q7ch K–B1 (50. . . . K–K1 51. R–QR7 RxPch 52. K–K6 K–B1 53. P–Q6 and wins) 51. P–Q6 RxPch 52. K–K6 RxP 53. R–Q8ch K–N2 54. P–Q7 and wins.

50. . . .	K–N2
51. P–B4	. . .

Fruitless for White is 51. K–K6 on account of 51. . . . P–K5 52.
P–B4 (52. PxP RxPch 53. K–B5 R–K6) RxP 53. P–Q6 R–Q6 54.
R–B5 P–R5 55. R–KR5 P–R6 56. P–Q7 P–K6 57. RxP P–K7 58.
R–R1 R–Q8, etc.

51. . . .	PxP
52. PxP	P–R5
53. R–N6ch	K–B2

If 53. . . . K–R2 54. R–N4 winning easily.

54. R–KR6	P–R6
55. P–Q6	K–N2
56. R–N6ch	K–B2
57. R–R6	K–N2
58. R–R4	K–B2
59. R–R5	. . .

So that if 59. . . . K–N2 60. P–Q7 R–Q6 61. K–K6, etc.

| 59. . . . | R–Q6? |

Missing the opportunity for the half point. Najdorf took a long
time for the text move, overlooking the following draw: 59. . . .
R–K3! 60. P–Q7 (60. R–R7ch K–N1 61. KxR KxR and draws)
60. . . . R–Q3 61. RxP K–N2! (Najdorf saw only 61. . . . RxP 62.
R–R7ch K–K1 63. RxR and wins), regaining the pawn and
drawing easily.

| 60. K–K5 | . . . |

Now White has some winning chances, but Black can still hold.

| 60. . . . | R–R6 |
| 61. P–Q7 | . . . |

If 61. R–R7ch K–N1 62. P–Q7 R–Q6 and draws.

61. . . .	K–K2
62. R–R7ch	K–Q1
63. P–B5	R–K6ch

Not 63. . . . R–R4ch 64. K–B6 R–R3ch 65. K–B7 with a book
win.

64. K–B4	R–K8
65. RxP	KxP
66. K–N5	K–K1?

Here Najdorf throws away his last chance to draw: 66. . . .
K–K2! 67. R–R7ch K–B1 68. K–B6 (if 68. K–N6 R–N8ch 69. K–B6

K–N1 70. R–QR7 R–KB8 with a book draw) 68. . . . K–N1 69.
R–N7ch K–R1 70. R–N2 R–QR8 71. R–K2 K–R2 72. K–B7
R–R2ch 73. R–K7 R–R1 74. P–B6 R–QN1, and White can make
no progress. For example, 75. K–K6ch K–N3 76. P–B7 (76.
R–N7ch K–R3 77. R–N2 R–N3ch, etc.) 76. . . . R–N3ch 77. K–K5
K–N2 and draws.

67. K–B6	. . .

This position is of a type known to be lost for Black.

67. . . .	K–Q2
68. R–R7ch	K–K1
69. R–R8ch	K–Q2
70. R–KB8	R–KR8
71. K–N7	R–N8ch
72. K–B7	R–KB8
73. P–B6	Resigns

Game 57

Knight versus Multiple Passed Pawns

The Knight is renowned for, among other things, its suitability
as a blockader. As a unit of relatively low value (compared
especially to a Rook or Queen) it is not wasted in such a role;
and because its strength lies in short-range operations it is not
uncomfortable standing in a single spot for long periods, as the
Bishop is. This last quality, however, is also the Knight's weakness: since it does not perform well at great distances it is not
effective—in fact it is almost useless—in trying to stop passed
pawns separated by more than two files.

In this game, White obtains some advantage in space and
better piece placement. A few Black errors place him in an unfavorable endgame. When White sacrifices a piece to get a mass
of passed pawns, Black's Knight is driven over the edge.

Compare this ending with that of Reshevsky–Seidman, game
10.

Palma de Majorca, 1969

ENGLISH OPENING

B. Larsen	**M. Bobotsov**
1. P–QB4	P–QB4
2. P–KN3	P–KN3
3. B–N2	B–N2
4. N–QB3	N–QB3
5. N–B3	. . .

Smyslov prefers 5. R–N1 followed by P–QR3 and P–QN4. He places his KN at K2 after playing P–K3. Smyslov's setup is more difficult for Black to meet.

| 5. . . . | P–K4 |

A good alternative is 5. . . . P–K3 followed by . . . KN–K2.

6. 0–0	KN–K2
7. P–Q3	0–0
8. P–QR3	P–Q3
9. R–N1	P–N3

To be considered is 9. . . . P–QR4, preventing White from continuing P–QN4. Access by White's Knight to his QN5 is insignificant in this type of position.

10. P–QN4	B–N2
11. PxP	QPxP
12. B–N2	Q–Q2
13. N–Q2	N–Q5
14. BxB	QxB
15. P–K3	N–K3
16. P–K4	. . .

Enabling White to post his Knight at Q5, while permitting Black to do the same. Chances at this point are approximately equal. In the absence of Black's QB, the weakness of the light squares near White's King is not easily exploitable.

| 16. . . . | P–B4 |

Since White's strategy will evidently be to obtain play by advancing his QRP, Black correctly attempts to get counterplay on the Kingside.

| 17. N–Q5 | QR–K1 |

A slight inaccuracy. Preferable is the immediate 17. . . . N–B3, aiming to post a Knight at Q5.

| 18. P–QR4 | N–B3 |
| 19. B–B3 | Q–Q2 |

Preventing P–R5.

| 20. R–N2 | . . . |

A useful waiting move, to see what Black will do. White retains the option of doubling Rooks on the QN-file or the KB-file.

| 20. . . . | P–B5 |

Too committal and too early. Wiser is 20. . . . N/K–Q5 followed by . . . R–B2 and . . . R/K–KB1.

| 21. Q–N4! | . . . |

Black was threatening 21. . . . N–N4 followed by . . . P–B6.

21. . . .	Q–KB2
22. N–B3	P–KR4
23. Q–R3	PxP

If 23. . . . P–KN4 24. P–N4 would end Black's activity on the Kingside. 23. . . . N/B–Q5 would be met by 24. BxN KPxB 25. P–R5 with advantage.

| 24. BPxP | P–KN4 |
| 25. Q–N2 | . . . |

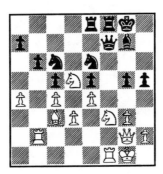

After 25. P–N4 P–R5, Black's chances are enhanced because his Knight then has access to his KB5.

| 25. . . . | **P–N5?** |

Too anxious to simplify, Black drifts into an unfavorable endgame. Correct is 25. . . . Q–N3 followed by doubling Rooks on the KB-file.

| **26. N–R4** | . . . |

This Knight is now activated and aims for an excellent post at KB5.

26. . . .	QxRch
27. QxQ	RxQch
28. KxR	R–B1ch
29. R–B2	RxRch
30. KxR	K–B2
31. N–B5	B–B3
32. K–N2	B–N4?

In order to prevent White from advancing his KRP, 32. . . . N–N4 is imperative, for then White would have a difficult task if he wanted to win.

| **33. P–R3** | K–N3 |
| **34. P–R4!** | . . . |

Putting Black completely on the defensive since his pieces are not able to penetrate White's position via KN4. Unproductive is 34. PxP PxP 35. N/Q–K3 K–R4, and White is unable to make headway.

| 34. . . . | B–Q1 |
| 35. K–B2 | . . . |

Having stabilized matters on the Kingside, White's monarch is ready to go to the other wing where a breakthrough is in the offing. White's Bishop is better than Black's because it has a good target, White's are the dominant Knights, and his King, having a clear objective (the Queenside breakthrough), is more active. White's technical problems, however, are considerable.

35. . . .	K–B2
36. N–Q6ch!	. . .

Preventing the King from reaching the Queenside.

36. . . .	K–N3
37. N–N7	K–B2
38. N–Q6ch	. . .

Gaining time to make the forty-move time control.

38. . . .	K–N3
39. K–K1	B–B3

Unavailing is 39. . . . B–B2 40. N–B5, and Black's monarch could not reach Q2 because of N–B6ch, winning the RP.

40. K–Q1	B–Q1

A better try is 40. . . . N/K–Q5, preventing White's King from reaching QB1 because of . . . N–K7ch.

41. K–B2	B–B2

Waiting for the end. Black should try 41. . . . N/K–Q5ch 42. K–N2 N–K7 43. B–K1 N–N5 44. NxN PxN 45. N–B8 P–R4 46. B–B2 K–B2 with some chance of holding the game.

42. N–B5	. . .

Black's pieces have no targets on which to concentrate. Four of his pawns are on squares controlled by White's Bishop. Still worse for Black is the fact that White's Knights occupy important squares, Q5 and KB5, where they have great mobility.

42. . . .	K–B2

43. P–R5 . . .

White's only possibility if he is to attempt to score the point. His opening strategy seems to have been based on the prospect of this breakthrough.

43. . . . **PxP**

If 43. . . . NxP 44. BxN PxB 45. K–N3 B–Q1 46. K–R4 P–R3 47. N–Q6ch K–B1 48. N–N7 K–K1 49. NxB KxN 50. KxP and wins.

44. K–N3 **K–K1?**

Also possible is 44. . . . N–N5 45. NxB NxN 46. BxP N–K3, and White's task would still be very difficult: for instance, if 47. P–Q4 N–B3; if 47. K–B3 P–R5; and, finally, if 47. K–R4 NxP 48. B–B3 N–B7 49. P–K5 N–K5 50. N–Q6ch (50. B–K1 N–Q5) NxN 51. PxN K–K1.

45. K–R4 **B–Q1**
46. N–Q6ch **K–Q2**
47. N–KB7 **B–B2??**

The losing move. Black could hold his own with 47. . . . N/K–Q5!. If 48. NxB KxN with equality, for if 49. N–B6 K–K2 50. NxRP K–B2–N3 trapping the Knight. If 48. BxN BPxB 49. NxB (49. K–N5 P–R3ch) KxN 50. K–N5 N–N5 51. NxN PxN 52. KxP K–B2 and draws.

48. NxB **KxN**
49. NxP **N/B–Q5**

After 49. . . . NxN 50. BxNch K–N3 51. B–B3, Black's resistance would collapse quickly.

50. BxN **NxB**

51. NxP!   . . .

The winning idea. The poor Black Knight cannot cope with White's passed pawns. A Knight is usually an excellent blockader of a single passed pawn (see the next game), but it can't handle a swarm.

	51. . . .	PxN

If 51. . . . N–K7 52. N–B6 NxP 53. KxP, etc.

52.	P–R5	N–K3
53.	KxP	K–Q3
54.	P–R6	N–N4
55.	K–N5	P–R3ch
56.	KxP	K–B3
57.	P–K5	N–R2
58.	K–R5	N–B1
59.	P–K6	K–Q3
60.	K–N6	KxP
61.	KxP	N–Q2ch
62.	K–N5	Resigns

Game 58

Knight versus One Passed Pawn

Despite its faults, the Knight excels in certain roles, one of which is blockader of a passed pawn. In the last game we saw how the Knight's short range limits its effectiveness in blockading separated passed pawns; in the present game the Knight has to deal only with one of them. Although White's passed pawn is in fact an extra pawn, and although White has the advantage of a Bishop against a Knight, and although the White pieces are conducted by the great Tal, still Black's Knight can hold the game. It should, anyway. Unfortunately, Gligoric gets the idea that he can force perpetual check by sacrificing the Knight, one of the worst ideas the normally steady Gligoric ever had.

Candidates' Match
Belgrade, 1968

RUY LOPEZ

M. Tal	S. Gligoric
1. P–K4	P–K4
2. N–KB3	N–QB3
3. B–N5	P–QR3
4. B–R4	N–B3
5. 0–0	B–K2
6. R–K1	P–QN4
7. B–N3	P–Q3
8. P–B3	0–0
9. P–Q4	. . .

Resorting to a variation favored by Korchnoi. In the first and fifth games of the match, Tal continued with the popular 9. P–KR3 but failed to obtain any advantage. It is, therefore, understandable that he decides to pursue a different course.

9. . . .	B–N5
10. B–K3	PxP
11. PxP	N–QR4
12. B–B2	N–B5?

Not the best course for equality. Correct is 12. . . . P–B4 13. QN–Q2 PxP 14. BxP N–B3 15. B–K3 P–Q4 16. PxP N–N5.

13. B–B1	P–B4
14. P–QN3	N–QR4

Bad is 14. . . . N–N3 15. QN–Q2 PxP 16. P–KR3 B–R4 17.
P–KN4 B–N3 18. NxP with P–B4 to follow, putting Black's QB
out of commission.

       15. P–Q5   . . .

Blocking the center and immobilizing Black's Knight at QR4.
If White continues, as in the previous note, with 15. QN–Q2,
Black can put pressure on White's QP by 15. . . . N–B3, and if
16. P–Q5 N–Q5 17. B–Q3 N–Q2, followed by either . . . B–B3
or . . . N–K4!

15. . . .	N–Q2
16. QN–Q2	B–B3
17. R–N1	N–K4

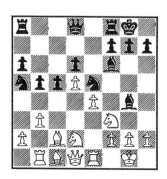

A good alternative is 17. . . . B–B6 18. P–KR3 BxN/6 19. QxB
Q–B3 20. R–K3 B–Q5 21. QxQ NxQ, as in the Korchnoi–Portisch
game in Sousse 1967, with approximate equality. The text move is
playable.

18. P–KR3	NxNch
19. NxN	BxN
20. QxB	R–K1
21. B–B4	B–K4
22. B–Q2	. . .

White wisely avoids trading Bishops. After 22. BxB PxB, Black
would be in a position to activate his lifeless Knight with . . .
N–N2–Q3. White's passed pawn would be of no value.

22. . . .	N–N2

Obviously the Knight is Black's headache. It cannot find an effective square. Also unappetizing is 22. . . . P–B5 23. P–QN4 N–N2 24. P–QR4.

23. Q–K2	**. . .**

Intending P–B4 to promote P–K5.

23. . . .	**Q–B3**
24. QR–Q1	**B–B5**
25. Q–B3	**B–N4?**

Bad is 25. . . . BxB 26. QxQ PxQ 27. RxB with the superior endgame because of Black's poorly posted Knight. Correct is 25. . . . B–K4 26. Q–Q3 P–N3. The text allows White to undertake enterprising action in the center.

26. Q–Q3	**BxB**

Forced, for if 26. . . . P–N3 27. P–B4 B–R3 (if 27. . . . BxP 28. R–KB1, and if 27. . . . B–R5 28. P–N3) 28. P–K5 with a winning position, since if 28. . . . PxP 29. PxP Q–N2 30. BxB QxB 31. P–Q6, etc.

27. P–K5!	**Q–R3**

27. . . . PxP is out of the question because of 28. QxPch K–B1 29. RxB followed by R/2–K2 with too much pressure.

28. RxB	**P–B5**

The only try. Hopeless is 28. . . . PxP 29. R/2–K2 regaining the pawn with advantage, for if 29. . . . P–B3 30. P–Q6 (threatening Q–Q5ch) K–R1 31. P–B4.

29. NPxP	**NPxP**
30. Q–QB3	**. . .**

After 30. QxP PxP followed by N–Q3, Black's position would be solid.

      30. . . .   **RxP**

If 30. . . . PxP 31. R/2–K2 P–B3 32. QxBP, and Black's Queen would be badly out of play. Black hopes that an exchange of Rooks will ease the defense.

      31. RxR   **PxR**

Now White has his passed pawn. But on the next move Black establishes a blockade with his Knight, which, despite Black's eventual loss of a pawn, should hold the game—especially since Black has a passed pawn of his own.

      32. R–K2   **N–Q3**
      33. QxKP   **Q–B8ch**
      34. K–R2   **Q–R6**

Black's Queen is now active and protects the Knight at the same time. White still enjoys a slight advantage, but it is quite another matter to demonstrate a win.

      35. Q–B4   . . .

      35. . . .   **R–K1**

Fearing the penetration of White's Rook at K7, Black decides to give up a pawn. A good alternative is 35. . . . P–N3 (not 35. . . . R–Q1 because of 36. BxPch KxB 37. Q–R4ch, winning the Exchange) 36. R–K7 R–Q1, and it is most difficult for White to make progress because of Black's threats on the Queenside with his passed pawn.

36. RxRch	NxR
37. QxP	. . .

37. Q–N8 can be met by 37. . . . K–B1.

37. . . .	P–N3
38. B–N3	N–Q3
39. Q–Q4	Q–B8
40. Q–QR4	P–QR4
41. Q–Q4	. . .

Obviously 41. QxP Q–B5ch leads to a perpetual check.

41. . . .	N–B4
42. Q–Q1	Q–N7
43. K–N1	N–Q3
44. Q–N4	Q–K4
45. P–N3	P–R4
46. Q–QR4	. . .

46. . . .	N–B4??

The final blunder. All Black has to do is play a waiting game, for White has no means to make progress, even though he is a pawn ahead. The correct continuation is 46. . . . Q–B6; then if 47. Q–B6 Q–K4, or if 47. Q–KB4 Q–B4. The Knight blockade would be unbreakable. The text mistakenly envisions a forced perpetual check by sacrificing the Knight.

47. QxP	NxP
48. PxN	QxPch
49. K–B1	QxPch

50. K–K2	**Q–N5ch**
51. K–Q3	**Q–N6ch**
52. K–B4	**P–R5**
53. K–B5	**Q–K6ch**

Neither is 53. . . . P–R6 more promising. There could follow 54. Q–R8ch K–N2 55. P–Q6 P–R7 56. B–Q5 Q–N8ch 57. K–N5 Q–N8ch 58. K–R5, and Black soon runs out of checks.

54. K–B6	**Q–K1ch**
55. K–N7	**P–R6**
56. Q–B7	**K–N2**
57. Q–B3ch	**P–B3**
58. QxP	**Q–N4ch**
59. K–B7	**Q–B4ch**
60. K–Q7	**Q–R2ch**
61. K–K8	**Q–N1ch**
62. K–K7	**Q–K4ch**
63. Q–K6	**Q–B2ch**
64. Q–Q7	**Q–K4ch**
65. K–Q8ch	**K–B1**
66. K–B8	**Resigns**

Game 59

A Passive Rook

The only good Rook is a working Rook! Due to an error on his 22nd move, White finds his Queen Rook standing uselessly while the battle rages. Deprived of this Rook's participation, White gradually gets the worst of the struggle.

Black's Rooks, on the other hand, maneuver their way into White's camp, making various mating threats and finally forcing decisive material gain. Note especially the great skill with which Smyslov, a former World Champion, handles his Rooks against White's dangerous Bishops. Everybody knows Rooks are stronger than Bishops; in a virtuoso performance Smyslov shows why.

Skopje, 1969

QUEEN'S GAMBIT ACCEPTED

J. Sofrevski	V. Smyslov
1. N–KB3	P–Q4
2. P–Q4	N–KB3
3. P–B4	PxP
4. P–K3	P–KN3

One of Smyslov's pet defenses against the Queen's Gambit. Black's setup does not have a good reputation, but that does not deter Smyslov.

5. BxP	B–N2
6. 0–0	0–0
7. N–B3	P–QR3
8. P–QR3	KN–Q2
9. P–K4	. . .

A good alternative is 9. B–K2 N–N3 (9. . . . P–K4 or 9. . . . P–QB4 10. P–Q5 with good play) 10. P–R3 (preventing . . . B–N5) with P–K4 to follow.

9. . . .	N–N3
10. B–K2	B–N5
11. B–K3	N–B3
12. P–Q5	. . .

Of little value to White is 12. P–K5 Q–Q2 13. Q–Q2 KR–Q1 14. KR–Q1 B–K3 with good play.

12. . . .	BxKN
13. BxB	. . .

If 13. PxB N–R4 14. R–B1 N/4–B5 with the superior chances because of White's weakened King position.

13. . . .	N–K4
14. B–K2	N/4–B5
15. B–B1	P–QB3
16. Q–N3	. . .

To be considered is 16. PxP QxQ (16. . . . PxP 17. Q–N3 N–R4 18. Q–N4 N–Q2 19. B–KN5 with advantage) 17. NxQ PxP 18. R–R2 KR–Q1 19. P–QN3 N–K4 20. R–B2 with the better game.

| 16. . . . | N–R4 |
| 17. Q–N4 | N–Q2 |

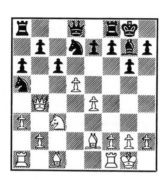

18. B–KN5 . . .

Interesting is 18. PxP NxP (if 18. . . . PxP 19. B–KN5 P–B3 20. B–KB4 P–K4 21. B–K3 R–N1 22. Q–Q6 RxP 23. KR–Q1 with great advantage) 19. QxNP N–Q5 20. B–QB4 N–QB4 21. Q–Q5 Q–N3 22. Q–N5, and it is questionable whether Black has sufficient compensation for the pawn.

18. . . .	P–QB4
19. Q–R4	P–N4
20. Q–B2	P–R3
21. B–K3	. . .

Preferable is 21. B–R4 in order to tie the Queen down to the protection of the KP, if only temporarily. The plausible 21. . . . N–K4 can be met by 22. P–B4 N/K–B5 23. P–K5 N–K6 24. Q–K4 NxR 25. RxN with good attacking possibilities for the Exchange or by 22. P–QN3 followed by P–B4.

| 21. . . . | Q–B2 |
| 22. QR–N1? | . . . |

A bad move that serves no purpose at all. The Rook belongs on QR1 where it will be of value after . . . P–QN5 and the exchange of pawns, when it will attack the Knight at QR5. The correct continuation for White is the aggressive 22. P–B4 followed by P–K5. If Black plays (after 22. P–B4) 22. . . . P–N5 or 22.

. . . B–Q5, White would continue 23. N–Q1 with the better position.

Note that this Rook remains passively placed on the QN-file throughout the middlegame and is therefore a contributing factor in Black's success.

22. . . .	**KR–B1**
23. N–R2	**. . .**

This too wastes valuable time and posts the Knight on an unfavorable square. Again, P–B4 is indicated.

23. . . .	**N–K4**

Smyslov now begins to assert himself.

24. K–R1	**N/K–B5**
25. B–B1	**Q–Q2**
26. P–B4	**N–Q3**
27. B–B3	**P–N5**

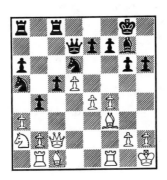

28. PxP?	**. . .**

This gives Black's forces, particularly his Rooks, a chance to come into play rapidly. Correct is 28. Q–B2 followed by P–K5 with chances for both sides.

28. . . .	**PxP**
29. Q–Q3	**. . .**

Better is 29. Q–Q1 to prevent Black's next move. Black may then eventually double Rooks on the QB-file.

29. . . .	**Q–R5**

After White's inaccuracy, Smyslov seizes the initiative and never permits his opponent to recover. Already White's bad Rook move (22. QR–N1) is giving him problems. After he wins a pawn, Smyslov will force the exchange of Queens to reduce the opponent's counterplay possibilities and to bring the favorable endgame closer. However, the intricate piece play that ensues, and continues to the end, taxes the abilities of both players.

3C. P–K5   . . .

The only course, for if 30. B–Q2 QxN 31. R–R1 QxNP 32. RxN N–B5, winning material.

30. . . .   **QxN**

Too smart to fall prey to greed, Smyslov resists the temptation to win a piece; instead, he is satisfied to remain a pawn ahead. Faulty is 30. . . . N–B4 31. P–Q6 QxN 32. P–Q7 R–Q1 33. BxR with a won position for White.

Black's continuation also guarantees activity for his King Bishop, now that he no longer has to worry about White's P–K5.

31. PxN   **PxP**
32. P–B5   **Q–B5!**

Virtually forcing the exchange of Queens, thereby reducing White's hope of an attack.

33. B–K2   . . .

If 33. Q–Q1 PxP 34. B–K2 or 34. B–R5 Q–B7, leading to approximately the same position as in the game.

33. . . .   **QxQ**
34. BxQ   **PxP**
35. BxBP   . . .

Worse is 35. RxP N–B5 36. R–B4 (36. P–QN3 N–R6!) 36. . . . N–K4 37. B–B5 R–B5 38. RxR NxR 39. B–Q3 R–K1!.

35. . . .   **R–B2**
36. B–Q2   . . .

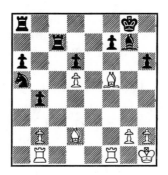

36. . . .   **R–N1**

Tempting but unsound is 36. . . . N–B5 37. BxNP R–N1 38. B–B3 N–K6 39. BxB! NxR 40. BxP, and the Knight is trapped!

37. P–QN3   **R–N4**

38. KR–K1   **K–B1**

Not 38. . . . RxP? 39. R–K8ch B–B1 40. BxRP and wins. The text keeps White's Rook out of K7 and therefore releases the Black Rook on B2 from that duty.

39. B–B4   **. . .**

White should hold on to his QP. 39. B–K4 is very much indicated, and if 39. . . . R–K2 (this is probably what White feared) 40. B–B4 N–N2 (if 40. . . . R–N3 41. B–B2 and White escapes from the pin) 41. B–Q3 RxP (41. . . . RxRch? 42. RxR RxP 43. B–K4 R–QN4 44. B–B6!) 42. BxQRP N–B4 43. B–B4 R–Q5 44. RxR KxR 45. B–K3 R–K5 46. BxN with good drawing chances.

39. . . .   **RxP**

40. P–N4   **B–K4**

Returning one of the pawns voluntarily. Black had to meet the immediate threat of 41. R–K4 followed by QR–K1 and R–K8 mate. If 40. . . . P–R4 41. B–K4 R–Q5 42. PxP R–K2 43. P–R6 B–B3 (if 43. . . . R/2xB 44. RxR RxR 45. BxPch K–N1 46. R–KN1) 44. R–R1 NxP 45. RxP R/2xB 46. RxR RxR 47. BxPch K–N1 48. BxP RxB 49. RxB (threatening to draw with P–R7ch) R–KR5 50. K–N2 N–B4, and Black wins the endgame since he gains the advanced pawn by force; but Smyslov may not have seen this possibility in all its intricacy (this was the last move before the

time control and time pressure may have played a part), or he
may not have trusted it. Alternatively, after 40. . . . P–R4 White
can continue 41. R–K4 PxP 42. QR–K1 B–K4 43. B–R6ch K–K2
44. RxQNP with good drawing chances. There is also the possibility of 40. . . . R–K2, but after 41. KR–Q1 RxRch 42. RxR B–K4
43. BxPch K–K1 44. R–QB1 with the annoying threat of R–B8
mate (if 44. . . . P–B3 45. R–B8ch K–B2 46. R–B8 mate). And
finally, Black can consider 40. . . . N–N2, but this is unappetizing
because of 41. QR–B1 RxR 42. RxR N–B4 (42. . . . N–Q1 43.
R–B8) 43. BxPch, etc.; or White has 41. B–K4 R–Q5 42. QR–Q1
RxR 43. RxR with good play. In view of these possibilities,
Smyslov decides to return a pawn and pursue aggressive action.

In all of these variations, White's Bishops function well, as
Smyslov knew they would, and his judgment told him that, since
he would have to give back a pawn anyway, he should do it so
as to give White as little counterplay as possible. Black's Rooks
cannot be prevented from invading the White position in the
long run.

41. BxPch   K–K2

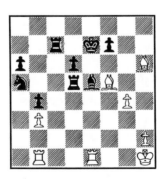

42. R–K4?   . . .

Overlooking the strong rejoinder on which Smyslov was relying.
To obtain counterchances, Sofrevski should play 42. B–N5ch P–B3
43. B–K3 R–B6 44. P–N5 PxP (if 44. . . . NxP or 44. . . . RxP
45. P–N6 is too strong) 45. BxPch K–K1 (45. . . . K–B2 46.
R–KB1 K–N2 47. R–N1, etc.) 46. B–K6 R/4–Q6 47. R–K4 with

a good position. If 42. . . . K–B1 43. B–K4 R/4–B4 (43. . . .
R–N4 44. B–Q3) 44. B–Q2 B–B6 45. B–R6ch K–N1 46. R–K2
with good play. If 42. . . . K–N1 43. R–K4, which makes 43. . . .
R–B6 unplayable because of 44. RxP R–R6 45. R–N8 mate. If
Sofrevski had seen Smyslov's plan, he might have hit upon my
suggested continuation.

| 42. . . . | R–B6 |

Black's plan depends on the fact that White's King is more
exposed than Black's. Black's Rooks begin to make a gradual
incursion into White's territory, endangering the monarch's
safety. But Black must continue to play accurately, for a single
slip can be disastrous.

| 43. RxP | . . . |

43. B–B4 can be met by 43. . . . N–B3.

| 43. . . . | R–R6! |
| 44. B–N5ch | . . . |

44. B–B4 offers no relief on account of 44. . . . BxB 45. RxB
R–Q7 46. R–K1ch K–Q1, and the Black King is safe, the White
King seriously endangered.

44. . . .	K–B1
45. B–K4	R–B4
46. R–N6	. . .

Nothing is achieved by 46. R–N8ch K–N2 47. P–N4 because
of 47. . . . RxPch 48. K–N1 R–B5 49. B–B3 N–B3 50. R–QB8
N–Q5 (or simply . . . RxQNP) 51. RxR NxBch 52. K–B1 NxB.

46. . . .	RxPch
47. K–N1	R–K7
48. B–Q3	R–QR7
49. B–R6ch	. . .

49. P–N4 is out of the question because of 49. . . . B–Q5ch 50.
K–B1 RxB 51. PxN R–B7ch 52. K–K1 RxNP with the threat of
. . . R–N8ch.

| 49. . . . | K–K2 |
| 50. R–N8 | . . . |

If 50. P–N4 R–B6, and if 50. RxRP B–Q5ch 51. K–R1 R–B6,
denying White the Rook check at QR7.

| 50. . . . | R–B6 |

Here comes the other Rook!

51. R–Q1   . . .

Finally this Rook gets in the game, but Black's Knight, now no longer needed to keep White's Rook on the QN-file, also joins the battle.

51. . . .   **N–B3**

There is practically no hope for victory in 51. . . . RxP 52. B–B8ch K–Q2 (if 52. . . . K–B3 53. R–B1ch K–N4 54. B–K7ch K–R3 55. B–B8ch B–N2 56. RxR NxR 57. R–B6ch) 53. RxR NxR 54. B–B4 R–N7 55. BxBP, when White's pawn gives him counter-play. And 51. . . . NxP 52. B–B8ch K–Q2 (52. . . . K–K3 53. RxN RxR 54. B–B4ch) 53. B–B5ch K–B2 54. R–B8ch K–N2 55. RxR BxR 56. BxP offers no prospects. White's two Bishops are ex-tremely dangerous in such open positions. Black must tame them by maintaining his initiative.

52. R–N7ch   . . .

After 52. B–B8ch K–B3 53. R–B1ch K–N4, White would not have the important B–K7ch at his disposal.

52. . . .   **K–K1**

53. B–KN5   . . .

Futile is 53. B–QB4 R–N6ch 54. K–B1 R–KR6 55. BxPch K–Q1 56. B–N5ch K–B1, etc.

53. . . .   **N–Q5**

54. K–B1   . . .

54. R–KB1 is faulty because of 54. . . . RxB 55. R–K7ch K–B1 56. R/7xPch K–N1 57. R–B8ch K–N2 58. R/1–B7ch K–N3, with no more checks.

54. . . .   **R–R7**

55. B–K4   . . .

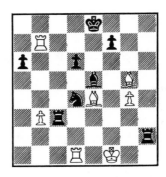

55. . . .   **K–B1**

Getting the King out of danger. Not 55. . . . N–B6 56. R–N8ch K–Q2 57. B–B5ch K–B2 (57. . . . K–K3? 58. B–B5 mate) 58. R–B8ch K–N3 (58. . . . K–N2 59. RxR BxR 60. B–K4ch) 59. RxR BxR 60. RxPch. Smyslov's patience is commendable. He is in no rush to end the fight quickly if this means endangering his own safety. Instead he prefers to play cautiously and increase his pressure gradually. Little by little White's tactical threats are dealt with until a few exchanges finally give Smyslov the endgame he wants.

56. B–Q5   **N–K3**
57. B–Q2   **. . .**

If 57. B–K7ch K–N1 58. BxN PxB, and Black's QP is immune to capture: 59. BxP BxB 60. RxB R–B8ch, etc.

57. . . .   **R–N6**
58. B–N4   **. . .**

Black has a sufficient reply to 58. B–K1 RxKNP 59. BxN PxB 60. R–B1 R–B5ch! 61. K–N1 R–B2, etc. 58. P–N5 fails to 58. . . . B–Q5 with the threat of immediate mate.

58. . . .   **RxKNP**
59. BxN   **. . .**

Black can meet 59. R–B1 by 59. . . . R–Q5, and if 60. BxN R–R8ch followed by 61. . . . RxR.

59. . . .   **R–R8ch**
60. K–K2   **R–K5ch**
61. K–B3   **R–B5ch**

62. K–K2	RxR
63. KxR	PxB

Black now has an easily won endgame, ahead two connected passed pawns.

64. K–B2	K–K1
65. R–N6	K–Q2
66. B–Q2	R–B7
67. K–Q3	R–B6ch
68. K–B2	. . .

If 68. K–K4 R–R6 69. P–N4 R–R6, and after guarding his QRP, Black can advance his QP at will.

68. . . .	B–B5!
69. B–K1	. . .

69. BxB RxB 70. RxP P–K4, and the two connected passed pawns cannot be stopped.

69. . . .	P–Q4

This pawn advances surprisingly fast.

70. RxRP	P–Q5
71. R–R2	P–Q6ch
72. K–Q1	R–B8
Resigns	

A well-deserved point for the former champion.

Game 60

Queen for a Day

Queens are pieces, too, and like other pieces there are good Queens and bad Queens.

Because of their great range and power, Queens thrive on open lines. In this game notice how White's Queen, abetted by center squares under White's control, harasses the enemy King, whereas Black's Queen, without center control in its favor, plays a more passive role. The situation demonstrates the interdependence of the elements of chess, particularly the effect of pawn structure on the mobility of the pieces.

USSR vs. the Rest of the World
Belgrade, 1970

QUEEN'S GAMBIT DECLINED

M. Najdorf	M. Tal
1. N–KB3	N–KB3
2. P–B4	P–K3
3. N–B3	P–Q4
4. P–Q4	P–B4
5. BPxP	NxP
6. P–K3	N–QB3
7. B–B4	. . .

A good alternative is 7. B–Q3.

7. . . .	PxP
8. PxP	B–K2
9. 0–0	0–0
10. R–K1	NxN

Better chances for equality are offered by either 10. . . . N–B3 or 10. . . . B–B3. The text gives Black a slightly better pawn structure but leaves White with greater central control. Also, the exchanged Black Knight would have been very useful for King-side defense, as the sequel shows.

11. PxN	P–QN3
12. B–Q3	B–N2
13. Q–B2	P–N3

Forced, for if 13. . . . P–KR3 14. R–K4 with a strong attack. With Black's Knight on KB3, this weakening would not have been necessary.

14. B–KR6	R–K1
15. Q–Q2!	R–QB1

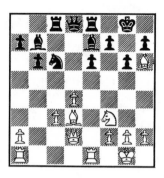

16. P–KR4   . . .

White initiates action on the Kingside despite his weak pawn structure on the Queenside. That single pawn move by Black (13. . . . P–N3) is a red cape before White's eyes.

   16. . . .   **N–R4**

The pawn is immune to capture: if 16. . . . BxP 17. NxB QxN 18. B–N5 Q–N5 (18. . . . Q–R4 19. B–K2) 19. R–K4 Q–B4 20. R–R4 (or 20. R–K5 Q–N5 21. B–K2) Q–R4 21. B–B6 and wins because of the terrific threat of Q–R6. Black must not give up his King Bishop so long as White still has his Queen Bishop.

   17. N–N5   . . .

White has to prevent . . . BxN.

   17. . . .   **B–B1**

Black has to reckon with 18. Q–B4. It is a victory for White— albeit a small one—that Black's KB has disappeared and left weak spots at KB3 and KR3.

   18. BxB   **RxB**
   19. P–R5   **N–B5**

Tal falters defensively. He should seriously consider 19. . . . P–KR3, and if 20. NxKP PxN 21. QxP (21. RxP R–KB3) Q–B3 22. PxP R–QB2, and White has sufficient compensation for the piece. If in this line 20. NxBP RxN 21. PxP R–KB3 22. QxP R–QB2, once again White has adequate play for the piece. Finally, if 20. N–K4 P–KN4 with a reasonable game since White's initiative would be slowed and Black would be ready to proceed with his counterplay on the QB-file.

20. BxN	RxB
21. PxP	RPxP
22. Q–B4	. . .

Threatening Q–R4.

22. . . .	Q–Q4
23. P–B3	K–N2
24. N–K4	. . .

24. R–K5 accomplishes nothing: 24. . . . Q–Q2 (not 24. . . . Q–Q3 25. Q–R4 R–KR1 26. QxRch KxQ 27. NxPch) 25. R–QB1 R–B1 with pressure against the QBP.

24. . . .	Q–KB4

If 24. . . . P–B3 25. K–B2 (not 25. N–Q6? P–K4!) followed by the strong R–R1.

25. Q–N3	BxN
26. PxB	. . .

And now White has excellent play on the KB-file. Black is hoping that White's exposed King will provide opportunities. But White's center is a strong factor, and the pawn that now appears on his K4 controls KB5, an important square in Black's defense.

26. . . .	Q–QR4?

A strategical error which keeps the Queen away from the Kingside where it is needed for defense. Tal obviously underrates White's attacking potential. Correct is either 26. . . . Q–KR4 followed by 27. . . . R–KR1 or 26. . . . Q–B3 27. R–KB1 Q–K2, and it is difficult to say whether White can make any headway.

Perhaps Tal's error is also psychological in part: Tal loves to attack and dislikes defense. There is no doubt that this preference has contributed to his very great achievements, but it can also blind a player to the need for defensive play when truly called for.

27. R–K3	KR–B1
28. R–KB1!	. . .

A very fine conception. Najdorf, undaunted by Tal's reputation for ferocity, sacrifices a pawn for mounting pressure against the Black monarch.

28. . . .	RxBP
29. R/3–B3!	R/1–B2

If 29. . . . RxR 30. QxR R–B2 (30. . . . P–B4 31. PxP followed by Q–N7ch) 31. Q–B6ch K–R2 (31. . . . K–N1 32. Q–Q8ch) 32. R–B4 and wins.

30. Q–B4	K–N1
31. Q–Q6!	. . .

Najdorf handles this position in grand style. The text move threatens 31. Q–Q8ch K–N2 32. Q–B6ch K–N1 33. RxR QxR 34. R–B3 with the winning threat of R–KR3. Black's position is untenable (those dark squares!).

31. . . .	RxR
32. Q–Q8ch	K–N2
33. RxR	Q–K8ch
34. K–R2	R–B6

If 34. . . . QxP 35. Q–B6ch (35. QxR also wins) K–N1 36. R–KR3 and wins.

35. Q–B6ch	K–R3
36. Q–B4ch	K–R2
37. QxPch	K–R3
38. Q–B4ch	K–R2
39. Q–B7ch	K–R3
40. Q–B8ch	K–R4

If 40. . . . K–N4 41. Q–B4ch K–R4 42. P–N4ch K–R5 43. Q–R6ch KxP 44. R–B4 mate.

41. Q–R8ch	K–N4

41. . . . K–N5 42. Q–R3ch winning the Rook.

42. Q–K5ch	**K–R3**
43. Q–B4ch	**K–R2**

44. R–B1! . . .

The winning continuation, found after adjournment.

44. . . . **Q–K7**

Unavailing is 44. . . . Q–K6 because of 45. Q–R4ch K–N2 (45. . . . K–N1 46. Q–Q8ch K–N2 47. Q–B8ch K–R2 48. R–B7 mate; if in this line 46. . . . K–R2 47. R–B7ch K–R3 48. Q–R4 mate) 46. R–B4! with Black defenseless against the threat of Q–B6ch or Q–K7ch followed by R–R4ch and mate.

45. Q–B7ch	**K–R3**
46. Q–B8ch	**K–R4**
47. R–B4	. . .

And now Black does not have any check at his disposal, unlike the position when Black's Queen was at his K8.

47. . . .	**Q–K8**
48. Q–R8ch	**K–N4**
49. Q–K5ch	**K–R3**
50. R–N4	**Resigns**

For if 50. . . . K–R2 51. Q–B6 and wins.

Game 61

Unbalanced Forces

Any general evaluation of the pieces begins with the pawn as the basic unit. It is then usually estimated that the Knight is "worth" three pawns, the Bishop slightly more than three, the Rook five pawns (some experts prefer 4½), and the Queen nine pawns (some say eight). Thus, Rook, Bishop, and pawn should be roughly equal to a Queen, and this is usually borne out in practice. The addition of a single pawn to either part of the formula, however, can radically affect the practical chances. In this game, for instance, the ending after White's 53rd move would be drawn if White did not have his KRP; with it he has winning chances.

The game illustrates the problems faced by both sides in this type of ending. This type is not rare; so the student is well advised to examine the variations closely.

Chess Olympics

Lugano, 1968

ENGLISH OPENING

S. Reshevsky	J. Kostro
1. P–QB4	P–QB4
2. N–QB3	P–KN3
3. P–KN3	B–N2
4. B–N2	N–QB3
5. P–Q3	P–K3
6. P–K4	KN–K2
7. KN–K2	0–0
8. 0–0	P–Q3
9. R–N1	P–QR3
10. P–QR3	R–N1
11. P–QN4	PxP
12. PxP	P–QN4
13. PxP	. . .

White cannot very well break the symmetry on the Queenside. Against 13. P–B5, Black can obtain a promising position with 13. . . . PxP 14. PxP P–N5 15. N–R4 Q–R4 followed by . . . R–Q1 with annoying pressure against the QP. Also unappetizing for White is 13. B–QR3 PxP 14. PxP N–K4 15. P–B5 (15. Q–N3 Q–B2 N–B5 with the superior chances.

13. . . .	PxP
14. P–Q4	P–Q4
15. B–B4	. . .

When making this move, I decided to sacrifice a pawn in order to create complications. To be considered is 15. P–K5 N–B4 16. Q–Q3 Q–K2 17. B–QR3 B–QR3 18. N–R2 with an effort to post this Knight at QB5 via QB1–N3.

15. . . .	R–N3
16. Q–N3	. . .

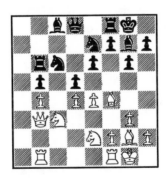

16. . . .	PxP
17. NxKP	N–B4

The QP is immune to immediate capture. 17. . . . BxP 18. NxB NxN 19. Q–N2 with the advantage because of Black's weakened King position without his KB. Also inadvisable is 17. . . . NxQP on account of 18. NxN BxN (18. . . . QxN 19. B–K3 winning the Exchange) 19. KR–Q1, and Black would be unable to extricate himself from the nasty pin without suffering material loss.

18. B–N5	P–B3
19. B–K3	QNxQP

After 19. . . . NxB 20. PxN, White would be on top because
of Black's weak KP.

20. NxN	**NxN**
21. BxN	. . .

Unproductive is 21. Q–N2 P–K4 22. KR–Q1 P–B4.

21. . . .	**QxB**
22. KR–Q1	**Q–K4**

Better than 22. . . . Q–B5 23. Q–K3 R–N1 24. N–B5, cutting
off the Queen, preventing Black's QB from developing, and
exerting considerable pressure against the KP.

White's compensation for the sacrificed pawn is the much
greater activity for his pieces, compared with Black's, and the
somewhat weakened condition of Black's KP. Also, White has
the initiative and good pressure against Black's QNP.

23. Q–K3	**R–R3**
24. Q–B5	. . .

Here I considered 24. P–B4 Q–N1 25. N–B5, but after 25. . . .
R–Q3 there is no satisfactory continuation for White.

24. . . .	**P–B4**

If 24. . . . QxQ 25. PxQ R–R4 26. N–Q6 B–QR3 (26. . . . B–Q2
27. N–N7) 27. P–B6 with good prospects of winning.

25. N–Q6	**B–Q2**

26. B–B1	. . .

I considered 26. P–B4 but discarded it because of 26. . . . Q–K7
(threatening 27. . . . R–R7) 27. R–K1 Q–Q7 28. QR–Q1 Q–N7

with no promising continuation for White. Also unproductive is
26. Q–B7 B–K1 27. Q–K7 B–KB3. And finally, if 26. NxBP QxQ
27. PxQ RxN 28. RxB RxQBP with an even position.

26. . . .	QxQ
27. PxQ	R–N1
28. NxBP	. . .

An alternative is 28. NxNP BxN 29. RxB RxR 30. BxR R–R4
31. R–N1 (or 31. R–Q8ch K–B2 32. R–QN8 B–Q5 33. P–B6
B–K4 with difficulty for White to make progress) 31. . . . K–B2
32. P–B6 R–R2 or 32. . . . B–K4 with little chance for White to
win.

28. . . .	NPxN
29. RxB	R–B3
30. RxP	RxR
31. BxR	RxP
32. B–R4	. . .

The position looks drawish but there are still some pitfalls.
Black's pawns are a little weaker than White's which means,
although this alone is not enough to win, that Black has to be
careful.

32. . . .	R–K4
33. B–N3	. . .

Threatening 34. R–K7.

33. . . .	B–B1
34. R–QB7	P–R3
35. K–N2	R–K8
36. R–N7	R–K7
37. K–B3	R–K8
38. P–R3	. . .

Waiting for my opponent to blunder. He obliges.

38. . . .	B–B4?

Correct is 38. . . . R–K4 with little chance for White to make
progress.

39. R–N5	B–K2

Black has to lose a pawn. If 39. . . . R–K4 40. BxPch RxB 41.
RxB with a clearly won endgame.

40. RxP	K–N2

| 41. R–B4 | R–K4 |
| 42. P–R4? | . . . |

Permitting Black to draw. Imperative is 42. B–B2.

| 42. . . . | B–B4? |

The sealed move. Black can draw with 42. . . . R–B4. There
would follow 43. BxP RxRch 44. KxR B–N5 45. K–N4 B–K8
46. P–B4 B–Q7 47. K–B3 B–B8 48. P–N4 B–Q7 49. P–N5 (without this advance, White cannot hope to make any progress) 49.
. . . PxP 50. RPxP (if 50. BPxP B–B8 51. K–N4 B–Q7 52. P–R5
BxP and draws) 50. . . . B–N5 51. K–N4 B–K2 52. P–B5 B–Q1
and draws since 53. P–B6ch is answered by . . . BxP.

43. B–B2	B–K2
44. B–Q3	R–QR4
45. K–N2	B–Q3
46. R–B4	. . .

Unavailing is 46. R–N4ch K–B2 47. R–N6 B–B1. The text
move threatens 47. R–B6.

| 46. . . . | K–B2 |
| 47. P–B4 | . . . |

This exposes the White King to checks but is indispensable if
White is to make any headway.

| 47. . . . | R–QB4 |
| 48. R–K4 | . . . |

Threatening to win the KP with 49. B–B4.

| 48. . . . | K–B3 |

| 49. P–N4 | R–Q4 |
| 50. P–N5ch | K–B4 |

Another possibility is 50. . . . PxP 51. BPxPch (if 51. RPxPch K–B4 52. R–Q4ch K–N5 and draws) 51. . . . K–B2 (better than 51. . . . K–B4 52. B–B2, placing the Black King in an uncomfortable situation; of course, 52. . . . R–Q7ch fails because of 53. R–K2ch) 52. B–B4 R–K4 53. R–Q4 with some chance for a win.

51. PxP! ...

51. R–Q4ch K–N5 52. RxR PxR 53. P–N6 B–B1 54. P–B5 B–N2 leads to a dead draw. Interesting however is 51. R–K3ch KxP 52. R–B3ch (52. R–K4ch K–B4 53. R–Q4ch K–K4 and draws) 52. . . . K–N5 (but not 52. . . . K–K4 53. P–N6 and wins) 53. P–N6 B–K4 and draws. The text move leads to a different type of endgame with a ray of hope for victory. White's Queen would only draw against Black's Rook and Bishop were it not for this RP.

51. . . . **RxB**

Practically forced, for if 51. . . . B–B1 52. R–K3ch! K–B3 (52. . . . KxP 53. R–B3ch, etc.) 53. P–R7 B–N2 54. K–B3 or 54. B–B4 with excellent winning chances.

52. P–R7	KxR
53. P–R8=Q	R–Q7ch
54. K–R3	BxP

White's chance to win lies in the promotion of the RP—a difficult task in view of the unfavorable position of White's King since there is a constant threat of a perpetual check. White's next several moves attempt to extricate the King from this threat.

55. Q–R8ch	K–B4
56. Q–B8ch	K–K5
57. Q–N4ch	K–B4
58. Q–N1ch	K–K4
59. Q–N8ch	. . .

Better than 59. K–N4 R–N7ch 60. K–B3 R–N6ch 61. K–B2 R–KR6 62. Q–R7 R–R7ch 63. K–B3 R–R6ch 64. K–K2 (futile is 64. K–N4 R–N6ch 5. K–R5 K–B3, when White's pawn can never advance) 4. . . . R–R7ch 65. K–Q3 R–R6ch 66. K–B4 K–B3 with drawing chances.

59. . . .	K–B4
60. Q–N1ch	K–K4
61. Q–N5ch	K–K5
62. Q–N7ch	K–K4

Imperative is 62. . . . K–B4, after which I would have to choose between 63. Q–N1ch K–K4 64. K–N4 and 63. Q–B7ch K–K4 64. P–R5 R–R7ch 65. K–N4 R–N7ch 66. K–B3 R–N6ch 67. K–B2 R–KR6 68. Q–N7ch K–B4 69. Q–N6ch K–K4 70. Q–N4. In either case, White would have very few winning possibilities.

63. K–N4	. . .

The point is that now Black has been deprived of the very important check at KN7. In addition, White's immediate threat of winning the Bishop compels Black to bring his Rook to the fifth rank, making it infeasible for this piece to get behind White's pawn. This fact is very instrumental in White's ability finally to promote the pawn. Rooks belong behind passed pawns!

63. . . .	R–Q5
64. Q–N8ch	K–Q4
65. Q–N5ch	K–Q3
66. K–B3	P–K4

Black lacks an adequate defense. If 66. . . . B–K4, then 67. P–R5 R–B5ch 68. K–K3 R–B3 (68. . . . R–B1 loses to 69. Q–N4ch, and 68. . . . R–KR5 fails to 69. Q–N8ch K–Q4 70. Q–Q8ch) 69. Q–N8ch K–Q4 70. Q–Q8ch K–B3 71. K–K4 R–B4 72. Q–K7 and wins (72. . . . RxP 73. Q–K8ch).

67. P–R5	K–K3
68. Q–K8ch	K–Q4
69. Q–N6	. . .

Preventing . . . R–Q6ch and at the same time making the pawn's advance possible.

69. . . .	R–N5
70. P–R6	R–N6ch

The endgame after 70. . . . BxP 71. QxB is interesting. If Black's pawn were at K2 instead of K4, the endgame would be drawn. With the pawn at K4, White can make progress as follows: 71. . . . R–B5ch 72. K–N3 R–Q5 73. Q–B6 R–KB5 74. Q–K7 R–Q5 75. Q–Q7ch K–K5 (if 75. . . . K–B4 76. Q–K6 forcing 76. . . . P–K5, after which White wins with 77. K–B4 because White's King is now in a position to exert telling pressure) 76. Q–KB7 (threatening Q–B3 mate), forcing 76. . . . R–Q6ch 77. K–N4 which enables White's King to enter the fray effectively. A possible continuation is 77. . . . K–Q5 78. Q–R7ch K–K5 79. Q–N7ch K–Q5 80. K–B5 R–K6 81. Q–Q7ch (forcing a separation between King and Rook) K–B6 82. Q–Q1 P–K5 83. K–K5 and wins.

71. K–K2	R–N7ch
72. K–Q3	R–Q7ch
73. K–B3	R–KR7
74. P–R7	P–K5
75. Q–N8ch	Resigns

For if 75. . . . K–Q3 76. Q–N8ch, and if 75. . . . K–B3 76. P–R8=Q.

Index to Openings

(Numbers refer to games)